Is Massa Day Dead?

ORDE COOMBS was born in St. Vincent, British West Indies. He studied at Yale University, Clare College, Cambridge, England, and New York University. His articles and essays have appeared in many of this country's leading magazines, and he is the author of *Do You See My Love for You Growing?*

Is Massa Day Dead?

BLACK MOODS IN THE CARIBBEAN

EDITED AND WITH AN INTRODUCTION BY
ORDE COOMBS

Anchor Books
ANCHOR PRESS/DOUBLEDAY • GARDEN CITY, NEW YORK
1974

Library of Congress Cataloging in Publication Data

Coombs, Orde, comp.
  Is Massa Day dead?

  Includes bibliographical references.
  CONTENTS: Walcott, D. The muse of history.—Brathwaite,
E. Timehri.—Millette, J. The Black revolution in the Caribbean.
[etc.]
  1. Negroes in the British West Indies. 2. West Indies, British—
Social conditions. I. Title.
F2131.C73 917.29′06′96
ISBN 0-385-07947-8
Library of Congress Catalog Card Number 73–16501

The Anchor Books edition is the first publication of IS MASSA
DAY DEAD?

Anchor Books Edition: 1974

Grateful acknowledgment is made to the following contribu-
tors for permission to reprint the material contained within
this anthology:

Edward Brathwaite for *Timehri*, which appeared in *Savacou 2*,
  Kingston, 1970. Reprinted by permission of the author.
Locksley Edmondson for *The Internationalization of Black*

Power, which appeared in *Mawazo*, Makerere University, Kampala, Uganda, vol. 1, 1968. Reprinted by permission of the author.

Merle Hodge for *The Shadow of the Whip*. Reprinted by permission of the author.

Eva Hodgson for *Bermuda and the Search for Blackness*. Reprinted by permission of the author.

Timothy O. McCartney for *What Is the Relevance of Black Power to the Bahamas?* Reprinted by permission of the author.

James Millette for *The Black Revolution in the Caribbean*, which was first published by Moko Enterprises, Trinidad, 1971. Reprinted by permission of the author.

Gordon Rohlehr for *History as Absurdity*, which first appeared in *Tapia*, vol. 1, nos. 11 & 12, Trinidad, 1970. Reprinted by permission of the author.

John Stewart for *Where Goes the Indigenous Black Church?* Reprinted by permission of the author.

Clive Y. Thomas for *Black Exploitation in the Caribbean*. Reprinted by permission of the author.

Derek Walcott for *The Muse of History*. Reprinted by permission of the author.

To Rona Liverpool,
who succeeded

and to Andrew W. Abrahams, M.D.,
who understood

CONTENTS

INTRODUCTION

The development of the style, trappings, and rhetoric of black power that touched the consciousness of many West Indians at the beginning of the seventies should have been foreseen by the politicians of the region who thought that they understood their people. But in April 1970, when black power activists in the Trinidad army mutineered, they sent island leaders into a spin of analysis from which they have only recently begun to recover.

For a time they could not understand how the young men and women whose parents they knew could shout so violently in their faces. They could not believe that all the work they had done to prepare their islands for independence meant so little to the corner "limers" and the swelling ranks of GCE* holders. It was as if their British pretensions and West Indian hypocrisies were no longer to be the fulcrums from which they could manipulate their paradoxically easygoing but litigious people.

It should not be believed that these politicians were at a far remove from the smell of poverty of their constituents or, that having once fought against white privilege, they considered their jobs finished with the playing of a new national anthem. In fact, all that one can say in retrospect is

* General Certificate of Education.

that they forgot, momentarily, that all the English-speaking islands of the Caribbean archipelago are really appendages of the colossus to the north.

To the untutored eye this fact may be, at first, difficult to see since historical and educational bonds tie these rocks to England. On close examination, however, one sees that the bonds have become frayed because of the American cultural juggernaut that smashes its way into the willing or unwilling psyches of all the islanders. It goes without saying that from this cultural onslaught, what most affects the West Indian sensibility are the rhythms, shadings, and styles of black America.

It was only a matter of time, then, that the black American's search for himself would lead West Indian activists to look with raised eyebrows at their own blackness, to think about the concentration of economic power in non-black hands, and to wonder, finally, about the meaning of their vaunted independence.

When they began to do these things, there could be no pause in the building of the scenario until the activists had come on stage, taken their bows, and departed. And these actors would know, even as they left the theater, that they were leaving behind them an audience that would alternately sit on its hands and then wildly applaud although the curtains had long since closed. For West Indian society is essentially a "pappyshow" society in which serious thought and dreadful calamities are acknowledged with the briefest of attention so that one can go about the business of one's business. It is this refusal to be unduly upset by events, to joke about tragedy, and to find melodrama in the croaking of a frog that makes the rural West Indian proletariat take himself less seriously than his politicians want him to. He understands, even if his leaders do not, that West Indian mothers raise their sons knowing that they will lose them to cities around the world. And they refuse to be sentimental about this, for they know that islands of magnificent beauty exact a penalty from their inhabitants by making wayfarers out of them. History and economics have determined this and no talk of black power can change that.

The West Indian also knows that he must be careful about waging vendettas against his fellow islanders. His home is so small that he knows how quickly allegiances are made, how Byzantine family relationships can be, how necessary it is to know someone who can grant favors. This matrix does not lend itself easily to festering hatreds, for in such a non-private society, one's vulnerability is an acknowledged fact of life. It is true that every day ex-friends take each other to court, that hungry lawyers take the pittance of peasants who file suit against their fellow sufferers because of imagined slights. But this is all a sort of pageantry, a *divertissement* from the rigors of poverty, a chance to be on center stage and to hold the pristine attention of men in magisterial wigs and gowns. An exercise, really, of the "pappyshow" mentality. So while words are thrown from generation to generation, while many people do not speak to each other for reasons they have long since forgotten, no serious calumnies are uttered, no blood spilled in the name of an idea or in defense of family honor. The people remain, therefore, steeped in hearsay and gossip, but relatively free of malevolence.

The West Indian's refusal to search for retribution and his ready acceptance of apology show, I think, the difficulty of the black power philosophy ever becoming in these islands anything more than sloganeering and a cheap device to frighten the pompous white fools of the area who insist on living in limbo on islands that have bestowed on them prestige and omniscience far out of proportion to their intrinsic worth. This does not mean that the West Indian is content with his poverty, that he does not clench his teeth during the hazardous climb from class to class, that he does not boil at the tyranny of light skin. It only means that he can be placated by so little even when this little comes late. "I want satisfaction. I must have my satisfaction," the wronged West Indian woman cries nine months after some feckless brother has dropped his load in her womb and departed. And very often all this woman wants is an acknowledgment of her lover's paternity and the odd dollar thrown her way.

The tourists and journalists who thought that the marches, the chants, the black fists raised against the sky meant that the West Indies would become a caldron of spewed hatred against whites did not understand the character of the islanders. And because they knew the depths of world-wide white barbarism against blacks, they assumed that the rhetoric of Caribbean black power carried the same weight as its progenitor from the north.

But what at bottom is the black power activist in the West Indies saying? Since the symbols of political power are already in black hands, he can only accuse these hands of having betrayed the people's trust. A common enough occurrence all over the world. He can raise his voice against the monopoly of economic power in the white and mulatto hands in his country, and here he will find more than slum dwellers urging him on in his fantasies of expropriation. "Tax them until they bleed" is one cry leveled against the white arbiters of the islands. "Cut up their lands and give them to the people" goes another that is directed against the large estate holders. These snarls are uttered in the bourgeois West Indian bastions of Woodbrook, Cane Garden, and Beverly Hills. But the black inhabitants of these areas who denounce white privilege know that through education, back-slapping, and hard work, they have put their children beyond poverty. And they know, too, that they will fight with tooth and claw against their fellow blacks if *their* properties are threatened. For it does not take long to see that the more powerful black members of the West Indian bourgeoisie only want to replace whites in the scheme of things. They only want to be recognized as the new bosses in a new order. They want to be free to rail against white venality while hiding their dirty brown hands. And it is their present ambiguity—caused by their resentment of white snobbery since they are far better educated than the whites around them and scorn for the poverty and unpredictability of the black masses—that makes them assiduously try to establish outworn prerogatives when most of the rest of the world is retreating from social Maginot lines. "Massa Day" it seems, never ends in the West Indies. It only grows blacker.

It is no easy fate to be a West Indian of sensibility and live in the Caribbean today. Many of the more serious thinkers of these islands who want to usher in a just society, who want to abolish privileges based on race or class, see themselves scorned as foolish utopians. Moreover, they have become victims of the plague of contemporaneity. They are washed with attention and then ignored as some new "hula hoop" presents itself to be promoted. Their ideas are not analyzed, but they themselves are put under a blaze of lights and their foibles and weaknesses exposed. They become the butt of everyone's humor and their effectiveness is destroyed.

It is during this period of retrenchment, this time of trying to exorcise, forever, the West Indian tendency to genuflect in front of white altars, that our artists may have something to say that we may be ready to hear. The writers in this book have traveled many roads and have searched hard for the measure of themselves. They present to us shards of thought on present black moods in the Caribbean. They know, as all artists must, that life is not worth living if it is unexplored and that any country that embraces its artists nurtures the genesis of revolution. For it is the duty of these men and women to see the decaying stem of the rose and to smell the manure that makes the oleander bloom.

And so Derek Walcott, a man of glowing talent and sensibility, whom Robert Graves notes "handles English with a closer understanding of its inner magic than most (if not any) of his English-born contemporaries," writes in *The Muse of History*, a eulogy to the fruit born of the pain of the middle passage. He looks at the people we have become and concludes: "I say to the ancestor who sold me, and to the ancestor who bought me, I have no father, I want no such father, although I can understand you, black ghost, white ghost, when you both whisper 'history,' for if I attempt to forgive you both I am falling into your idea of history which justifies and explains and expiates, and it is not mine to forgive, my memory cannot summon any filial love, since your features are anonymous and erased and I have no wish and no power to pardon. . . . but to you, inwardly forgiven grandfathers, I, like the more honest of my race, give a strange thanks. I give the strange and bitter and yet ennobling thanks for the monumental groaning and soldering of two great worlds, like the halves of a fruit seamed by its own bitter juice, that exiled from your own Edens you have placed me in the wonder of another, and that was my inheritance and your gift."

Edward Brathwaite states in *Timehri* that "the problem of and for West Indian artists and intellectuals is that having been born and educated within [a] fragmented culture, they start out in the world without a sense of 'wholeness.'" He looks at the experience of the Guyanese artist Aubrey Williams who, in gazing at the *timehri* (rock signs, paintings, petroglyphs, etc.) of the Warraou Indians of his native Guyana, understood how this primordial life—almost unknown to him—had been an influence on his sensibility and style. And Brathwaite bids us all journey into the past to find the African and Amerindian in us, for only then can we become ourselves and measure the rhythm of our own creativity.

James Millette and Gordon Rohlehr both teach at the University of the West Indies, St. Augustine, Trinidad. Millette tries to explain the currents of anxiety that are abroad in contemporary Trinidad. He looks at the heightened expectation of the poor who seem to demand that independence should mean more than a flag and a newly rich bourgeoisie, and he says that "the final answer to the problems of many people all over the world, who have the same experience that we have, involves in general a universal attack on the system which has created the poverty and dispossession that has made necessary the black revolution in Trinidad and Tobago."

Rohlehr's *History as Absurdity* is really a literary critique of *From Columbus to Castro* and other writings of the Prime Minister of Trinidad and Tobago, Dr. Eric Williams. Rohlehr says that this book "is meant to be both the historian's bible for the new era, and the great work from with the national movement in Trinidad and Tobago will derive its intellectual dynamic against the deepening pressures of this age of neo-colonialism." He feels, however, that Williams' writing of history "has hardly developed since *Capitalism and Slavery*, [and that] he still sees his job as the gathering together of a stockpile of facts to be hurled like bricks against dead and living imperialists." The work is deficient, states Rohlehr, because the author cannot see himself as merely part of a historical link in the fight against colonialism. He must make grandiose claims and assume heavy burdens because he feels that no one else is capable of writing history or deftly playing politics. And so Rohlehr ends on a somber and pessimistic note. He says that "the 1930s generation has run its time and is slowly taking its place as just another link in the common chain. The 1950s generation will soon begin its mistakes. The people of the forties seem to be quite bewildered, caught as they are, between the embarrassing frenzy of an aging rebel and the posturing of youth, who also cannot recognize themselves as simple common links in the chain. In the struggle for power which characterizes the end of this era, as of any other, what is being lost is the sense of historical continuity."

Merle Hodge reminds us of the inequality of the sexes in the West Indies. In *The Shadow of the Whip* she notes that Massa Day will never end in the West Indies until there is equality of the sexes. For the West Indies is still a male-dominated society in which women quickly learn their place, where man's infidelities are encouraged and woman's indiscretions denounced.

Clive Y. Thomas argues in *Black Exploitation in the Caribbean* that it is foolish to think that in buying 51 per cent of "the local expression of a multinational corporation" one is controlling that plant. Local plants have no say in the price, for example, of bauxite, in the levels of investment, or in their own output. Consequently, says Thomas, national control can only begin at the point of outright ownership. "It is only when there is effective national ownership that there is opportunity to develop a strategy of control. In other words, the history of these institutions precludes a divorce of ownership and control. Foreign ownership means foreign control."

Eva Hodgson writes movingly about growing up black in Bermuda among black islanders who thought themselves superior to their kinsmen further south while they bowed in submission to the myths of white infallibility. And Timothy O. McCartney wonders about the relevance of black power to the tourist-oriented society of the Bahamas.

John Stewart, who left the Caribbean years ago and is now an academician in California, returns spiritually to his birthplace, Trinidad, and evokes for us the kinds of religious experiences that so many of us have refused to give voice to. In his piece *Where Goes the Indigenous Black Church?* Stewart paints a moving portrait of the nearly illiterate preacher who, because he accepted the call of the church from his father, will try to pass on that devotion to his sons. But *they* will definitely find no reward in belonging to a proletarian church, and they will almost certainly make their own overtures to the churches of the bourgeoisie.

It is left to Locksley Edmondson to remind us that the search for black power is world-wide and cannot now be stopped. In *The Internationalization of Black Power* he informs us that it is not an example of contemporary sentimentality to talk fervently about Pan-Africanism. For although we do not move as one, although there are disparate sounds among us, black people have begun not only to probe their commonality, but to understand that the bonds that bind us are greater than the shibboleths that separate us.

There is no reason, then, not to relish the "Africanness" of West Indian society, for the children of Africa are in the majority there, and while one approves of the diversity of the many cultures of the area, to try to stifle the African in us because we are years removed from the immediate sounds of drums is to stifle ourselves.

Here, then, are the views of ten West Indians as they face the questions of color and identity in their native lands—lands that for too long refused to face the spider of prejudice as it spun its web in the face of dark-skinned people and told them that the barriers they observed were economic rather than racial. West Indian artists are not yet cherished and their vision is taken lightly. But they will continue to try to touch the sensibilities of their people until the day comes when no black child in soaring fantasy will silently recite with Virtue in *The Blacks:* "I am white, it's milk that denotes me, it's the lily, the dove, quicklime and the clear conscience, it's Poland with its eagle and snow!"

Derek Walcott

THE MUSE OF HISTORY: AN ESSAY

> *History is the nightmare from which
> I am trying to awake.*
> Joyce

I

The common experience of the New World, even for its
patrician writers whose veneration of the Old is read as the
idolatry of the mestizo, is colonialism. They too are victims
of tradition, but they remind us of our debt to the great
dead, that those who break a tradition first hold it in awe.
They perversely encourage disfavor, but because their sense
of the past is of a timeless, yet habitable, moment, the New
World owes them more than it does those who wrestle with
that past, for their veneration subtilizes an arrogance which
is tougher than violent rejection. They know that by openly
fighting tradition we perpetuate it, that revolutionary literature is a filial impulse, and that maturity is the assimilation
of the features of every ancestor.

When these writers cunningly describe themselves as clas-
sicists and pretend an indifference to change, it is with an

irony as true of the colonial anguish as the fury of the radical. If they appear to be phony aristocrats, it is because they have gone past the confrontation of history, that Medusa of the New World.

These writers reject the idea of history as time for its original concept as myth, the partial recall of the race. For them history is fiction, subject to a fitful muse, memory. Their philosophy, based on a contempt for historic time, is revolutionary, for what they repeat to the New World is its simultaneity with the Old. Their vision of man is elemental, a being inhabited by presences, not a creature chained to his past. Yet the method by which we are taught the past, the progress from motive to event, is the same by which we read narrative fiction. In time every event becomes an exertion of memory and is thus subject to invention. The further the facts, the more history petrifies into myth. Thus, as we grow older as a race, we grow aware that history is written, that it is a kind of literature without morality, that in its actuaries the ego of the race is indissoluble and that everything depends on whether we write this fiction through the memory of hero or of victim.

In the New World servitude to the muse of history has produced a literature of recrimination and despair, a literature of revenge written by the descendants of slaves or a literature of remorse written by the descendants of masters. Because this literature serves historical truth, it yellows into polemic or evaporates in pathos. The truly tough aesthetic of the New World neither explains nor forgives history. It refuses to recognize it as a creative or culpable force. This shame and awe of history possess poets of the Third World who think of language as enslavement and who, in a rage for identity, respect only incoherence or nostalgia.

II

The great poets of the New World, from Whitman to Neruda, reject this sense of history. Their vision of man in the New World is Adamic. In their exuberance he is still capable of enormous wonder. Yet he has paid his accounts to Greece and Rome and walks in a world without monuments and ruins. They exhort him against the fearful magnet of older civilizations. Even in Borges, where the genius seems secretive, immured from change, it celebrates an elation which is vulgar and abrupt, the life of the plains given an instant archaism by the hieratic style. Violence is felt with the simultaneity of history. So the death of a gaucho does not merely repeat, but is, the death of Caesar. Fact evaporates into myth. This is not the jaded cynicism which sees nothing new under the sun, it is an elation which sees everything as renewed. Like Borges too, the poet St.-John Perse conducts us from the mythology of the past to the present without a tremor of adjustment. This is the revolutionary spirit at its deepest, it recalls the spirit to arms. In Perse there is the greatest width of elemental praise of winds, seas, rains. The revolutionary or cyclic vision is as deeply rooted as the patrician syntax. What Perse glorifies is not veneration but the perennial freedom; his hero remains the wanderer, the man who moves through the ruins of great civilizations with all his worldly goods by caravan or pack mule, the poet carrying entire cultures in his head, bitter perhaps, but unencumbered. His are poems of massive or solitary migrations through the elements. They are the same in spirit as the poems of Whitman or Neruda, for they seek spaces where praise of the earth is ancestral.

III

New World poets who see the "classic style" as stasis must see it also as historical degradation, rejecting it as the language of the master. This self-torture arises when the poet also sees history as language, when he limits his memory to the suffering of the victim. Their admirable wish to honor the degraded ancestor limits their language to phonetic pain, the groan of suffering, the curse of revenge. The tone

of the past becomes an unbearable burden, for they must
abuse the master or hero in his own language, and this implies self-deceit. Their view of Caliban is of the enraged
pupil. They cannot separate the rage of Caliban from the
beauty of his speech when the speeches of Caliban are equal
in their elemental power to those of his tutor. The language
of the torturer mastered by the victim. This is viewed as
servitude, not as victory.

But who in the New World does not have a horror of the
past, whether his ancestor was torturer or victim? Who, in
the depth of conscience, is not silently screaming for pardon
or for revenge? The pulse of New World history is the rac-
ing pulse beat of fear, the tiring cycles of stupidity and
greed. The tongues above our prayers utter the pain of entire races to the darkness of a Manichean God: *Dominus
illuminatio mea*, for what was brought to this New World
under the guise of divine light, the light of the sword blade
and the light of *dominus illuminatio mea*, was the same
iridescent serpent brought by a contaminating Adam, the
same tortured Christ exhibited with Christian exhaustion,
but what was also brought in the seeded entrails of the
slave was a new nothing, a darkness which intensified the
old faith.

In time the slave surrendered to amnesia. That amnesia
is the true history of the New World. That is our inheritance,
but to try and understand why this happened, to condemn
or justify is also the method of history, and these explana-
tions are always the same: This happened because of that,
this was understandable because, and in days men were such.
These recriminations exchanged, the contrition of the master replaces the vengeance of the slave, and here colonial
literature is most pietistic, for it can accuse great art of
feudalism and excuse poor art as suffering. To radical poets
poetry seems the homage of resignation, an essential fatalism.
But it is not the pressure of the past which torments great
poets but the weight of the present:

> there are so many dead,
> and so many dikes the red sun breached,
> and so many heads battering hulls
> and so many hands that have closed over kisses
> and so many things that I want to forget.
>
> Neruda

The sense of history in poets lives rawly along their nerves:

> My land without name, without America,
> equinoctial stamen, lance-like purple,
> your aroma rose through my roots
> into the cup I drained, into the most tenuous
> word not yet born in my mouth.
>
> *Neruda*

It is this awe of the numinous, this elemental privilege of naming the new world which annihilates history in our great poets, an elation common to all of them, whether they are aligned by heritage to Crusoe and Prospero or to Friday and Caliban. They reject ethnic ancestry for faith in elemental man. The vision, the "democratic vista," is not metaphorical, it is a social necessity. A political philosophy rooted in elation would have to accept belief in a second Adam, the re-creation of the entire order, from religion to the simplest domestic rituals. The myth of the noble savage would not be revived, for that myth never emanated from the savage but has always been the nostalgia of the Old World, its longing for innocence. The great poetry of the New World does not pretend to such innocence, its vision is not naïve. Rather, like its fruits, its savor is a mixture of the acid and the sweet, the apples of its second Eden have the tartness of experience. In such poetry there is a bitter memory and it is the bitterness that dries last on the tongue. It is the acidulous that supplies its energy. The golden apples of this sun are shot with acid. The taste of Neruda is citric, the *Pomme de Cythère* of Césaire sets the teeth on edge,

the savor of Perse is of salt fruit at the sea's edge, the sea
grape, the "fat-poke," the sea almond. For us in the archipelago the tribal memory is salted with the bitter memory of
migration.

To such survivors, to all the decimated tribes of the New
World who did not suffer extinction, their degraded arrival
must be seen as the beginning, not the end of our history.
The shipwrecks of Crusoe and of the crew in *The Tempest*
are the end of an Old World. It should matter nothing to
the New World if the Old is again determined to blow itself
up, for an obsession with progress is not within the psyche
of the recently enslaved. That is the bitter secret of the
apple. The vision of progress is the rational madness of history seen as sequential time, of a dominated future. Its
imagery is absurd. In the history books the discoverer sets a
shod foot on virgin sand, kneels, and the savage also kneels
from his bushes in awe. Such images are stamped on the
colonial memory, such heresy as the world's becoming holy
from Crusoe's footprint or the imprint of Columbus' knee.
These blasphemous images fade, because these hieroglyphs
of progress are basically comic. And if the idea of the New
and the Old becomes increasingly absurd, what must happen
to our sense of time, what else can happen to history itself,
but that it too is becoming absurd? This is not existentialism. Adamic, elemental man cannot be existential. His first
impulse is not self-indulgence but awe, and existentialism is
simply the myth of the noble savage gone baroque. Such
philosophies of freedom are born in cities. Existentialism is
as much nostalgia as is Rousseau's sophisticated primitivism,
as sick a recurrence in French thought as the isle of Cythera,
whether it is the tubercular, fevered imagery of Watteau or
the same fever turned delirious in Rimbaud and Baudelaire.
The poets of the "new Aegean," of the Isles of the Blest,
the Fortunate Isles, of the remote Bermudas, of Prospero's
isle, of Crusoe's Juan Fernandez, of Cythera, of all those
rocks named like the beads of a chaplet, they know that the
old vision of paradise wrecks here.

I want to hear a song in which the rainbow breaks
and the curlew alights among forgotten shores
I want the liana creeping on the palm-tree
(on the trunk of the present 'tis our stubborn future)
I want the conquistador with unsealed armour
lying down in death of perfumed flowers,
the foam censing a sword gone rusty
in the pure blue flight of slow wild cactuses

Césaire

But to most writers of the archipelago who contemplate only the shipwreck, the New World offers not elation but cynicism, a despair at the vices of the Old which they feel must be repeated. Their malaise is an oceanic nostalgia for the older culture and a melancholy at the new, and this can go as deep as a rejection of the untamed landscape, a yearning for ruins. To such writers the death of civilizations is architectural, not spiritual, seeded in their memories is an imagery of vines ascending broken columns, of dead terraces, of Europe as a nourishing museum. They believe in the responsibility of tradition, but what they are in awe of is not tradition, which is alert, alive, simultaneous, but of history, and the same is true of the new magnifiers of Africa. For these their deepest loss is of the old gods, the fear that it is worship which has enslaved progress. Thus the humanism of politics replaces religion. They see such gods as part of the process of history, subjected like the tribe to cycles of achievement and despair. Because the Old World concept of God is anthropomorphic, the New World slave was forced to remake himself in His image, despite such phrases as "God is light, and in Him is no darkness," and at this point of intersecting faiths the enslaved poet and enslaved priest surrendered their power. But the tribe in bondage learned to fortify itself by cunning assimilation of the religion of the Old World. What seemed to be surrender was redemption. What seemed the loss of tradition was its renewal. What seemed the death of faith was its rebirth.

IV

Eliot speaks of the culture of a people as being the in-
carnation of its religion. If this is true, in the New World
we have to ask this faceted question: (1) Whether the religion taught to the black slave has been absorbed as belief,
(2) whether it has been altered by this absorption, and (3)
whether wholly absorbed or absorbed and altered, it must
now be rejected. In other terms, can an African culture
exist, except on the level of polemical art or politics, without an African religion, and if so, which African religion?

The spectacle of mediocre talents raising old totems is
more shameful than the faith of the convert which they
ridicule, but the flare of a literary religion is brief, for faith
needs more than style. At this stage the polemic poet, like
the politician, will wish to produce epic work, to summon
the grandeur of the past, not as myth but as history, and to
prophesy in the way that Fascist architecture can be viewed
as prophecy. Yet the more ambitious the zeal, the more
diffuse and forced it becomes, the more it roots into research, until the imagination surrenders to the glorification
of history, the ear becomes enslaved, the glorifiers of the
tom-tom ignoring the dynamo. These epic poets create an
artificial past, a defunct cosmology without the tribal faith.

What remains in the archipelago is the fragmentation
into schisms, the private cosmology of the wayside preacher.
Every day in these islands the sidewalk blossoms with such
victims, minds disfigured by their attempt to comprehend
both worlds unless they create a heaven of which they are
the center. Like the wayside prophets, the "epic" poet in
the islands looks to anthropology, to a catalogue of forgotten
gods, to midden fragments, artifacts, and the unfinished
phrases of a dead speech. These engage in masochistic rec-
ollection. The epic-minded poet looks around these islands
and finds no ruins, and because all epic is based on the visible presence of ruins, wind-bitten or sea-bitten, the poet

celebrates what little there is, the rusted slave wheel of the sugar factory, cannon, chains, the crusted amphora of cut-throats, all the paraphernalia of degradation and cruelty which we exhibit as history, not as masochism, as if the ovens of Auschwitz and Hiroshima were the temples of the race. Morbidity is the inevitable result, and that is the tone of any literature which respects such a history and bases its truth on shame or on revenge.

And yet it is there that the epic poetry of the tribe originates, in its identification with Hebraic suffering, the migration, the hope of deliverance from bondage. There was this difference, that the passage over our Red Sea was not from bondage to freedom, but its opposite, so that the tribes arrived at their New Canaan chained. There is this residual feeling in much of our literature, the wailing by strange waters for a lost home. It survives in our politics, the subdued search for a Moses. The epic concept was compressed in the folk lyric, the mass longing in chanter and chorus, couplet and refrain. The revivalist poems drew their strength from the self-hypnotic nature of their responses, interminable in monody as the tribal hope.

> I know moonrise, I know star-rise,
> Lay this body down,
> I go to my Lord in the evening of the day,
> Lay this body down.

But this monody is not only resigned but martial:

> Joshua fit de battle of Jericho,
> Jericho, Jericho,
> Joshua fit de battle of Jericho,
> And the walls come tumbling down.

The epic poem is not a literary project. It is already written; it was written in the mouths of the tribe, a tribe which had courageously yielded its history.

V

While the Old Testament epics of bondage and deliverance provided the slave with a political parallel, the ethics of Christianity tempered his vengeance and appeared to deepen his passivity. To his masters this world was not new but an extension of the old. Their vision of an earthly paradise was denied him, and the reward offered in the name of Christian suffering would come after his death. All this we know, but the phenomenon is the zeal with which the slave accepted both the Christian and the Hebraic, resigned his gaze to the death of his pantheon, and yet deliberately began to invest a decaying faith with a political belief. Historians cannot chronicle this, except they go by the statistics of conversion. There is no moment of a mass tribal conversion equal to the light's unhorsing of Saul, what we were told to believe instead was a slow, massive groan of surrender, the immense laborious conversion of the defeated into good niggers, or true Christians, and certainly songs such as this one seem to be the most contemptible expression of the beaten:

> I'm going to lay down my sword and shield,
> Down by the riverside, down by the riverside . . .
> I ain't going study war no more,
> Study war no more . . .

How can we teach this as history? Aren't those the words of the whitewashed, the defeated, isn't this the Christian treachery that seduces revenge, that led the exhausted tribes to betray their gods? A new generation looks back on such conversion with contempt, for where are the songs of triumph, the defiance of the captured warrior, where are the nostalgic battle chants and the seasonal songs of harvest, the seeding of the great African pastoral? This generation sees in the epic poetry of the work song and the early blues self-contempt and inertia, but the deep truth is that pinioned and humiliated in body as the slave was, there is, beyond simple fortitude, a note of aggression, and what a later generation sees as defeat is really the willing of spiritual victory, for the captured warrior and the tribal poet had chosen the very battleground which the captor proposed, the soul:

> I am a warrior, out in the field,
> And I can sing, and I can shout,
> And I can tell it all about that Jesus died for me,
> When I get over yonder in the happy paradise,
> When I get over yonder in the field.

What was captured from the captor was his God, for the subject African had come to the New World in an elemental intimacy with nature, with a profounder terror of blasphemy than the exhausted, hypocritical Christian. He understood too quickly the Christian rituals of a whipped, tortured, and murdered redeemer, though he may have recoiled at dividing and eating his flesh for in primal cultures gods defeat each other like warriors and for warriors there is no conversion in defeat. There are many such warriors in the history of the archipelago, but the true history is of the tribe's conversion, and it is this which is our concern. It returns us to Eliot's pronouncement, that a culture cannot exist without a religion, and to other pronouncements irradiating that idea, that an epic poetry cannot exist without a religion. It is the beginning of the poetry of the New World. And the language used is, like the religion, that of the conqueror of the God. But the slave had wrested God from his captor.

In tribal, elemental poetry, the epic experience of the race is compressed in metaphor. In an oral tradition the mode is simple, the response open-ended so that each new poet can add his lines to the form, a process very much like weaving or the dance, based on the concept that the history of the tribe is endless. There is no dying fall, no egotistical signature of effect, in short, no pathos. The blues is not pathos, not the individual voice, it is a tribal mode, and each new oral poet can contribute his couplet, and this is based on the concept that the tribe, inured to despair, will also survive: There is no beginning but no end. The new poet enters a flux and withdraws, as the weaver continues the pattern, hand to hand and mouth to mouth, as the rock-pile convict passes the sledge:

> Many days of sorrow, many nights of woe,
> Many days of sorrow, many nights of woe,
> And a ball and chain, everywhere I go.

No history, but flux, and the only sustenance, myth:

> Moses lived till he got old,
> Where shall I be?

The difference is in the intensity of celebration. The pietistic rhythm of the missionary is speeded to a martial frenzy which the slave adapts to a triumphal tribal mode. Good, the missionary and merchant must have thought, once we've got them swinging and clapping, all will be peace, but their own God was being taken away from merchant and missionary by a submerged force that rose at ritual gatherings, where the subconscious rhythm rose and took possession and where in fact the Hebraic-European God was changing color, for the names of the sub-deities did not matter, Saint Ursula or Saint Urzulie; the Catholic pantheon adapted easily to African pantheism. Catholic mystery adapted easily to African magic. Not all accepted the white man's God. As prologue to the Haitian Revolution, Boukman was invoking Damballa in the Bois Cayman. Blood sacrifices, warrior initiations, tortures, escapes, revolts, even the despair of slaves who went mad and ate dirt, these are the historical evidence, but what is finally important is that the race or the tribes were converted, they became Christian. But no race is converted against its will. The slave-master now encountered a massive pliability. The slave converted himself, he changed weapons, spiritual weapons, and as he adapted his master's religion, he also adapted his language, and it is here that what we can look at as our poetic tradition begins. Now began the new naming of things:

Epic was compressed in the folk legend. The act of imagination was the creative effort of the tribe. Later such legends may be written by individual poets, but their beginnings are oral, familial, the poetry of firelight which illuminates the faces of a tight, primal hierarchy. But even oral literature forces itself toward hieroglyph and alphabet. Today, still in many islands, the West Indian poet is faced with a language which he hears but cannot write because there are no symbols for such a language and because the closer he brings hand and word to the precise inflections of the inner language and to the subtlest accuracies of his ear, the more chaotic his symbols will appear on the page, the smaller the regional dialect, the more eccentric his representation of it will become, so his function remains the old one of being filter and purifier, never losing the tone and strength of the common speech as he uses the hieroglyphs, symbols, or alphabet of the official one. Now two of the greatest poets of this archipelago have come from French-patois speaking islands. St.-John Perse, born and reared until late adolescence in Guadeloupe, and Aimé Césaire, the Martiniquan. Both have the colonial experience of language, one from privilege, the other from deprivation. Let it not be important for now that one is white, the other black. Both are Frenchmen, both are poets who write in French. Well, to begin with it is Césaire's language which is the more abstruse, more difficult, more surrealist, while Perse's French is classic. Césaire has not written his great poem, *Cahier d'un Retour au Pays Natal*, in dialect, but we must pay attention to its tone. For all the complexity of its surrealism, its sometimes invented words, it sounds, to at least one listener familiar with French patois, like a poem written tonally in Creole. Those tonal qualities are tartness and impatience, but the language of Césaire in this great revolutionary poem, or rather a poem partially appropriated by revolutionaries, is not proletarian. The tone of Perse is also majestic, it marches a path of inevitable conquest appropriating as it proceeds, and to the reader trying to listen purely to the language of either poet without prejudice, without subliminal whispers of history, they have at least one thing in common: authority. Their diction has other similarities, for instance, form. In *Cahier d'un Retour au Pays Natal*, as well as in the prose poems of Perse from the Antillean *Éloges* to *Chronique* and beyond, there is a strict, synonymous armature shared within the tradition of the metropolitan language, and which both must have felt to be an inheritance despite their racial and social differences, despite the distance of Perse from the dialect of house servants and of fishermen, despite the fealty of Césaire to that dialect. The sources of that diction are both ancient and contemporary: the Bible and the tribal ode as well as French surrealist poetry, the proletarian hymns of Whitman, and the oral or written legends of other civilizations, for Perse the East and the Mediterranean, for Césaire the Hebraic Mediterranean and Africa. In visual structure the poetry of both shares the symmetry of the prose ode, the appearance of translation from an older epic which invests their poems with an air of legend. Now here are two colonials, or more precisely, two poets whose formative perceptions, whose apprehension of the visible worlds of their very different childhoods, were made numinous by their elation in the metropolitan language, and whose very different visions created indisputable masterpieces, and, here is the point, without doing violence to the language itself, in fact perpetuating its grandeur through opposite beliefs, Perse through prophecy and nostalgia, Césaire through nostalgia and polemic. Yet, as a translator, I would rather attempt an equivalent in English to Perse than to Césaire, for the simple reason that Perse is perhaps simpler, for where his language grows abstruse in the vocabularies of archaeology, marine biology, botany, and so forth, the language of Césaire skims the subtleties of modern surrealism. Yet as an Antillean, I feel more akin to Césaire's tone.

I do not know if one poet is indebted to the other, but whatever the bibliographical truth is, one acknowledges not an exchange of influences, not imitation, but the tidal advance of the metropolitan language, of its empire, if you like, which carries simultaneously, fed by such strong colonial tributaries, poets of such different beliefs as Rimbaud, Char, Claudel, Perse, and Césaire. It is the language which is the empire, and great poets are not its vassals but its princes. We continue to categorize these poets by the wrong process, that is, by history. We continue to fiddle with the obvious limitations of dialect because of chauvinism, but the great poem of Césaire's could not be written in a French Creole dialect because there are no words for some of its concepts, there are no equivalent nouns for its objects, and because even if these were suddenly found, they could not be visually expressed without the effort of an insane philologist. Both poets manipulate a supreme, visionary rhetoric that carries over into English. Sometimes they sound identical:

(1)   Narrow path of the surge in the blur of fables . . .

(2)   Wandering, what did we know of our ancestral bed, all blazoned
      though it were in that speckled wood of the Islands?
      . . . There
      was no name for us in the ancient bronze gong of the old
      family house. There was no name for us in our mother's oratory
      (jacaranda wood or cedar), nor in the golden antennae quivering
      in the head-dresses of our guardians, women of colour. We were
      not in the lute-maker's wood, in the spinet or the harp: nor . . .

(3)   I want to hear a song in which the rainbow breaks
      and the curlew alights along forgotten shores

I want the liana creeping on the palm-tree
(on the trunk of the present 'tis our stubborn
   future)
I want the conquistador with unsealed armour
lying down in death of perfumed flowers,
the foam censing a sword gone rusty
in the pure blue flight of slow wild cactuses.

(4)   Master of the three roads a man stands before you
        who
           walked much,
        Master of the three roads a man stands before you
           who walked on hands who walked on feet who
           walked on the belly who walked on the
           behind.
        Since Elam. Since Akkad. Since Sumer.
        Master of the three roads a man stands before you
        who
           has carried much.
        And truly, friends, I carried since Elam, since Akkad,
           since Sumer.

Perse and Césaire, men of diametrically challenging back-
grounds, racial opposites to use the language of politics, one
patrician and conservative, the other proletarian and revolutionary, classic and romantic, Prospero and Caliban, all such
opposites balance easily, but they balance on the axis of a
shared sensibility, and this sensibility, with or deprived of the
presence of a visible tradition, is the sensibility of walking to
a New World. Perse sees in this New World vestiges of
the old, of order and of hierarchy, Césaire sees in it evidence
of past humiliations and the need for a new order, but the
deeper truth is that both poets perceive this New World
through mystery. Their language tempts us to endless quotation, there are moments when one hears both voices simultaneously, until the tone is one voice from these different
men. If we think of one as poor and the other as privileged
when we read their addresses to the New World, if we must

see one as black and one as white, we are not only dividing this sensibility by the process of the sociologist, but we are denying the range of either poet, the power of compassion and the power of fury. One is not making out a case for assimilation and for the common simplicity of all men, we are interested in their differences, openly, but what astonishes us in both poets is their elation, their staggering elation in possibility. And one is not talking of an ideal possible society, for you will find that only in the later work of Perse, a society which is inaccessible by its very grandeur, but of the elation in presences which exists in *Éloges* and in *Pour Fêter une Enfance*, the possibility of the individual Caribbean man, African, European, or Asian in ancestry, the enormous, gently opening morning of his possibility, his body touched with dew, his nerves as subtilized to sensation as the mimosa, his memory, whether of grandeur or of pain, gradually erasing itself as recurrent drizzles cleanse the ancestral or tribal markings from the coral skull, the possibility of a man and his language waking to wonder here. As the language of Perse later becomes hammered and artificial, so does the rhetoric of Césaire move toward the heraldic, but their first great work is as deeply rooted and supple as a vine.

But these poems are in French. The fact that they have now begun to influence English poetry from the archipelago is significant because they are powerful works and all power attracts to itself, but their rhetoric is unmanageable for our minor "revolutionary" poets who assume a grandeur without a language to create it, for these imitators see both poems through history, or through sociology; they are seduced by their subjects. Therefore there is now a brood of thin, querulous fledglings who steal fragments of Césaire for their own nests, and yet these fledglings will condemn Perse as a different animal, a white poet. These convulsions of bad poetry appear when the society is screaming for change.

Because we think of tradition as history, one group of anatomists claims that this tradition is wholly African and that its responses are alerted through the nostalgia of one race, but that group must allow the Asian and the Mediterranean the same fiction, and then the desolate terraces of Perse's epic memory will be as West Indian to the Middle Easterners among us as the kingdoms of the Guinea Coast are to Césaire or the poetry of China is to the Chinese grocer. If we can psychologize, divide, trace these degenerations easily, then we must accept the miracle of possibility which every poet demonstrates. The Carribbean sensibility is not marinated in the past. It is not exhausted. It is new. But it is its complexity, not its historically explained simplicities, which is new. Its traces of melancholy are the chemical survivals of the blood which remain after the slave's and the indentured worker's convalescence. It will survive the malaria of nostalgia and the delirium of revenge just as it survived its self-contempt.

Thus, while many critics of contemporary Commonwealth verse reject imitation, the basis of the tradition, for originality, the false basis of innovation, they represent eventually the old patronizing attitude adapted to contemporaneous politics, for their demand for naturalness, novelty, originality, or truth is again based on preconceptions of behavior. They project reflexes as anticipated as the exuberance, spontaneity, and refreshing dialect of the tribe. Certain performances are called for, including the fashionable incoherence of revolutionary anger, and everyone is again appeased, the masochist-critic by the required attack on his "values," the masochist-poet by the approval of his victim. Minstrel postures, in their beginnings, are hard to identify from private truths, but their familiarity soon establishes the old formulae of entertainment. Basically, the anger of the black is entertainment, or theater, if it makes an aesthetic out of anger, and this is no different in its "naturalness" than the legendary joy or spontaneous laughter of the minstrel. It is still nightclub and cabaret, professional fire-eating and dancing on broken bottles. The critic-tourist can only gasp at such naturalness. He wouldn't care to try it himself, really. We are back to Dr. Johnson's female preacher.

The liberal warms to the speech of the ghetto in a way

quite contemptible to the poet, for the benignity of the liberal critic perpetuates the sociological conditions of that speech, despite his access to anger. What he really preaches again, but this time through criticism, is the old separate-but-equal argument. Blacks are different, and the pathos is that most blacks have been led to believe this, and into the tragedy of proclaiming their difference. The theories clash, for the radical seeks to equate the deprived up to the status of the privileged, while the liberal and his unconscious accomplices, the poets of the ghetto and of "revolutionary rhetoric," fear to lose "their own thing" if they let thought and education widen by materialist benefits. Often it is the educated and privileged poet who masks his education and privilege behind a fake exoticism of poverty and the pastoral. They write one way and speak another. There has been the treason of clerks, and now we have the treason of the intellectuals.

The degeneration of technique, when technique is an open question, hides itself in originality. Bad verse written by blacks is better than good verse written by whites, because, say the revolutionaries, the same standards do not apply. This is seen as pride, as the opposite of inferiority. So too, one can isolate in this writer's general demeanor of style that belligerent naïveté or a joy unqualified which characterizes a pubescent literature. One which accepts subconsciously a condition of being praised or corrected, which may resist but also insinuates by resistance, the correctives of a "superior" or at least an older discipline or tradition. It is a flaw which also sees history as a ladder of achievement, but it is a competitive energy which either fails often from exhaustion or amazes by its prolixity. It is manic, it is inferior, but it is certain of its direction and challenges. It engages its peers. For purity, then, for pure black Afro-Aryanism, only the unsoiled black is valid, and West Indianism is a taint, and other strains adulterate him. The extremists, the purists, are beginning to exercise those infections, so that a writer of "mixed," hence "degenerate," blood can be nothing stronger than a liberal. This will develop a rich individualism through a deeper bitterness, it will increase egocentricity and isolation, because such writers and poets already have more complex values. They will seem more imperialistic, nostalgic, and out of the impetus of the West Indian proletariat, because they cannot simplify intricacies of race and the thought of the race. They will become hermits or rogue animals, increasingly exotic hybrids, broken bridges between two ancestries, Europe and the Third World of Africa and Asia, in other words, they will become islands. Because of this isolation their ironic fate will be to appear inaccessible, irrelevant, remote. The machinery of radicalism which makes culture-heroes of more violent writers and which makes a virtue of immediacy will not include them. They are condemned to middle age.

And all of this has sprung, at the root, from a rejection of language. The new cult of incoherence, of manic repetition, glorifies the apprentice, and it also atrophies the young who are warned against assimilation. It is as if the instinct of the black is still escape, escape to the labyrinth, escape to a special oblivion removed from the banalities of poverty and from the weight of a new industrial imperialism, that of absentee "power structures" who control the archipelago's economy. That there will always be abrupt eruptions of defiance is almost irrelevant itself because the impulse of such eruptions, their political philosophy, remains simplistic and shallow. That all blacks are beautiful is an enervating statement, that all blacks are brothers more a reprimand than a charter, that the people must have power almost their death wish, for the real power of this time is silent. Art cannot last long in this shale. It crumbles like those slogans, fragments and shards of a historical fault. Power now becomes increasingly divided and tribal when it is based on genetics. It leads to the righteous secondary wars of the Third World, to the self-maiming of civil wars, the frontier divisions of third-rate, Third World powers, manipulated or encouraged by the first powers. Genocides increase, tribal wars increase and become increasingly hallucinatory and remote. Nigeria, Bangla-

desh, Vietnam, the Middle East, Greece, the Spains of our
era. The provincial revolutions can only spare a general compassion because they know who manages or stages such things.
They believe that the same manipulation is beneath them.

The revolution is here. It was always here. It does not
need the décor of African tourism or the hip postures and
speech of metropolitan ghettos. Change the old word "slum"
for the new word "ghetto" and you have the psychology of
funk, a market psychology that, within a year of the physical
revolution, has been silently appropriated by Mediterranean
and Asian merchants. Soul is a commodity. Soul is an outfit.
The "metropolitan" emphasis of the "revolution" has
clouded the condition of the peasant, of the inevitably
rooted man, and the urban revolutionary is by imitation or
by nature rootless and a drifter, fashionably so, and in time a
potential exile. The peasant cannot spare himself these city
changes. He is the true African who does not need to pro-
claim it.

ON HISTORY AS EXILE

Postures of metropolitan cynicism must be assumed by
the colonial in exile if he is not to feel lost, unless he prefers
utter isolation or the desperate, noisy nostalgia of fellow
exiles. This cynicism is an attempt to enter the sense of
history which is within every Englishman and European, but
which he himself has never felt toward Africa or Asia. There
develops the other sense, that the history of Africa or of
Asia is inferior, and we see how close we draw to madness
here, for this sense qualifies not the significance of an event,
but the event itself, the action of the event as second class.
The exile will not be argued out of this. He has chosen to
see history this way, and that is his vision. The simplifica-
tions of imperialism, of the colonial heritage, are more dignified, for these gave brutish tribes their own dignity. But
even less honest than the colonial in exile is the generation
after him, which wants to effect a eugenic leap from im-

perialism to independence by longing for the ancestral dignity of the wanderer-warrior. Mysterious customs. Defunct gods. Sacred rites. As much as the colonial, however, they are children of the nineteenth-century ideal, the romance of redcoat and savage warrior, their simplification of choosing to play Indian instead of cowboy, filtered through films and adolescent literature, is the hallucination of imperial romance, the posture is melodramatic, the language of its stances idealized from the literature of exploration remembered from Captain Marryat, Kipling, or Rider Haggard. It continues the juvenile romance of savage drums, tribal rites, barbarous but sacred sacrifices, golden journeys, lost cities. In the subconscious there is a black Atlantis buried in a sea of sand.

The colonial is tougher. He sees history for what it is in the world around him, an almost inexpressible banality. He sees the twentieth century without self-deceit and juvenile fantasy. The other curses the banality and chooses myth. Poets of the second group now begin to see poetry as a form of historical instruction. Their target is the officialized literature of the schools, the sociologists, their fellow historians, and above all, the Revolution. They become fascinated with the efficacy of poetry as an aspect of power not through its language but through its subject. Their poetry becomes a kind of musical accompaniment to certain theses, and as history it is forced to exclude certain contradictions, for history cannot be ambiguously recorded. Whatever its motive, either this happened or it did not. All piety is seen as villainy, all form as hypocrisy.

Inevitably, these poets grow obsessed with the innovation of forms, but this innovation is seen as critical strategy, for it will need to attack others as well as defend its position, if it is to be seen as spontaneous choice. Conservatively, it imitates what it believes to be the tribal mode, and it makes no distinction between the artificiality of the high style of tribal ceremony and the language which it employs to achieve this. It may even use fragments of the original language to adorn itself, even if such language is not its natural tongue.

A new conservatism now appears, a new dignity more reactionary and pompous than the direction of the language
used. It moves manically between the easy applause of
dialect, the argot of the tribe and ceremonial speech, the
"memory" of the tribe, that is, between the new dignity and
the popular, and in between there is nothing. The normal
voice of the poet, his own speaking voice is lost, and no
language is writ.

No, if we look for the primal imagination in West Indian
literature, its "revolutionary" aspect, we find it crucially
evolving in West Indian fiction, the poetic principle is more
alert in our best prose, and whatever ethnic impulse drives
this imagination examines the roots of contemporary man
with the same force as poets of a different race using English.
In *Other Leopards* there is this passage:

> Now, having removed my body and the last
> traces of it, I am without context clear. Going
> up this new tree, picking the thorns bare, one
> by one, I am in a darkness nowhere at all, I
> am nothing, nowhere. This is something gained.
> Hughie has not found me; I have outwitted him.
> I have achieved a valuable state: a condition out-
> side his method. Only remains now to remove
> my consciousness. This I can do whenever I
> wish. I am free of the earth. I do not need to go
> down there for anything.

In *Wodwo* by Ted Hughes there is:

> What am I? nosing here turning leaves over
> following a faint stain on the air to the river's edge
> I enter water . . .
>   I seem
> separate from the ground not rooted but dropped
> out of nothing casually I've not threads
> fastening me to anything I can go anywhere
> I seem to have been given the freedom
> of this place what am I then . . .

which, excuse the broken quotations, is the tone of the whole poem, language, tone, hesitation, and assurance, the deliberate picking out of names, the numinous process in Williams of a man reduced, in Hughes of a man evolving, the passage from the novel and the whole of Hughes's poem are the same. They are not merely the same in subject, anthropology, in fact they are different in structure obviously, and there is absolutely no question of exchanged influences except Hughes had read Williams, whose book appeared some years before, but what is there is the displaced, searching psyche of modern man, the reversion of twentieth-century man whether in Africa or in Yorkshire to his pre-Adamic beginning, to pre-history, and this shared contagion of madness exists universally in contemporary poetry, and particularly in a poet like Samuel Beckett.

The words jerk, the search is anguished, the pronouncing of chosen nouns, the cynical or violent rejection of the named thing itself, or the primal or the final elation of the power or of the decadence of the Word itself, the process is shared by three utterly different writers, one Guyanese-African, one English-Celtic, the third Irish-Celtic. What is shared is more than the language, it is the drilling, mining, molelike or mole-cricketlike burrowing into the origins of life or into its detritus, which, pardon the paradox, is the same. Logos as excrement, logos as engendering spasm. In the sense that these three are black writers we can only use the term "black" to imply a malevolence toward historical system. The Old World, or visitors to the Old World, or those who exist in the Old World, whether it is Africa, or the Yorkshire submarine world deep as England, or Beckett's unnamed, unnamable gray world of a wrecked civilization, these who are embittered by those worlds write blackly, with a purging pessimism which goes beyond the morbid. In the New World there is the same process in writers with an optimistic or visionary force, there is the same slow naming. This exists wholly in Wilson Harris. But this blackness is luminous. The black in Williams returns in his madness to beginning again. He climbs his thorn tree, he reverts to the anthropological origins of all mankind, no doubt he will descend again, and like Hughes's medieval monster undergoing his thrilling metamorphosis from demon to man as he begins to name things, and he may wreck and destroy civilization and its languages again like those crawlers through primordial and postatomic mud in Beckett, but these three elemental cycles are the common agony of three racially different writers. These crude cycles are the poet's knowledge of history. So what does this prove? It proves that the truest writers are those who see language not as linguistic process but as a living element, it more closely demonstates the laziness of poets who confuse language with linguistics and with archaeology. It also annihilates provincial concepts of imitation and originality. Fear of imitation obsesses minor poets. But in any age a common genius almost indistinguishably will show itself, and the perpetuity of this genius is the only valid tradition, not the tradition which categorizes poetry by epochs and by schools. We know that the great poets have no wish to be different, no time to be original, that their originality emerges only when they have absorbed all the poetry which they have read, entire, that their first work appears to be the accumulation of other people's trash but that they become bonfires, that it is only academics and frightened poets who talk of Beckett's debt to Joyce or of Pinter's to Beckett.

The tribe requires of its poets the highest language and more than predictable sentiment. Now pardon this excursion into autobiography. I know, from childhood, that I wanted to become a poet, and like any colonial child I was taught English literature as my natural inheritance. Forget the snow and the daffodils. They were real, more real than the heat and the oleander, perhaps, because they lived on the page, in imagination, and therefore in memory. There is a memory of imagination in literature which has nothing to do with actual experience, which is, in fact, another life, and that experience of the imagination will continue to make actual the quest of a medieval knight or the bulk of a white whale, because of the power of a shared imagination. The world of

poetry was natural and unlimited by what no child really
accepts as the actual world, and of course, later disenchant-
ment and alienation will come. But these are not altogether
important, they become part of maturity. To simplify: once
I had decided to make the writing of poetry my life, my
actual, not my imaginative life, I felt both a rejection and a
fear of Europe while I learned its poetry. I have remained
this way, but the emotions have changed, they are subtler,
more controlled, for I would no longer wish to visit Europe
as if I could repossess it than I wish to visit Africa for that
purpose. What survives in the slave is nostalgia for imperial
modes, Europe or Africa. I felt, I knew, that if I went to
England, I would never become a poet, far more a West
Indian, and that was the only thing I could see myself becoming, a West Indian poet. The language I used did not
bother me. I had given it, and it was irretrievably given, I
could no more give it back than they could claim it. But I
feared the cathedrals, the music, the weight of history, not
because I was alien, but because I felt history to be the
burden of others. I was not excited by continuation of its
process but by discovery, by the plain burden of work, for
there was too much to do here. Yet the older and more
assured I grew, the stronger my isolation as a poet, the more
I needed to become omnivorous about the art and literature
of Europe to understand my own world. I write "my own
world" because I had no doubt that it was mine, that it was
given to me, by God, not by history, with my gift. At that
time nobody anatomized the honesty of my commitment,
nobody urged me to reject old values, but such people would
have to go through an anguish of rejection and arrogant self-
assertion later. These are qualifications of faith, but they are
important. We are misled by new prophets of bitterness who
warn us against experiences which we have never cared to
have, but the mass of society has had neither the interest nor
the opportunity which they chose. These preach not to the
converted, but to those who have never lost faith. I do not
mean religious faith but reality. Fisherman and peasant know
who they are and what they are and where they are, and

when we show them our wounded sensibilities we are, most of us, displaying self-inflicted wounds.

I accept this archipelago of the Americas. I say to the ancestor who sold me, and to the ancestor who bought me I have no father, I want no such father, although I can understand you, black ghost, white ghost, when you both whisper "history," for if I attempt to forgive you both I am falling into your idea of history which justifies and explains and expiates, and it is not mine to forgive, my memory cannot summon any filial love, since your features are anonymous and erased and I have no wish and no power to pardon. You were when you acted your roles, your given, historical roles of slave seller and slave buyer, men acting as men, and also you, father in the filth-ridden gut of the slave ship, to you they were also men, acting as men, with the cruelty of men, your fellowman and tribesman not moved or hovering with hesitation about your common race any longer than my other bastard ancestor hovered with his whip, but to you, inwardly forgiven grandfathers, I, like the more honest of my race, give a strange thanks. I give the strange and bitter and yet ennobling thanks for the monumental groaning and soldering of two great worlds, like the halves of a fruit seamed by its own bitter juice, that exiled from your own Edens you have placed me in the wonder of another, and that was my inheritance and your gift.

DEREK WALCOTT was born in St. Lucia. He is a playwright, poet, and founder-manager of the Trinidad Theatre Workshop. His plays, which have been produced in the Caribbean, New York, Toronto, London, Paris, and Ibadan, include Drums and Colours, Franklin, Harry Dernier, Henri Christophe, The Sea at Dauphin, Ti-Jean, The Wine of the Country, and Dream on Monkey Mountain. His books of poetry are In a Green Night, Selected Poems, The Castaway, The Gulf and Other Poems, and Another Life. He has won a Rockefeller Foundation Fellowship, the Guinness Award for Poetry, the Royal Society of Literature Award, and the Cholmondeley Poetry Award. He now lives in Trinidad.

Edward Brathwaite

TIMEHRI

The most significant feature of West Indian life and imagination since Emancipation has been its sense of rootlessness,
of not belonging to the landscape; dissociation, in fact, of
art from the act of living. This, at least, is the view of the
West Indies and the Caribbean that has been accepted and
articulated by the small but important "intellectual elite"
of the area; a group—call it the educated middle class—ex-
planter and ex-slave—that has been involved in the post-
plantation creolizing process that made our colonial polity
possible. To understand the full meaning of this dissociation of the sensibility, and why it has primarily affected our
middle classes and the so-called "intellectual elite," it will
be necessary, in the first place, to look briefly at our colonial
heritage within the context of the process of creolization.

The concept and process of creolization has been treated
in some detail by (among others) Richard N. Adams in a
paper, "The Relation Between Plantation and Creole Culture," in *Plantation Systems of the New World*.[1] "Creolization" is a sociocultural description and explanation of the
way the four main culture carriers of the region—Amerindian, European, African, and East Indian—interacted with

each other and with their environment to create the new societies of the New World. Two main kinds of creolization may be distinguished: a mestizo-creolization, the inter-culturation of Amerindian and European (mainly Iberian) and located primarily in Central and South America; and mulatto-creolization, the interculturation of Negro-African and European (mainly Western European) and located primarily in the West Indies and the slave areas of the North American continent. The crucial difference between the two kinds of creolization is that whereas in mestizo-America only one element of the interaction (the European) was immi-grant to the area, in mulatto-America both elements in the process were immigrants. In mestizo-America there was a host environment with an established culture which had to be colonized mainly by force—an attempted eradication of Amerindian spiritual and material structures. In mulatto-America, where the indigenous Indians were fewer and more easily destroyed and blacks were brought from Africa as slaves, colonizing Europe was more easily able to make its imprint both on the environment (the plantation, the North American city) and the cultural orientation of the area. As the effects of force began to wear off in mestizo-America, the process of creolization began to reverse itself: Europeans be-came Indianized. In mulatto-America, where force had always been a more secondary factor or had, in a sense, been exerted by remote control, the process of creolization began to alter itself with the waning of the colonial regime. It simply fragmented itself into four main sociocultural orientations: European, African, indigeno-nationalist, and folk.

The problem of and for West Indian artists and intel-lectuals is that having been born and educated within this fragmented culture, they start out in the world without a sense of "wholeness." Identification with any one of these orientations can only consolidate the concept of a plural society, a plural vision. Disillusion with the fragmentation leads to a sense of rootlessness. The ideal does not and can-not correspond to perceived and inherited reality. The re-sult: dissociation of the sensibility. The main unconscious concern of many of the most articulate West Indian intellectuals and artists in the early postcolonial period was a description and analysis of this dissociation: C. L. R. James's *Minty Alley*, the work of George Lamming, V. S. Naipaul, and Orlando Patterson, and M. G. Smith's *The Plural Society in the British West Indies*. The achievement of these writers was to make the society conscious of the cultural problem.[2] The second phase of West Indian and Caribbean artistic and intellectual life, on which we are now entering, having become conscious of the problem, is seeking to transcend and heal it.

My own artistic and intellectual concern is, I think, not untypical of this new departure in West Indian and Caribbean cultural life. As such, I shall briefly describe it, since I believe that in doing so, I will be able to throw some direct and personal light upon our present stage and forum. I was born in Barbados, from an urban village background, of parents with a "middle-class" orientation. I went to a secondary school originally founded for children of the plantocracy and colonial civil servants and white professionals[3]; but by the time I got there, the social revolution of the thirties was in full swing, and I was able to make friends with boys of stubbornly non-middle-class origin. I was fortunate, also, with my teachers. These were (a) expatriate Englishmen, (b) local whites, (c) black disillusioned classical scholars. They were (with two or three exceptions) happily inefficient as teachers, and none of them seemed to have a stake or interest in our society. We were literally left alone. We picked up what we could or what we wanted from each other and from the few books prescribed like Holy Scripture. With the help of my parents, I applied to do modern studies (history and English) in the sixth form. Since modern studies had never been taught at this level before (1948), and there were no teachers to teach it, I (with about four others) was allowed to study the subject on my own with only token supervision and succeeded, to everyone's surprise, in winning one of the Island Scholarships that traditionally took the ex-planters' sons "home" to Oxbridge or London.

The point I am making here is that my education and background, though nominally "middle class," is, on examination, not of this nature at all. I had spent most of my boyhood on the beach and in the sea with "beach-boys" or in the country, at my grandfather's, with country boys and girls. I was therefore not in a position to make any serious intellectual investment in West Indian middle-class values. But since I was not then consciously aware of any other West Indian alternative (though in fact I had been living that alternative), I found and felt myself "rootless" on arrival in England and, like so many other West Indians of the time, more than ready to accept and absorb the culture of the mother country. I was, in other words, a potential Afro-Saxon.

But this didn't work out. When I saw my first snowfall,[4] I felt that I had come into my own; I had arrived; I was possessing the landscape. But I turned to find that my "fellow Englishmen" were not particularly prepossessed with me. I was the experience later to be described by Mervyn Morris, Kenneth Ramchand, and Elliot Bastien in *Disappointed Guests* (Oxford University Press, 1965). I reassured myself that it didn't matter. It made no difference if I was black or white, German, Japanese, or Jew. All that mattered was the ego trip, the self-involving vision. I read Keats, Conrad, Kafka. I was a man of Kulture. But the Cambridge magazines didn't take my poems. Or rather, they only took those which had a West Indian—to me, "exotic"—flavor.[5] I felt neglected and misunderstood.

Then, in 1953, George Lamming's *In the Castle of My Skin* appeared and everything was transformed. Here breathing to me from every pore of line and page was the Barbados I had lived. The words, the rhythms, the cadences, the scenes, the people, their predicament. They all came back. They all were possible. And all the more beautiful for having been published and praised by London, mother of metropolises.

But by now this was the age of the emigrant. The West Indies could be written about and explored. But only from a point of vantage outside the West Indies. It was no point going back. No writer could live in that stifling atmosphere of middle-class materialism and philistinism. It was Lamming again who gave voice to the ambience in *The Emigrants* (1954) and in *The Pleasures of Exile* (1960). His friend Sam Selvon made a ballad about it in *The Lonely Londoners* (1956), and Vidia Naipaul could write, in *The Middle Passage*:

> I had never wanted to stay in Trinidad. When I was in the fourth form I wrote a vow on the endpaper of my Kennedy's *Revised Latin Primer* to leave within five years. I left after six; and for many years afterwards in England, falling asleep in bedsitters with the electric fire on, I had been awakened by the nightmare that I was back in tropical Trinidad . . . I knew [it] to be unimportant, uncreative, cynical . . . (p. 41)

For me, too, child and scion of this time, there was no going back. Accepting my rootlessness, I applied for work in London, Cambridge, Ceylon, New Delhi, Cairo, Kano, Khartoum, Sierra Leone, Carcassonne, a monastery in Jerusalem. I was a West Indian, rootless man of the world. I could go, belong, everywhere on the world-wide globe. I ended up in a village in Ghana. It was my beginning.

Slowing, slowly, ever so slowly; obscurely, slowly but surely, during the eight years that I lived there, I was coming to an awareness and understanding of community, of cultural wholeness, of the place of the individual within the tribe, in society. Slowly, slowly, ever so slowly, I came to a sense of identification of myself with these people, my living diviners. I came to connect my history with theirs, the bridge of my mind now linking Atlantic and ancestor, homeland and heartland. When I turned to leave, I was no longer a lonely individual talent; there was something wider, more subtle, more tentative; the self without ego, without I, without arrogance. And I came home to find that I had not really left. That it was still Africa; Africa in the Caribbean. The middle passage had now guessed its end. The connection between my lived but unheeded non-middle-class boyhood and its great tradition on the eastern mainland had been made.

The problem now was how to relate this new awareness to the existing, inherited non-African consciousness of educated West Indian society. How does the artist work and function within a plurally fragmented world? How can a writer speak about "the people," when, as George Lamming dramatizes in *In the Castle of My Skin*, those to whom he refers have no such concept of themselves?

"I like it," I said. "That was really very beautiful."

"You know the voice?" Trumper asked. He was very serious now.

I tried to recall whether I might have heard it. I couldn't.

"Paul Robeson," he said. "One of the greatest o' my people."

"What people?" I asked. I was a bit puzzled.

"My people," said Trumper. His tone was insistent. Then he softened into a smile. I didn't know whether he was smiling at my ignorance, or whether he was smiling his satisfaction with the box and the voice and above all Paul Robeson.

"Who are your people?" I asked. It seemed a kind of huge joke.

"The Negro race," said Trumper. The smile had left his face, and his manner had turned grave again . . . He knew I was puzzled . . . At first I thought he meant the village. This allegiance was something bigger. I wanted to understand it . . . (p. 331)

What kind of product will emerge from this gap and dichotomy; from conscious vision and the unwillingly envisioned? It is a problem that Derek Walcott, never leaving

the Caribbean and aware of it from his very first lines in
1949, was increasingly to face.[6] On the one hand, aware of
the material and restricting influences around him, he
wanted, as *Letter to Margaret* (*Bim*, No. 12, 1955) suggests,
to cut himself off:

> Daily, my gift to a nervous crowd of roars
> Conceals raw anger under lip-thin laughter,
> As when the pavilion of pigments applauds after
> Some skin-surpassing stroke, I itch to scratch the sores
>
> Under the green epidermis of the lawn.
> But single, am helpless . . .

On the other hand, in *Hic Jacet* (*The Gulf and Other
Poems*, 1969) he seems certain in the knowledge that the
source of his art was and is with the people, and now, "Convinced of the power of provincialism," he says:

> Commoner than water I sank to lose my name . . .

But Walcott is a brilliant exception, creatively expressing
through his work the pressures and dilemmas of his plural
society. He is a humanist in the sense that the scholars and
artists of the Italian Renaissance were humanists. He is concerned with converting his heritage into a classical tradition,
into a classical statement. But as the folk movement from
below his outward-looking position begins to make itself felt,
there is heard, in the title poem, *The Gulf*, a growing note of
alienation and despair:[7]

> Yet the South felt like home. Wrought balconies,
> the sluggish river with its tidal drawl,
> the tropic air charged with the extremities
>
> of patience, a heat heavy with oil,
> canebrakes, that legendary jazz. But fear
> thickened my voice, that strange, familiar soil

prickled and barbed the texture of my hair,
my status as a secondary soul
The Gulf, your gulf, is daily widening,

each blood-red rose warns of that coming night
where there's no rock cleft to go hidin' in
and all the rocks catch fire, when that black night,

their stalking, moonless panthers turn from Him
whose voice they can no more believe, when the black
    X's
mark their passover with slain seraphim.

So the question of communal, as opposed to individual
wholeness still remains. And returning to London late in
1965, I was more than ever aware of this. For there were the
West Indian writers and artists, still rootless, still isolated,
even if making a "name." It seemed that flung out centrifu-
gally to the perimeter of their possibilities, our boys were
failing to find a center. Andrew Salkey's *Escape to an Autumn Pavement* (1960) and *The Adventures of Catullus
Kelly* (1968), Naipaul's *The Mimic Men* (1967), and Orlando Patterson's *An Absence of Ruins* (1967) were moving
witnesses to this realization.

Then, in 1966–67, two events of central importance to the
growth and direction of the West Indian imagination took
place. Stokely Carmichael, the Trinidadian-born American
black power leader, visited London and magnetized a whole
set of splintered feelings that had for a long time been seeking a node. Carmichael enunciated a way of seeing the black
West Indian that seemed to many to make sense of the entire history of slavery and colonial suppression, of the African
diaspora into the New World. And he gave it a name. Links
of sympathy, perhaps for the first time, were set up between laboring immigrant, artist/intelletual, and student.
Sharing, as he saw it, a common history, Carmichael produced images of shared communal values. A black International was possible. West Indians, denied history, denied

heroes by their imposed education, responded. From London
(and black America) the flame spread to the university
campuses of the archipelago. It found echoes among the
urban restless of the growing island cities. Rastafari art,
"primitive" art, dialect and protest verse suddenly had a
new urgency, took on significance. Walter Rodney published
Groundings with My Brothers (1969); Marina Maxwell
started the Yard Theatre; Olive Lewin's Jamaican Folk
Singers began to make sense; Mark Matthews in Guyana in
poems like *Portia Faces Life* was doing with the dialect of
the tribe what critics like Louis James[8] had declared to be impossible. The artist and his society, it seemed, were coming
close together.

The second event, of late 1966, was the founding, in London, of the Caribbean Artists Movement (CAM). The object of CAM was first and foremost to bring West Indian
artists "exiled" in London into private and public contact
with each other. It was a simple thing, but it had never happened before. The results were immediate, obvious, and
fruitful. Painters, sculptors, poets, novelists, literary and art
critics, publishers for the first time saw and could talk to
each other. Wilson Harris and Aubrey Williams, both of
Guyana, both working on the same kind of theme, had
never met each other. Now they could engage in long dia-
logues. Harris and Michael Anthony, natural opposites, met
and talked and talked. John Hearne and Orlando Patterson
clashed.[9] We all heard and came out of it the richer. Jerry
Craig was invited to illustrate Andrew Salkey's *Jonah Simp-
son* (1969); Williams, for the first time in his life, was asked
to provide a cover for a West Indian publication, *The Islands
in Between*. After this, he collaborated with Sam Selvon over
the illustrations for *A Drink of Water* (1968), and with
Longman's for a school edition of Jan Carew's *Black Midas*
(1969). Conferences were held at the University of Kent in
1967 and 1968 and at the West Indian Students Center in
1969. Academics interested in West Indian art and literature
came into the picture. Some who knew nothing about us became interested. Art exhibitions of West Indian work—

never seen collectively before—were arranged in a variety of places: the West Indian Students Center, the Theatre Royal, the universities of Kent and Sussex, the House of Commons, and in Birmingham. New artists like Clifton Campbell and Errol Lloyd made their appearance; grand old men like Ronald Moody, creator of "The Savacou," a sculpture of the Carib bird placed outside the Epidemiological Research Unit at the Mona campus [of the University of the West Indies, in Jamaica], made their reappearance. Poetry readings were held almost monthly. West Indian students and their friends became interested; joint sessions were held between CAM and the West Indian Society at the London School of Economics. The West Indian Students Center became CAM headquarters; its presence rejuvenated the place. Soon CAM-like organizations were being formed at the Students Center, in Nottingham, Edinburgh, and later in some of the London ghettos. A relationship between artist and audience had become possible. And John La Rose's bookshop, his book service, and finally his New Beacon Publications venture were all, too, to come out of this new mood and movement.

All this was possible because CAM came at a time when several artists and writers then in London had something new to say. I was about to start publishing my trilogy of long poems, influenced by those resurrectionary years in Ghana and tightened by my contact with Jamaican society with its black consciousness and its controlled rage and implosive violence, the sound of ska, rock-steady, reggae, and Orlando Patterson's *The Children of Sisyphus* (1964). John La Rose was about to launch the New Beacon Press with his own collection of poems, *Foundations*. Patterson had completed his second novel *An Absence of Ruins* (1967) and was working on *The Sociology of Slavery* (1967). Andrew Salkey, already moving to new directions with *The Late Emancipation of Jerry Stover* (1968), was soon to visit Cuba and return with an urgent sense of the Third World revolution, which he connected with Stokely Carmichael's ideas. Marina Maxwell was working on "Violence in the Toilets" (*Race Today*,

Sept. 1969), "Play Mas'," and "Towards a Revolution in the Arts of the Caribbean." All these artists were concerned primarily with the ex-African black experience, slavery, the plantation, and their consequences.

But there was also Harris and Aubrey Williams, both black, both from Guyana, who were contributing if not a different vision, then at least a different approach to that vision. Coming from mainland South America, they found themselves involved not with the problem of mulatto-creolization, but with mestizo-creolization. Their starting point, was not the Negro in the Caribbean, but the ancient Amerindian. Williams, speaking at a CAM symposium in June 1967, said:

> In art, I have always felt a wild hunger to express the rather unique, human state in the New World . . . I find there an amalgam of a lot that has gone before in mankind, in the whole world. It seems to have met there, after Columbus, and we are just on the brink of its development. The forces meeting in the Caribbean . . . will eventually, I feel, change this world . . . not in the sense of a big civilization in one spot, but as the result of the total of man's experience and groping for the development of his consciousness.[10]

In articulating this faith in the Caribbean and in emphasizing roots rather than "alien avenues," Williams was connecting with what many West Indian writers are now trying to do. And in emphasizing the importance to himself of primordial man, *local* primordial man, he, like Harris, was extending the boundaries of our sensibility. Most of us, coming from islands, where there was no evident lost civilization—where, in fact, there was an "absence of ruins"—faced a real artistic difficulty in our search for origins. The seed and root of our concern had little material soil to nourish them. Patterson's view was that we should accept this shallow soil (we begin from an existential absurdity of nothing) and grow our ferns in a kind of moon dust. Fertility would come later; if not, not. Naipaul refused to plant at all.[11] He watered the waste with irony. But Williams, coming from Guyana, where he had lived intimately for long periods with the Warraou Indians of the northwest district, had a more immediate and tactile apprehension of artistic soil.

It was not only a matter of getting to know the people— although that was a crucial element in his growth. He didn't only come to an understanding of tribal custom and philosophy—although that too was essential to him as continuing creator. But he could actually *see* the ancient art of the Warraou Indians. Living with them placed him in a significant continuum with it; for high up on the rocks at Tumatumari, at Imbaimadai, people who were perhaps of Maya origin— the ancestors of the Warraou and others in the area—had made marks, or *timehri:* rock signs, paintings, petroglyphs; glimpses of a language, glitters of a vision of a world, scattered utterals of a remote *Gestalt;* but still there, near, potentially communicative. Sometimes there were sleek brown bodies that could have been antelope or ocelot; there were horns and claws of crabs. There were triangular forms that might have been the mouths of cenotes. But hints only; gateways to intuitions; abstract signals of hieroglyphic art. To confirm that these marks were made by man, imprints of the etcher's palm were left beside the work; anonymous brands in living stone, imperishable witnesses from past to conscious present. It is from these marks that Aubrey Williams' art begins:

> I feel that these pre-Columbian influences are so strong, that we couldn't possibly shut them off. We might be attracted to alien avenues, but we're not really trying to shake off primordial life; and this primordial life is still manifest in Caribbean life today and I hope that it will inform and strengthen what we will become.[12]

This vision, coming from these sources, has made Williams a unique artist. In the first place, he is grounded, in the

NOTES

1. Washington, D.C., 1959. See also Gilberto Freyre in *Casa Grande e Senzala* (Rio de Janeiro, 1933) and *Sobrados e Macambos* (Rio de Janeiro, 1936); Mavis Campbell, "Edward Jordan and the Free Coloureds: Jamaica 1800–1865." Ph.D. thesis, University of London, 1968; and my own *The Development of Creole Society in Jamaica 1770–1820* (London, 1971).

2. The achievement of Elsa Goveia, expressed in *A Study of the Historiography of the British West Indies to the End of the Nineteenth Century* (Mexico, D.F., 1956), is that she described the state of Caribbean disnomia without herself being trapped in its effects.

3. See Austin Clarke, "Harrison College and Me," *New World Quarterly*, Barbados Independence Issue (Bridgetown, 1966); Paule Marshall, *The Chosen Place, The Timeless People* (New York, 1969), p. 61.

4. See "The Day the First Snow Fell," *Caribbean Quarterly*, Vol. 5, No. 3 (April 1958), p. 128.

5. See "A Caribbean Theme," in *Poetry from Cambridge* (London, 1950).

6. See Derek Walcott, *25 Poems* (Bridgetown, 1949); *Epitaph for the Young* (Bridgetown, 1949).

7. For this, from two different points of view, see Gordon

Rohlehr's review of *The Gulf* in *The Trinidad Guardian*, Dec. 10, 11, 13, 1969; and Lloyd King, "Bard of the Rubbish Heap: The Problem of Walcott's Poetry," in *Tapia*, No. 5 (Feb. 1, 1970), pp. 7–8.

8. *The Islands in Between* (London, 1968). For a refutation at some length of the Euro-centered academic view of West Indian literature and society in this book, see my "Caribbean Critics," *New World Quarterly*, Vol. 5, Nos. 1–2 (1969); *The Critical Quarterly*, Autumn 1969.

9. See CAM *Newsletter*, Nos. 3, 4 (1967).

10. Aubrey Williams, CAM *Newsletter*, No. 3.

11. I make, however, an exception of Naipaul's major work so far, *A House for Mr. Biswas*. Here, despite the futility, it seems to me, there is clear evidence of planting.

12. Williams, CAM *Newsletter*, No. 3.

EDWARD BRATHWAITE *was born in Barbados in 1930 and was educated there and at Pembroke College, Cambridge, England, where he read for an honors degree in history. His first job was as an education officer in Ghana where he lived for eight years. During this time, among other things, he organized a children's theater and produced two books of plays—*Four Plays for Primary Schools *and* Odale's Choice. *In 1962 he returned to the West Indies to teach history at the University of the West Indies in Jamaica. His trilogy of long poems—*Rights of Passage *(1967),* Masks *(1968), and* Islands *(1969)—about the black diaspora have been published by the Oxford University Press. A second (prose) trilogy is now appearing—*The Development of Creole Society in Jamaica *(London, 1971),* White Power in Jamaica: The Interdynamics of Slave Control, *and* Africa in the Caribbean. *He has received an Arts Council of Great Britain Bursary (1967), the Cholmondeley Award (1970) and a Guggenheim Fellowship (1971) for creative writing in poetry.*

James Millette

THE BLACK REVOLUTION
IN THE CARIBBEAN

I should begin I suppose by gratefully acknowledging the invitation of Penn State University to speak today on a subject which I propose to call "The Historical Background to the Black Revolution in the Caribbean."

I suppose too that in speaking to an audience in the United States of America there are probably some things I should begin by specifically saying. One is that inevitably we have to make some adjustments, mainly psychological I believe, in relation to the conception of size. I come from an area where the scale of things is rather smaller than the scale is in the United States. In money terms, when I speak of dollars, Trinidad and Tobago dollars, I am speaking of currency which is worth, normally if you are lucky, about fifty cents of the United States dollar. I am also talking of a society, specifically with respect to Trinidad and Tobago, comprised of some 1,100,000 persons—a small society.

And also when I speak about black people in Trinidad and Tobago, I speak of two black races, not one. I speak of people who are drawn from Indian stock as well as people who are drawn from African stock. Also I think that it is useful for me to attempt some kind of justification for talking to you about the historical background to the black revolution in the Caribbean.

I believe in fact that the most important reason might well have to do with the existence today of a black revolution the world over. But I also think that there is a larger significance in the recent developments in Trinidad and Tobago and in the West Indies deriving from the fact that the history of the development of ex-colonial countries and territories into a state of independence has been one of the most profound developments of our time. And perhaps the most important significance of Trinidad and Tobago is that it provides us with an opportunity of examining, as it were, on a canvas the stages by which a single society moved from a colonial setting to independence and, in the view of some of us, back to a colonial state again.

We have had in our country a pretty unique experience. In Trinidad and Tobago today the administration in office has been in power for fifteen years. That is a claim which cannot really be matched by many other countries in the world. Also, the administration in office has been headed and has been dominated in fact by a single personality, the personality of Dr. Eric Williams—in a sense, a scholar in politics. In a sense, too, as he himself described himself, a colonial at Oxford in the 1930s. He has had a particular kind of background which was not unfamiliar in the 1930s and '40s and '50s and a background which in some ways excellently fitted him for the task of the '50s. But we are not so sure today that that background excellently fits him for the tasks of the '60s and '70s. What he did do, however, as an intellectual in politics, was to raise many of the important issues which are likely to confront and have confronted nations such as our own and also to confront the people with some of these issues. Unfortunately, the titillation that was involved in confronting the population with those issues was not entirely matched by an ability to fulfill the expectations of the people whom he titillated. And so today the black revolution in Trinidad and Tobago is to some extent a revolution based upon the frustration which has derived particularly from this kind of titillation and from the failure to fulfill.

There is another point of wider significance, and it has to do with the fact that in Trinidad and Tobago, in a sense, there have been two conflicting notions of development represented by two different people. One of these persons is Dr. Eric Williams himself. The other is a man by the name of C. L. R. James, who may be even better known at the international level. C. L. R. James has had a very checkered history. He is best known as the tutor and mentor in politics of some of the most important African politicians of our time. People like Nkrumah, people like Kenyatta, James Padmore, and other important West Indians of the period are among the men to have first extolled the notion of pan-Africanism. They are among the first black people to have envisioned the possibility of establishing independent black societies where formerly there were colonial societies, and C. L. R. James has a completely different vision of the possibilities for black people in the West Indies from that which Williams has. And that difference has intensified some of the conflicts in our society and has certainly intensified and has drawn attention to some of the contradictions. The contradictions in Trinidad today are the contradictions—political, economic, social, and psychological—of an ex-colonial society operating in what is basically a neo-colonialist capitalist environment and trying to fulfill, despite all the odds, some of the objectives which the people of Trinidad and Tobago would like to see fulfilled.

So much with respect to significance. In order to put you in the picture, I think I should also say something about the main features of West Indian society today. The main features of West Indian society are to my mind three.

First of all, West Indian society is overwhelmingly a black society. It is a society in which 90 to 95 per cent of the people are black people. Also it is a society which is overwhelmingly a dependent society. And it is a society, too, in which today there is a very pronounced movement toward the denial of whatever kind of democracy could be believed to have existed in the West Indies till now.

Insofar as blackness is concerned, the social characteristics associated with blackness in the West Indies developed as a result of the historical legacy of slavery and as a result of the historical legacy of East Indian indentureship. Slavery came via the sugar plantation in the seventeenth century and after. West Indian society based upon the capitalist production of sugar for the purpose of export was thoroughly transformed. For the capitalist, production of sugar involved the dispossession of the small white holders who had before that farmed tobacco and the substitution of this small farming class with large numbers of dispossessed black slaves who were slaves for life and who had no claim whatever to ownership and control in the West Indian environment. That setting entered a new phase in Trinidad and Tobago with the importation, after 1838 and the emancipation of the slaves, of whole hosts of East Indian laborers who came to the West Indies under indentureship and who existed in a condition of servitude different only in degree, and particularly in relation to the duration of that servitude, from that under which the slaves had existed.

The fact is that black people in the West Indies have never really been actors in their own environment. They have always been acted upon, and the whole psychological, social, economic, and other deprivations which they have experienced have given blackness in the West Indies a particular kind of character.

One character is that in large part West Indians who are black have learned to despise themselves. There is a very substantial self-contempt existing among black people in the West Indies. Also there is a very sharp realization that the West Indies have never really produced for black people the kind of benefits and advantages of which people believe the West Indies to be capable. We in the West Indies know wealth. We in the West Indies know happiness. We in the West Indies know conspicuous consumption. We know what it is to live well. But black people in the West Indies do not in the main know much of this from their own personal experience. Their experience of happiness and wealth and good living is a vicarious experience in that they see other people living well. They see other people being happy. They see other people driving around in the big cars and so on. This means that West Indians, that is, conscious West Indians, are also very knowledgeable about their relationship with other countries, the developed countries in particular. Over the years this has been a particularly disadvantageous relationship and has meant that the West Indian people have remained in an unequal confrontation with a world which is white, with a world which is self-confident. This world is largely European, Canadian, and American, and it is a world which in the view of many West Indians—myself included—is an increasingly exploitative world.

Insofar as the spectre of dependence is concerned, the most important conception is the conception of the plantation economy which is not only historically related with the plantation production of staple crops like sugar, at times coffee, bananas, citrus fruits, and cocoa, but also an economy which has never really existed for its own purposes and has never really been moved by its own stimulations.

It is not that the economy of the West Indies is unimportant; it has always been of the utmost importance, but the importance has derived from the fact that the West Indies has always been an enclave in a larger international society for whose advantage it existed. The West Indian economy has always been involved with the most lucrative items of international trading. In the eighteenth century the commodities that were most desired by the nations of the world were slaves, sugar, and precious metals, and the West Indian Islands either traded in those commodities or produced them. In the twentieth century the most important items or some of the most important items are oil, bauxite, sugar—always sugar—bananas, and of course the large financial transactions of the international banking system. So that the West Indies have not in any sense been a backwater of the international economy. They have always been very much involved in that economy. But though they have always been involved in it, they have been involved as passive instruments of the international economic system, acted upon by other people and never really acting of their own volition.

So these societies have remained in large part locations in which the important raw materials have been extracted, markets in which important manufacturing goods have been sold, territories in which decision making at a local level has been virtually absent, and in general areas with very little power to sustain themselves economically. There is hardly any West Indian country which has yet reached the stage which was described nearly a decade ago as the "take-off" point. The West Indian economics to a large extent are still monocultural. They are still primary-producing, and their people still have a very high propensity to import. That is to say that nearly every West Indian country is a substantial importer of goods produced overseas to such an extent that today one of the most important determinations of nearly every West Indian government concerned with change is to substitute some locally produced goods for imported goods. What it means, too, is that the processes of change have to be seen as involving, in my mind, the complete rupture of the relationships which have existed between ourselves and the developed countries of the world and which to a large extent explain the dependence of our society. It means, for example, creating new tastes. It means, for example, creating, to whatever extent that is possible, a new indigenous technology.

Insofar as the third feature is concerned—the increasing undemocratic nature of the West Indies—it would seem that this derives from a basic conflict between the enlarged hopes of the people and the failure of the governments to fulfill those hopes and aspirations. It is important here to emphasize that this tendency has developed very markedly in the period of independence. In fact, independence itself has sharpened the whole conflict. In my view independence— whether it is of the kind for which people have had to fight, as people are fighting in Angola and Mozambique today, as people will have to fight in South Africa, as people have fought in Algeria, or whether it is what some of us call the "tea party" variety of independence in which successive legions of West Indians have made the trip to Marlborough House or some other stately palace in London to sit down and discuss with British officials whether or not they were fit enough to govern themselves—whether or not independence is of one or the other variety, in my mind the establishment of independence in an ex-colonial society involves a revolutionary process. And it involves revolutionary consequences.

The essence of these consequences has to do with the fact that the locus of power is dramatically shifted from overseas to within the territory itself and this lays open all sorts of possibilities, one of the interesting possibilities being that political power can be seized by force. It is of course foolish to attempt to seize political power by force in Port of Spain if the locus of political power is overseas in London. You seize nothing, even if you are successful. But when the locus of power is in Port of Spain, the revolutionary possibilities are completely different. Moreover, the whole process of independence involved in many of these countries for the first time the mobilization of a complete people. In Trinidad and Tobago many of us date the modern phase of political development from 1956, the period in which Dr. Eric Williams and others began to mobilize the country in order to establish self-government and independence within the confines of a West Indian federation. And Williams and his colleagues were not alone in doing this. This was being done in other West Indian countries. It was being done for example in Jamaica. It was being done in Barbados. And also it was either preceded or succeeded by similar movements in other parts of the world: in India, in Ceylon, in Pakistan, in Ghana, Nigeria and other African countries, and in other parts of the West Indies.

What all this political mobilization of the people meant was that the leaders had to hold out some new vision to the people concerned. Invariably, the vision involved new political perspectives. And this is what to a large extent the leadership was concerned with and concerned itself with portraying: the possibility of transferring political power from, say, London to Port of Spain or from Paris to Dakar or wherever the capital of the colonial territory happened to be.

All in all, what was involved was the specific elaboration and discussion of what were basically political objectives. And the people who benefited from independence in the first round were the people who were in the position either to seize political power for themselves or to benefit from the seizure of political power by others. That is to say that the people who have benefited from independence first and foremost in the West Indies today are the people who were first of all politicians.

Secondly, there was the bureaucracy and civil service— the people who succeeded the colonial administrators. And thirdly, there were those groups of indigenous businessmen who were able to move into those gaps that were created by the expulsion of the foreigner.

All this contrasted very sharply with the expectations of the people, because the expectations of the people were very basically social even though they collaborated in the whole political articulation of what the political objectives should be. What they were pre-eminently concerned with, even though they didn't say so, were social things. They were concerned with jobs, more money, greater happiness, and the elimination of those discriminations between black and white that still today are perpetuated in the West Indies.

So the governments of the West Indies have been faced in our time with an unceasing dilemma because if they are going to resolve the basic conflict between themselves and the people, then they have to do one of two things. Either they have to adopt policies which are increasingly unpalatable for many of them since they have become part of the vested interest themselves, or they have to oppress the people. In other words, they have to suppress a people who are asking for things which the governments simply cannot or will not provide; and this is the direction which the societies have been taking. The road which is being taken in the West Indies today is one of oppressing and intimidating and menacing and using the thousand and one resources at the command of government in order to keep a people mute and still and silent. This is what, in essence, is the cause of the basic conflict which has developed in recent times in a black power movement in Trinidad and Tobago.

The black power movement is perhaps the latest and most important manifestation of this. But there have been other manifestations. For example, it is true to say that over the last five or six years many people, some of them university people like myself, have had the very unfortunate experience of having their passports taken from them. Other people have been put under house arrest. C. L. R. James himself was put under house arrest in Trinidad on his return to that island in 1965. Guyana went into independence with several Guyanese citizens under political detention. In Dominica there is a new law of censorship which virtually restricts the newspapers to publishing only whatever the government wants. In Trinidad and Tobago there is no law of censorship, but the newspapers know their place anyhow. In Jamaica, in Barbados, in nearly every West Indian society you can think of, there have been over the years very clear signs of this movement toward repression, of the exertion of a greater authority or perhaps a greater authoritarianism in the affairs of governments in their relations with the people of the West Indies.

And the basic fact is that this is the consequence of those features which I have been talking about and which have really saddled the West Indian people with a very fundamental experience of poverty, dispossession, and oppression. All in all, West Indians own and control nothing. That is, the West Indian people as a whole—whether they are black or whether they are white—basically they have nothing. All the important industries are owned and controlled by foreigners. In Trinidad recently the government acquired a 51 per cent interest in sugar, so it is not true to say this any more for sugar, but the management contract is still in the hands of Tate & Lyle [the British-owned monopoly], and in any case oil, the principal foreign exchange earner is almost totally foreign owned. The tourist industry is still very much a foreign industry. The banking system is in real fact completely a foreign banking system.

What this means is that the society is economically manipulated to an extent which severely weakens even the political independence which we are supposed to have, so that the politicians themselves even if they are willing, find themselves operating within the constraints of an economic strait jacket which makes it very difficult for them to do the sorts of things and provide the kinds of policies which the West Indian people are expecting. But I think I must underline that the politicians are not particularly willing. Today, for example, there is a widespread realization in the West Indies, and most certainly in Trinidad and Tobago, that the road forward must begin in one way or the other with a reckoning with those international corporations operating in our midst and exploiting us. But between the population and the corporations stand the governments concerned. Remove the governments and you will have a reckoning in the West Indies tomorrow. But the governments have saddled themselves with the particular responsibility of adopting the interest of the foreigner and of defending the exploitative interest of the corporations against the interest of the local people.

Also I must point out that one of the factors which has exacerbated the problems of poverty and dispossession in the West Indies has had to do with the adoption in the English-speaking countries of a model of development known as the Puerto Rican model of development. That model of development originated in Puerto Rico in the 1950s, a country which, as you know, has a very intimate association both at the economic and political level with the United States of America and a country in which the problems of development seemed unlikely to be resolved without some positive new program in the 1950s. The positive new program that was adopted was based upon the invitation of foreigners to come into the country to invest and to bring with them the expertise to set up industries and do this under very important concessionary agreements. We in the West Indies, and in the English-speaking West Indies particularly, have been very much fascinated with the Puerto Rican model, so we have adopted the Puerto Rican model in the West Indies too. When Williams came to power in 1956, for example, one of his first acts was to invite to Trinidad and Tobago Dr. Teodoro Moscoso, who had had a lot to do with Operation Bootstrap in Puerto Rico. What did Operation Bootstrap mean in Puerto Rico and what has it meant in the West Indies. In brief, for us it means even less than it has meant for Puerto Rico because we have never had the same access to the American market, nor have our people the same physical access to the American continent that Puerto Ricans have had. Access to the American market and access to the American continent for the Puerto Ricans have represented certain important safety valves which have helped to sublimate the problems of poverty and dispossession in Puerto Rico. We have not had the same kinds of safety valves. And what the Puerto Rican model meant in Trinidad and Tobago is that we have been confronted all the time with the basic difficulties involved in trying to develop a country by giving the initiative in development to foreigners.

Let me show you what it means. Over the last fourteen or fifteen years, during which the pioneer schemes have been operating, we have provided about 14,000 new jobs in Trinidad and Tobago. This is a small number of jobs by our standards, because 14,000 new jobs is only the number of jobs which will provide for the incremental labor force available at the beginning of each year. That is to say that on January 1 next year we will need 15,000 new jobs or thereabouts if we are to hold unemployment simply at existing levels. Our unemployment at existing levels today in Trinidad and Tobago amounts to 15 or 20 per cent of the labor force. In the United States of America, in Canada, in the United Kingdom, when the unemployment levels reach

6 per cent there is a very important political and economic crisis. In Trinidad and Tobago, in all the West Indian countries, the level of unemployment for the last seven to ten years has existed at a 15 to 20 per cent level of the labor force and many of us believe that this is precisely a consequence of the strategy of development that has been adopted, because the strategy of development is based upon the importation of technological know-how which is fed by the presumptions of societies which are not exactly like ours, which have not the same kind of experience with labor surplus that we have. In other words, the developed societies of the world have had from time to time experiences with labor shortage. We in the West Indies have experiences with labor surplus. The technology that we have been importing into the West Indies to develop our societies has itself been creating unemployment.

For example, the pioneer industry schemes say that one of the things that new manufacturing industries are permitted to do is to import raw materials free of duty. The kind of raw materials that are imported are, for example, knocked-down automobiles, cars which are 70 to 80 per cent made overseas, packed into boxes, brought down to the West Indies, taken out of those boxes, and assembled. That is the manufacturing industry! Or let us take the even more notorious case of a factory that came into Trinidad and Tobago for the purpose of manufacturing socks. The Industrial Development Corporation was persuaded that it ought to permit this factory to import on a large scale the raw material needed for manufacturing socks, and so the factory was given the option of importing 100,000 dozen pairs of sock blanks. I don't know how many of you know what a "sock blank" is. A sock blank is a sock that is made up in all respects except that the sole is left open, and what you do when you import your raw material to make socks is simply to put the toe on the machine and sew it up and you've made a sock. In other words, the value added is about .1 per cent of the entire value of that commodity. The 99.9 per cent value which was added was added overseas. In other words, that kind of manufacturing industry creates employment overseas. It creates unemployment in Trinidad and Tobago.

But not only this. The population themselves have been forced to stand back and be witnesses to the growing disequality between themselves and the new group of manufacturers, very largely local whites and foreign whites, who have been making money and living conspicuously at the expense of the population. Nearly every new manufacturing industry established in Trinidad and Tobago involves a rise in price in relation to the commodity concerned. The basis upon which the industry is established is first of all the customary establishment of a monopoly over the local market. Secondly, it is in the nature of the situation that the local market is about the only market accessible to that industry. Such an industry cannot compete with the industries of the United Kingdom producing the same goods; it is possible to import a car from the United Kingdom and sell it cheaper in Trinidad and Tobago than a car which is, so to speak, manufactured in Trinidad and Tobago, that is to say, assembled. So the monopoly of the local market can only exist on two basic conditions. One basic condition is a rise in price and the other basic condition, which seems to be always a concommitant of the rise in price and the establishment of such industries, is the production of an inferior quality of goods. And the population pays for this. Not only does the population pay for this by having to put up with an inferior kind of commodity while at the same time paying more for it, but they pay for it too by having to suffer the obvious disequalities emerging between themselves and the local and foreign business elite. It is only too obvious that very many of these individuals are making a good deal out of the new manufacturing industries, and at the bitter expense of the rest of the population.

Another of the features of the new manufacturing industries, another of the concessions, is that the firms involved should enjoy a tax-free holiday of anything for five to ten years. In other words, they pay no taxes for five to ten years on corporate profit. What it means is that it is possible to establish a firm in Trinidad and Tobago under the Pioneer Aid schemes and recover the invested capital several times over during the span of income tax exemptions; and some firms in fact have simply recovered their capital several times and then have gone somewhere else to plunder.

Now these are some of the basic features which in a way explain the black revolution in the Caribbean today, and the features of the Puerto Rican model as exhibited in Trinidad are complemented by the inabilities of the society to provide for itself even in respect of some of the more important basic necessities of any society. Today, health is a problem in Trinidad and Tobago. Unemployment is a problem in Trinidad and Tobago. Education is a problem in Trinidad and Tobago. In fact, education and unemployment are in my view the most important problems of all. And education and unemployment have a lot to do with the specific character of the "black revolution" which has recently occurred in Trinidad and Tobago. The education which people get today hardly fits them for any employment whatever. In fact, the host of unemployed in Trinidad and Tobago have two very important characteristics. In a large degree the unemployed are concentrated in the urban areas of black population. Also this unemployed population is very largely a young population; 31 per cent of the unemployed labor force is between fifteen and nineteen years old. About 20 to 25 per cent of those between the ages of twenty and twenty-four looking for work, willing to work, and able to work are today unemployed. And not only are they unemployed but many of them are pretty well educated too. In fact, the education system in Trinidad and Tobago is in one sense a reasonable education system in that it teaches people to be literate, teaches them to read and write and very often to read and write very well. What it does not do is match education with the prospects for employment and to create and educate a society which is able to move into gainful employment.

This is not all. The prospects for educated people getting jobs in Trinidad and Tobago is complicated by a whole host of subtle discriminations which operate against black people. It is my experience and the experience of many other persons that white people with whom we went to school in Trinidad and Tobago, and who are in many ways educationally inferior to us, have had no difficulty whatever in becoming bank managers. Many of them make the most important decisions about the economy today insofar as those decisions are made in Trinidad and Tobago. In fact, the business elite in Trinidad and Tobago, to the extent that a local business elite exists, is composed of uneducated white people. The whites in Trinidad and Tobago are yet to produce a historian. They have yet to produce an economist. They have yet to produce people who can be singled out and distinguished on the objective criterion of ability alone. The people of ability, the people of creativity in Trinidad and Tobago, as in the whole of the West Indies, are not white people; and that is the price that whites are paying for privilege in Trinidad and Tobago because they have never really been called upon to exert themselves to earn what they have. They are a privileged class whose only basis for privilege is what we call in Trinidad and Tobago "contact," and contact involves having the right background, knowing the right people, and, principally, being white.

Now what this means is that people who are educated, even those who are well educated and for whom jobs would normally exist, have to compete with other people who are basically uneducated for those jobs, and very often they lose out. And this means that the whole black power revolution in Trinidad and Tobago today is based upon an increasing frustration among black people which is sharpened by this notion of poverty and dispossession and which in a sense is exacerbated by a feeling of betrayal between black and black.

At the moment I want simply to continue by pointing out that there have been many more reactions to poverty and dispossession in the West Indies besides the black power revolution. Some of these reactions have, in fact, begun to affect the economy. Sugar is the most important agricultural stand-by in the West Indies, and if you know how West Indian sugar is marketed, you would appreciate the plight that the sugar industry is in today. West Indian sugar is not sold freely on the world market. It is sold by negotiation with those persons, particularly in the United Kingdom, willing to purchase West Indian sugar at prices which are higher than the international market price. The strategy for selling West Indian sugar involves sitting down every four or five years and discussing with the United Kingdom Ministry of Food what price will be paid for West Indian sugar over the ensuing five years, and invariably it involves on the part of the West Indian sugar producers a commitment to produce a given tonnage of sugar which is called a "quota." Now that quota is very important. It is also a quota which is very highly prized, but it is an interesting fact of the sugar situation in the West Indies today that virtually no West Indian society has been able to fulfill the quota which it has received. Trinidad has been consistently producing short of its quota. Guyana has been consistently producing short of its quota, and the same holds true for Barbados and Jamaica.

The one important explanation of this has to do with the fact that the people who are employed in the sugar industry and for whom sugar is much more than a question of prices and quotas—people for whom sugar is a question of life and death and the kind of life they are going to live, the kind of life their children are going to be allowed to live—have turned upon the sugar industry. Sugar fires in Jamaica, Barbados, Guyana, and in Trinidad and Tobago are part of a way of life. Perhaps the problem is much more serious in Barbados and Jamaica than it is elsewhere, but in nearly every West Indian community with a sugar industry the people are turning upon sugar, and the problems involved in the establishment of a sugar society in the West Indies in the seventeenth, eighteenth, and nineteenth centuries are still problems with which the ordinary people involved in the production of plantation sugar are confronted. So that is one manifestation of the way in which people are reacting to poverty and dispossession in the West Indies.

Another manifestation is the increasing calls for radicalization of the economic system. People are calling for public ownership. People are calling for nationalization of industries and, as I have already pointed out, it is true to say that the real barrier to the establishment of these goals is the existence of the West Indian governments and the part which the West Indian governments elect to play in making it difficult for the people of the West Indies to fulfill their objectives in relation to these matters.

There is also another factor, which has to do with migration. Trinidad and Tobago has a unique place in the Caribbean insofar as migration is concerned. Trinidad has been, ever since the community began to be developed in 1783, a net receiver of persons. It has been a receiver of persons not only from the eastern Caribbean but from even farther afield, and it is only in recent times that we have started to export people out of Trinidad and Tobago. Today the migration figures out of Trinidad and Tobago amount to something like 10,000 to 15,000 persons per year out of a population of 1,100,000. But not only is the absolute figure significant in that the outward migration is recent, but also the people who are moving out of the society are, by and large, skilled people. People like doctors and nurses and other medical personnel. People like dentists. People with professional manufacturing and mechanical skills. These are the people who are moving out, and they are precisely the people which the country would have to rely upon in order to develop itself when the proper formula for development is found.

In addition to this, the black power movement has come as the sharpest possible reaction to the experience of poverty and dispossession. And speaking particularly of the black power movements in the West Indies, it is important to say, first of all, that even though the recent unrest manifested itself in Trinidad and Tobago alone, the historical basis for black power is such that black power must be regarded as a West Indian movement. In fact, the governments of the Caribbean and the reactionary people on the other side, as well as the people who are concerned with radicalization and reconstruction, recognize that there is not only a unity in the West Indian situation but that there must also be a unity in the West Indian response to that situation. We do not fool ourselves by believing that the problems of Trinidad and Tobago can be tackled in Trinidad and Tobago alone. We believe that these problems have to be tackled in the other West Indian territories too, and also outside of the West Indian territories. But basically the black power movement envisages the establishment of a new society in the West Indies on the basis of a general West Indian assault upon the present system existing in the West Indies. Indeed, it is not an overstatement to say that that system must be destroyed.

There is one other thing to be said which will put black power in a very particular Caribbean context. As a further reflection on the fact that the population of the Caribbean is 90 to 95 per cent black, many people do not understand why it is that a black power movement should originate in a country in which the government is black. People on the outside have told me, "It is obvious that you should have a black power movement in the United States of America where the blacks are a minority of the population, where they are oppressed and unlikely to get what they want except by fighting for it. But why do you have a black power movement in Trinidad and Tobago? What's all this black power business about?" The simple fact is, as any activist will tell you on the streets in Trinidad and Tobago, that black men in power do not connote black power. The fact is that today people feel in Trinidad and Tobago a sharper sense of betrayal precisely because they have been betrayed by blacks. It is one thing to be betrayed by whites. It is another thing to be betrayed as a black people by people who are black. There is a primeval character to the black power movement in the West Indies which feeds upon this one peculiarity—that here you have a society 90 to 95 per cent black in which the rewards of the society are very obviously going to those in the society who are not black, and this state of affairs is presided over, and indeed in some respects encouraged and perpetuated, by governments which are themselves black.

There are also other aspects to the black power situation in Trinidad and Tobago. One of the origins of the movement obviously has to do with the fact that in the West Indies there has been a continuing crisis drawn from the existence of a long historical process of poverty and dispossession. But over the last several years there has been a series of incidents which started with the exclusion of Walter Rodney in Jamaica in October 1968. Then, too, there was the fraudulent Guyana election of December 1968, involving a fraud perpetuated by the government of Guyana and applauded and assisted by nearly every other government in the West Indies. Also, there was the Sir George Williams University crisis in Canada. There was the Anguilla affair and also there was the positive creation of a new mood among the young people of Trinidad and Tobago. The new mood fed upon the extent to which young people in Trinidad and Tobago were determined to examine the old situation for themselves.

Finally, all of this leads to one conclusion on our part in Trinidad and Tobago. Today we see that the situation in our country is a situation with which not very many people would like to be confronted, because it seems as if all the most important problems which one could see in any society are concentrated in Trinidad and Tobago. Problems about the multinational corporation. Problems about the role of violence in political change. Problems about the legitimacy of the political party. Problems of dependence. And so on. And all of these are sharpened by the expectation of the people that what must be done must be done now. But that is the size of the problem and we are confronted with it. The whole thing is that the problems in Trinidad will not be resolved except in relation to what other people elsewhere are doing. And this means not only what black people are doing, but what other people who have some of the problems that we have are doing. I am also interested in the extent to which American capital is penetrating societies like the United Kingdom, penetrating societies like France and the European Common Market as a whole. And it seems to me that the final answer to the problems of many people all over the world, who have the same experience that we have, involved in general a universal attack on the system which has created the poverty and dispossession that has made necessary the black revolution in Trinidad and Tobago.

JAMES MILLETTE, a Trinidadian, is a historian and the head of the Department of History at the University of the West Indies, St. Augustine, Trinidad. He is also active in politics. He is general secretary of the United National Independence Party in Trinidad and has been one of the major influences behind the publication of Moko, the first of a growing series of radical newspapers published in the Caribbean and particularly in Trinidad and Tobago. He has also been associated with the New World Movement and is the author of one book, entitled The Genesis of Crown Colony Government, as well as of numerous articles and pamphlets.

Gordon Rohlehr

HISTORY AS ABSURDITY: A LITERARY CRITIC'S APPROACH TO *From Columbus to Castro* AND OTHER MISCELLANEOUS WRITINGS OF DR. ERIC WILLIAMS

From Columbus to Castro purports to be more than just another history book. Its subtitle, which makes it "The History of the Caribbean 1492–1969," implies that it is *the* definitive study of 477 years of history in these widely scattered islands. Apart from this fantastic claim is the fact that the book was written by Dr. E. E. Williams, the Prime Minister of a country which has been for some years in a state of silent turmoil. Thus the reader is particularly interested in the views of its author on the Caribbean past, his sense of how the past permeates and defines the present, and the perspectives which he offers for the future.

Since, too, *From Columbus to Castro* is presented as the fruit of over eighteen years' experience and research and succeeds an impressive list of books, monographs, pamphlets, and lectures, it is of particular interest as the intellectual climax of a long academic and political career and as the synthesis of a lifetime's experience in both the writing and making of West Indian history. Questions which engage the reader almost before he reads the book are, "What new things does Dr. Williams have to say about the Caribbean past?" and "How coherent will his vision turn out to be?" and "What, if any, is the connection between his scholarship and his politics?"

In addition to all this, *From Columbus to Castro* has already been used as the springboard from which the Prime Minister's party, the PNM [Peoples' National Movement], means to jump into the era of the swinging seventies. It has been welcomed by an exclusive dinner, which the publisher himself traveled from London to attend; by an adulatory speech made in worship of the author by a minister of his government who, from his lack of concrete references, seems not to have read the book; and by a meeting of the PNM at Queen's Park Savannah, in which Dr. Williams, fulfilling his multiple role of historian-politician and philosopher-king, unleased on an unsuspecting public the party's new charter, which contains (and I quote) "the most profound concept in contemporary political social and economic thought"—end of quote. I should add that more than once, Williams himself reviewed the book for television and radio. This seems rather like an attempt to oust Mr. Burnham of the Republic of Guyana in this game of Caribbean one-upmanship. Mr. Burnham had scored a first in the Caribbean by instituting the world's only co-operative republic in 1969. Now it is the Trinidad Magna Carta ushered in by a massive history book, which is certainly much more impressive than Mr. Burnham's *A Destiny to Mould*, which ushered in the co-operative republic.

From Columbus to Castro, then, is meant to be both the historian's bible for the new era and the great work from which the national movement in Trinidad and Tobago will derive its intellectual dynamic against the deepening pressures of this age of neo-colonialism. It is Dr. Williams' titanic attempt to bring up to date such thoughts and perceptions as are his, to revise old insights, to include fresh ideas, and to assemble both the archaic and the immediate visions in a single massive volume, which would show once and for all how West Indian history can be impressed into the service of decolonization; how the academic can become a politician and yet preserve his academic integrity, while at the same time reassuring former students of the now defunct "University of Woodford Square,"* that despite his years of hermitlike invisibility, the great brain is still solidly at work.

These days it is difficult to view without skepticism anything Dr. Williams has to say either as politician or as historian. His last two history books have been the objects of quite astringent criticism from professional historians at the University of the West Indies. Dr. K. O. Laurence, for example, views Dr. Williams' *History of the People of Trinidad and Tobago* as an excellent "manifesto of a subjugated people," but criticizes the author for a tendency to overstate his case and to omit a number of things which would significantly modify his conclusions. Dr. Laurence mentions in particular Dr. Williams' failure to credit the contribution of Albert Gomes; to assess the work of the Abolitionists; to treat the system of apprenticeship, the effect of World War II, and the American occupation on the islands; to consider the Moyne Report; or to see the long struggle for self-government as a continuous and unbroken process. He sees Williams' treatment of the post-1956 era as "frankly partisan" and ends with an implicit rejection of his methodology:

> However, it is obviously desirable that the books which will dictate the view of their own history which the peoples of the Caribbean will possess for the next generation should be written as *histories*, not as nationalist manifestoes. Otherwise it will be necessary for later generations to unlearn much of the "history" which the first generation learned, just as in the United

* A square in Port of Spain where Dr. Williams spoke to masses of Trindadians during the early years of the PNM.

States, for example, it has been necessary to rewrite the traditional views of the emergence of that great country in the eighteenth century.[1]

Dr. Laurence then goes on to define the problem as an imperfect marriage between the historian and the politician:

> Dr. Williams of course is both politician and historian, and if it be said that it is the politician who gives the book its punch, it is certainly the historian who gives it its authority. That authority needs frequently to be challenged, for the nationalist politician has from time to time led the historian to swerve dangerously; but the book is a great achievement.

One wonders whether the last statement is not defeated by all that precedes it.

Elsa Goveia's review of *British Historians and the West Indies*, first published in *Caribbean Quarterly* and since republished in John La Rose's *New Beacon Reviews No. 1*, is in its calm way a devastating piece of criticism. She thinks that Dr. Williams has misnamed his book and is able to show that he does not examine the work of seven or eight major British historians who wrote extensively about the West Indies, while he includes the work of an American who did not write about the West Indies at all. She mentions the "combination of omissions and hasty dogmatism which mars his present work" and concludes:

> Whether in education or history, good intentions are not enough, and the road to hell is paved with authoritative half-truths. No one is ever educated or liberated from the past by being taught how easy it is to substitute new shibboleths for old.[2]

She finds the book "disappointing and even somewhat irresponsible" and sees it as "just not good enough either for the people or for the students of the West Indies who are likely to read it." Later, she suggests that Dr. Williams write essays on the contemporary West Indian scene, which his experience as historian and politician could render valuable.

With these two warnings behind us, then, we cannot help but approach *From Columbus to Castro* with some degree of skepticism. Indeed, such skepticism is doubly necessary since Dr. Williams makes fantastic claims for the book and has been prepared to use its publication as a means of bolstering up his political position in Trinidad and Tobago. Dr. Williams states his purpose in a Preface (pp. 11–12):

> Few "colonials" have to date extended their nationalism to the cultural field and dedicated themselves to the task of writing—or rewriting, where necessary—their own history.
>
> The present work is designed to fill this gap and to correct this deficiency. Its scope is the entire West Indian area, including the Guianas—whether their connections have been or are British or French, Spanish or American or Danish. . . .
>
> Its goal is the cultural integration of the entire area, a synthesis of existing knowledge, as the essential foundation of the great need of our time, closer collaboration among the various countries of the Caribbean, with their common heritage of, subordination to, and dictation by outside interests.

From Columbus to Castro, then, has grown out of a belief that little is being done by West Indians in the rewriting of their own history, and its Preface is a direct criticism of the History Department of the University of the West Indies. Dr. Williams has now come to rescue historiography in the West Indies from the doldrums, as he claimed in 1956 to have rescued Trinidad from the Crown Colony system and from political anarchy and immorality in public affairs. He must have been living in a hermit's cell somewhere, bypassed by time. He clearly has taken no account of the growing number of unpublished theses in West Indian history, the fruit of hard work, serious scholarship, and at times nationalist pride. In this area, the lack of West Indian publishing houses willing to handle academic texts is a felt one.† Publishers know that relatively few West Indian historians will have Dr. Williams' ability to advertise their books on trips abroad, as well as on the local television and radio, since very few of them will be prime ministers of anywhere.

Apart from its messianic urge, the preface expresses Dr. Williams' very commendable aim of working toward "the cultural integration of the entire area." This indicates that he is one of an increasing band of creative writers in West Indies who sense the essential cultural similarity of the area. Dr. Williams, despite his abrupt withdrawal from the Federation after Jamaica left, has been an advocate of regional co-operation since the mid-forties. In the fifties, when he was lecturing about the necessity for a federation, George Lamming was producing *New World of the Caribbean*, a program of readings from British Caribbean writers which was federal in perspective, growing as it did out of the optimism of the British West Indian Federation. Now, *From Columbus to Castro* appears while Carifta is in its embryonic stage and while West Indian writers like Brathwaite and Walcott are annually widening their perspectives. Literature, history, and politics are thus quietly serving as a counterpoint to each other, and Dr. Williams is certainly not alone in the great task which he says that he has undertaken. It is therefore good to hear Dr. Williams mentioning the names of some of the region's creative writers in his final chapter, and in his Preface implying the identity of his quest with theirs, though it is by no means evident from some of his past and most of his recent political activities that he has

† Dr. Williams as a Caribbean leader could help to establish a Carifta (Caribbean Federation Trade Association) publishing house which would publish the growing volume of academic material on the West Indies, in reasonably priced editions.

applied their severe critiques and rejections of our sterile politics and Afro-Saxon attitudes to himself. It seems that he has read them to no end.

Dr. Williams' notion of writing history has hardly developed since *Capitalism and Slavery*. He still sees his job as the gathering together of a stockpile of facts to be hurled like bricks against dead and living imperialists. *Capitalism and Slavery*, like *The Negro in the Caribbean* (1942), was the product of the age when black intellectuals first began as a body to refute the stereotypes of the African which Europeans had for centuries been vending. Those two early works were the academic equivalent of Césaire's *Cahier* and Damas' *Pigments*, which the French banned and burned during World War II because these colonials had been able to show that France as a colonial power had been just as racist as Nazi Germany. Williams' early work was a significant advance in black consciousness. The fact that it is largely a reaction to white prejudice explains its extremely factual nature. Williams knew that if he aspired to alter the past, he could do so only by a true rediscovery of fact. The meticulous citation of facts and figures was a necessary defense against the accusation which is still being made about *Capitalism and Slavery*, that Williams, as a black man, was simply trying to write history as revenge. It was self that he sought to vindicate—his own self and the racial one—and the completeness of this self-vindication depended on the authenticity of the facts. Dr. Williams at this stage couldn't afford to write too much propaganda, since identity itself depended on his telling a substantial part of the truth.

When the victim of colonialism begins to tell his version of the truth, he normally shocks most the liberals within the ranks of the colonizing race. For the colonial, the study of his history is a journey into self rather than into time past; for the white liberal, it is more generally evasion of the deeper implications of racial and cultural contact under the artificial conditions of imperialism. Recently, Sylvia Wynter has argued that British critics of West Indian literature show

a similar capacity for evading its central issues and agonies.[3]
She identifies their failure as a failure to admit the part their
people played in West Indian history and to see how this
produced the rebellion of the West Indian mind in both its
positive and negative aspects. Her argument is that such rebellion leads to a totally different approach to art, which
critics brought up in a metropolitan tradition of criticism
judge from the standpoint of their own irrelevant or in-
adequate aesthetic. They therefore sidestep the judgment
which West Indian literature passes on both their culture and
their role in the sordid drama of empire, by concentrating on
the aesthetic flaws rather than the wider implications of
this literature.

Significantly, as Dr. Williams realizes, it is the Irish writers like Swift, Shaw, and Joyce and an Anglo-Indian such
as Orwell who come nearest to the corrosive irony which is
the peculiar gift of the colonial experience. "I understood
Britain's Irish policy and the Irish 'colonial' better after I
had read Swift, Shaw, and Joyce," he writes in Chapter 3 of
Inward Hunger. He also mentions with approval in *From
Columbus to Castro* Swift's scathing satire on British imperialism in *Gulliver's Travels.* Whites who have known the
pressures of colonialism themselves generally have an approach to history and to life which resembles that of their
black counterparts. Joseph Conrad, that Polish colonial,
sailor, and exile, in his *Heart of Darkness* was one of the few
Europeans who realized an idea that is a first principle with
black writers: that in the imperial collision, it was the West
that was on trial—western culture, values, mythology,
scholarship, tradition, and reputation for humanitarianism.
Heart of Darkness, a book which shows neither a love nor an
understanding of the African, is nevertheless a macabre
study of the decay of the West and ends up by expressing
a profound disillusion at the process of history itself.

The Williams of *Capitalism and Slavery* was part of this
international company of acrid ironists all bound together by
the futility of their colonial status.

In *Inward Hunger* Williams sees himself as the product of a largely irrelevant primary and secondary education who sets out to "conquer" Oxford. Chapter 3 of this book begins with an extremely lyrical description of Oxford's broad academic tradition. Dr. Williams' discovery of this heritage is seen almost as a fulfillment of self, the true discovery of his identity. Then there is a latish discovery of the pain and irrelevance, the non-identity, of being a colonial at Oxford —and a *black* colonial, at that. The second half of the chapter is decidedly less lyrical than the first. In it Dr. Williams describes how he moved from under the protective wing of his tutor and faced what he interprets as the racial prejudice of the institution as a whole, when he tried to qualify for a fellowship at All Souls. If a grim sort of humor informs his description of the ordeal of dinner parties, teacups, and choosing the correct piece of irrelevance that passes for wit in that incestuous world, it is a kind of naïve outraged innocence that informs the narration of a passage like this one:

The first incident occurred in the examination room. The examination included an oral translation from a foreign language. I chose French, Spanish not being available. The student had to enter a long room, in which he found some forty Fellows seated around a table. In the course of translation, I made a horrible mistake. The crowd roared. I received the distinct impression that the roar was aimed at me and not at the mistake. It sobered me at once. I lost all nervousness, I looked all around the room, at one individual member after the other until quiet had been restored. *I felt like a schoolmaster upbraiding by looks a group of unruly pupils.* Some began to pick their nails, one looked out of the window, one twiddled with a book in front of him. When there was absolute quiet I resumed translation in cold, unemotional voice. At the end I came to a passage of which I could not make head or tail. I declined to translate. The warden pressed me three times

to have a go at it. I refused. To set the matter at rest, I
told him on the final occasion that I did not wish to give
rise to another such guffaw as I had already listened to.
He thanked me for coming, and I took my leave.[4]

This is a remarkable passage precisely because it reveals
much more of Dr. Williams and the cultural predicament of
the Afro-Saxon colonial than he admits. Beguiled by the idea
that he had conquered Oxford merely because he had
proved himself their best history student in years, he had
dreamed briefly of joining the world of entrenched snobbery
and tradition. As he saw it, the world had replied by laugh-
ing at his blackness and his ignorance of one of its languages.
Dr. Williams' entire life since that period has been partly an
attempt to prove to the Fellows of All Souls that he is not
only their equal, but their superior; not anybody's pupil, but
everybody's schoolmaster.

How, for example, is the reader expected to take this account of the famous confrontation between Dr. Williams
and Mr. X of the Caribbean Commission, when, according
to him, they were trying to use his book *The Negro in the
Caribbean* as an excuse to dismiss him?

> Throughout the discussion I was conscious of two im-
> pressions: (a) that Mr. X was literally flabbergasted—
> I doubt that he ever expected any colonial to write or
> speak to him like that; (b) that morally and *physically*
> I was his superior. That he should be evasive and apolo-
> getic I fully expected. But he was more than that. At
> times he was quite incoherent . . . when we were
> through he had had enough; I could have gone on [talk-
> ing] for three hours.[5]

Here we find the daydream which the colonial always has
of humiliating Massa, his longing to ply the castigating whip
for a change. Beneath it lies the need to prove self and manhood, which can never be fulfilled unless there is an audience
of squirming colonizers and a chorus of applauding slaves.

There is a kind of triumphant pettiness about the passage which rings embarrassingly near to the core of the colonial psyche. All colonials have had the dream. In the case of Dr. Williams, though, a brilliant mind constantly satirizes itself. The last passage quoted reveals all the bitterness of the infighting of the late Crown Colony era, the loneliness of the individual whose dignity had always to be asserted as limits were placed on personality. V. S. Naipaul, who came a generation after Dr. Williams and also attended Oxford, found it a distinctly different place from the one Williams described. In contrast to philistine Trinidad, Naipaul tells us, England has been the only place where he has discovered "generosity—the admiration of equal for equal" (*The Middle Passage*, London, 1962, p. 42). England must have changed after twenty years; but under the strain of the thirties, the divided Afro-Saxon colonial psyche could scarcely be expected to cope without a weird unpredictable oscillation between its component halves. The victim learns to feel a simultaneous blend of love, hatred, and contempt for both black and white, and he swings unpredictably between these conflicting emotions. Sometimes he expresses *all* of them at the same time and in the same action. The result of this is generally irony of some sort, a peculiar rigor of mind, and a schoolmaster's desire to castigate and be respected.

In *From Columbus to Castro*, as in *Capitalism and Slavery*, one has the sense of a careful compilation and organization of fact to suit the exigencies of a central purpose. Examples of this accumulation abound in both books—the later book draws heavily on material from the former—and are especially to be seen in the chapters where Dr. Williams shows how the slave trade affected things like shipbuilding and the textile and iron industries in England. Here he mentions every minute article made from iron and used in the trade: fetters, axes, iron hoops, handcuffs, stoves, tools, guns, and a host of others. This accumulation of detail, which at times threatens to break down into absurdity, is, no doubt, meant to convey the impression of the enormity of the trade and is reinforced by a barrage of statistics, with which most other historians would have been satisfied. The device is semiliterary and semirhetorical. One merit of this kind of attention to detail is that with its direct reference notes, an adequate index, and the meticulous citation of sources, a work such as *Capitalism and Slavery* becomes a reference text and other scholars are able to benefit fully from the archivist activity of the pioneer historian. But G. R. Mellor on checking this work discovered that a few quotations had been taken out of context and edited to suit the main thesis. He concluded with the warning "that unless those who are engaged in research are very careful they will find what they are looking for."[6]

When, however, as in *From Columbus to Castro*, absolutely no indication is given as to the sources of the majority of facts and figures and there are few reference notes, the worth of the book is immediately in question. It cannot be safely used as the reference text it was intended to be, since the student has no immediate or remote means of checking either the facts or figures. He will never be able to ascertain unless he duplicated research already done by Dr. Williams (which would be rather a waste) whether the author is vending some of the same "authoritative half-truths" that both Drs. Laurence and Goveia have identified in his later work.

Lack of references must therefore be cited as a grievous flaw in *From Columbus to Castro*, especially since a substantial part of it is devoted to the presentation of bare statistics on the sugar industry throughout the ages. By constantly citing statistics without citing sources, Dr. Williams makes it impossible for the student to view these statistics in any context other than the one he himself provides. The quotation which he takes from Mark Twain about there being "lies, damned lies, and statistics" may well be true for his own work, for all the reader knows.

Another shortcoming is that at times fact seems to be indulged in for its own sake, until the pattern beneath the face of fact is obscured. Fact too often controls vision rather than vision fact. Perhaps this is because a sense of people as living complex beings rather than as economic, political, or sociological abstractions is generally missing from Dr. Williams' work. Elsa Goveia's comment on the West Indian historical experience is particularly apt here:

It is essential for West Indians to grasp in all its complexity the nature of the influence which slavery has exercised over their history. But they will not be able to do this until they can see the white colonists, the free people of colour, and the Negro slaves as joint participants in a human situation which shaped all their lives.[7]

Dr. Williams would probably dismiss this, as he dismisses Mellor's thesis, as the "idealist conception of history" (p. 540), though all that Dr. Goveia seems to be asking for is "understanding of the basic pressures inherent in the situation." She would, perhaps, prefer to be regarded as a humanist historian, which is the category in which she, in her Historiography, placed all those historians who not only accepted the humanity of Indian and African, but tried to understand the complex human situation created by West Indian history.

Truly creative writing about the West Indian past and present—whether it has been accomplished by poets like Césaire, Walcott, and Brathwaite, novelists such as Carpentier, Naipaul, and Lamming, historians such as Elsa Goveia, the C. L. R. James of The Black Jacobins, or Walter Rodney of A History of the Upper Guinea Coast; or a psychologist such as Fanon—has always been concerned with this need to understand and explore "the basic pressures inherent" in the West Indian situation. It has always been a question of trying to understand self, of self-knowledge. Ultimate deficiency in the historiography of the West Indies has, for both colonizer and colonized, almost invariably implied a failure in self-knowledge.

In the case of Dr. Williams, there is at times an almost deliberate abdication of the right to a self, an almost perverse reduction of experience to a rubbish heap of statistics about sugar. In his work, people seem to be conceived of as the sum of the facts and statistics concerning their lives—certainly a limited vision of experience, not calculated to fill anyone's inward hunger. One of the features about Swift's writing which has had little influence on Dr. Williams' vision is Swift's passionate protest, most evident in *A Modest Proposal*, at the economists' tendency, real then as well as now, to reduce people to statistics. In this respect the irony of the colonial experience has certainly turned against Dr. Williams. In order to counter the numerous damaging stereotypes which white people invented about black people, Dr. Williams adopts a method of obsessive factuality, which in the end also drains the black experience of its humanity.

The true historian of the West Indies in this era will need to have a strong sense of the West Indian people such as is seldom evident in *From Columbus to Castro*. For in the case of the Afro-West Indians more than even the poor whites and the East Indians, it was an entire race consisting of several peoples which was stereotyped as inferior and whose every aspect of being was invaded and violated. It is therefore necessary for the West Indian historian, who like Dr. Williams seeks to bring about "the cultural integration of the entire area" (p. 12), to do much more than present "a synthesis of existing knowledge" about the islands (which Dr. Williams does not do, in any case).

The historian of the seventies has a different role from the historian of the thirties, which Dr. Williams has remained. He will have to be something of a social anthropologist or a social psychologist and try to chart the enduring quality of mind which enabled people to survive the evil combination of circumstances. He will have to reject the idea that the blacks were simply the objects, and never the subjects, of their history until comparatively recent times. The blacks were the subjects of their history insofar as they negated the idea that they were less than human, insofar as they made repeated efforts at gaining their freedom, insofar as they took definite and unceasing action to help give their history its distinctive shape. They were its objects insofar as they were constantly at the mercy of their violators. Yet, as Dr. Williams himself notes, rebellion against their tormentors was as much part of the experience of black people as submission to them. The exceedingly repressive slave laws, as he says, bear eloquent witness of the fact. In rebelling, the slave was both expressing and vindicating a self. It is not enough, therefore, simply to mention the fact that such rebellions did occur and then to make a list of the corpses. It is necessary, if there is to be fresh vision, to do the same depth analysis of the dichotomy of rebellion and submission as has been done of the economics of slavery and sugar.

If the historian neglects to do this, he is bound to sink into the simple fatalism which informs Dr. Williams' huge work, in which the images of death and destruction are as pervasive as in Conrad's *Heart of Darkness*. Some of the most icily impressive chapters of the book narrate the tale of the terrible wastage of lives with a detachment that simply reinforces the blank brutality of the fact itself. Here at least the facts and figures are themselves frighteningly eloquent, and the factual method is fully justified in the face of the bleakness of the experience being described. In Chapter 4, it is the Spanish empire and the death of the Indians; later, it is to be seventeenth-century Barbados; then Jamaica and Haiti; then indentureship in Trinidad and Guyana with their phenomenal mortality rates; after that it is the malnutrition, hookworm, and malaria of the twentieth-century West Indies . . . As the Guyanese poet Martin Carter puts it in his poem *Black Friday 1962*,

> and everytime, and anytime,
> in sleep or sudden wake, nightmare, dream,
> Always for me the same vision of cemeteries, slow
>   funerals,
> broken tombs, and death designing all.

One does not have to travel far in West Indian literature to meet the image of death and abortion, though it is gradually being countered with images of the womb, birth, and resurrection.

It is as if the madness and eventual mysticism which Dr. Williams describes overtaking Columbus have also penetrated the very tissue of the historical experience of these islands. This is, of course, also a favorite idea with West Indian writers. Lamming writes in *In the Castle of my Skin*:

> A sailor called Christopher followed his mistake and those who came later have added theirs. Now he's dead, and as some say of the dead, safe and sound in the legacy of the grave. 'Tis a childish saying for they be yet present with the living. The only certainty these islands inherit was that sailor's mistake, and it's gone on from father to son 'mongst rich and poor.

This sense of fatality also informs Naipaul's *The Middle Passage*. It lies at the root of his irony, as much as it informs the acrid sarcasm which is part of Dr. Williams' response to the West Indian experience.

Time and again his conclusions about West Indian history closely resemble Naipaul's. As he traces the fierce international conflicts which took place in the sixteenth, seventeenth, and eighteenth centuries, it is the irony that time and time again engages his mind. Consider this passage, for example:

> From the territorial aspect, the West Indian colonies assumed an importance that appears almost incredible today, when one looks at those forgotten, neglected, forlorn dots on the map, specks of dust as de Gaulle dismissed them, the haggard and wrinkled descendants of the prima donnas and box office sensations of two hundred years ago (p. 88).

Ironic, if even a trifle inaccurate. The exploiters of this age preserve a much greater sense of propriety. But the bauxite of Jamaica, Guyana, and Surinam, the oil of Trinidad and Venezuela, and even the sunshine and the beaches of most of the islands still seem to be exploitable commodities and provide the enterprising descendant of the slave trader and planter with his adequate pound of flesh. It is not the decline of the West Indies that should engage our sentiment, but rather their endurance as a perennially fertile hunting ground for everyone except the people who live there. There are several passages in Brathwaite's most recent poetry which make this point with a kind of despair. Reviewing the sterile economics and politics of the area, he concludes [in *Islands*, title poem, p. 45] that:

> . . . the rope
> will never unravel
> its knots, the branding
> iron's travelling flame that teaches
> us pain, will never be
> extinguished. The islands' jewels:
> Saba, Barbuda, dry flat-
> tened Antigua, will remain rocks,
> dots, in the sky-blue frame
> of the map.

The difference between Brathwaite (who is professionally a historian and is about to publish one of those books on West Indian history which Dr. Williams claims that few people besides him are bothering to write) and Williams or Naipaul, who seem too paralyzed by the nightmare of West Indian history, is one of emphasis. Brathwaite is as much concerned with the fact and idea of survival as he is with the powerful fact of mortality and weakness. Naipaul, when, as in *A House for Mr. Biswas*, he does seriously consider the prospect of survival and rebellion, is concerned primarily with the interpenetration of rebellion and absurdity of identity and nonentity in the West Indian response to experience. In Naipaul the absurd West Indian situation leads to gestures at creative rebellion in the individual's efforts to arrange his meaningless world. These gestures may be Mr. Biswas' in his

attempts to build a house or Kripal Singh's in his attempts to
be Premier of a Crown Colony. In the small island the barriers between plebeian and patrician are really superficial.
All are caught in the circle of futility; thus rebellion itself,
because it is conducted by nowhere people, culturally and
economically both orphan and underprivileged, leads only to
a further dimension of absurdity.

It seems to me that Dr. Williams, both in his writing and
in his life, fulfills the Mohun Biswas syndrome. His sense of
the absurdity of West Indian history has led to a most relentless and sustained rebellion. But as a book like *Inward
Hunger* or a pamphlet like *My Relations with the Caribbean
Commission* proves, this rebellion remains painfully self-
conscious and at times betrays a longing to wield the same
schoolmaster's whip whose lash still burns across his memory. The need to prove mastery returns him and his rebellion
back to absurdity. An example will, perhaps, make my meaning clearer.

Massa Day Done, a speech which he made on March 22,
1961, has been considered one of his greatest. It had to be.
With elections in the offing, C. L. R. James inexplicably
fallen from grace, and the opposition forces growing daily
more vocal, Williams needed to maintain his reputation for
both rhetoric and intellect. Few Caribbean politicians would
have found the former difficult. Dr. Williams began with a
tirade of abuse against his political enemies which had the
distinct ring of robber-talk and *sans humanité* picong which
are both forms of folk rhetoric and must have pleased the
crowd no end:

> This pack of benighted idiots, this band of obscurantist
> politicians, this unholy alliance of egregious individual-
> ists, who have nothing constructive to say, who babble
> week after week the same criticisms that we have
> lived through for five long years, who, nincompoops as
> they are, think that they can pick up any old book the
> day before a debate in the Legislative Council and can
> pull a fast one in the Council by leaving out the

sentence or the paragraph or the pages which contradict their ignorant declamations—for people like these power is all that matters.[8]

The ending of the paragraph is rather a rhetorical anti-climax, but the string of explosive big words rhythmically building up to a kind of climax would have sounded good to the audience. Here was Dr. Williams, the national schoolmaster, fulfilling his dream which has become an obsession since the days of his humiliation before the Fellows of All Souls, Oxford. He was castigating unruly schoolboys by a display of his intellectual superiority. It doesn't matter that professional historians have shown that Dr. Williams too tends to omit passages which contradict his argument; that was not the irony anyone would have been likely to notice at the time. Throughout the speech he stressed his intellectual superiority. To attack his ideas, he said, was to attack "twenty years of assiduous research" and to jeopardize the interests of "our national community." He accused the opposition of "intellectual dishonesty" while he and his University of Woodford Square were "dedicated to the pursuit of truth and to the *dispassionate discussion of public issues.*" (Italics mine)

He then delivers a very fine lecture on the role of Massa in West Indian society. Massa was the one who historically brutalized black people and who was always opposed to their independence. He sought power for his own ends just like the house slaves in the opposition party. In Trinidad, Massa met his match with the advent of the PNM (Dr. Williams' party) which had done so much to set right some of the major injustices which had been historically perpetrated by Massa. Next follows a list of the party's achievements in the areas of agriculture and lands, housing, health, education, and so on.

The real surprise comes at the end when Dr. Williams boasts about the projected visit of Sir Winston Churchill to the island and expresses his pleasure that it is the PNM government which would proudly show him what local diplomacy had achieved in Chaguaramas, in begging him for "protection for West Indian products," and in "making representations to live in respect of West Indian migrators to the United Kingdom." It is amazing how easily all the bombast deflates itself and, miraculously, still remains bombast. After the long litany which showed that "Massa day done," Dr. Williams suddenly returns to the light of common day, where he depends on Massa's subsidies and Massa's open door.

But the irony goes even further than this, because if Massa, by Dr. Williams' own definition earlier in the speech, was, black or white, a man who was ultimately opposed to the independence of the colonized, one couldn't choose a better example of Massa than Churchill himself. It was Churchill who was most adamant on the matter of India's independence. He scornfully referred to Mahatma Gandhi as "a seditious Middle Temple lawyer posing as a fakir in dhoti" and asking for independence for his people. Churchill couldn't bear to think that anyone who studied in England should not be an Anglophile or should identify with his own oppressed people. Race pride and *imperium in imperio* received their embodiment in Churchill, for whom Dr. Williams was proud to unroll the red carpet a few minutes after defining the Churchill-phenotype as the enemy of his people. This apparent right-about-turn would be inexplicable to anyone who did not understand Dr. Williams' Oxford experience. For him it isn't really a right-about-turn at all. It is yet another opportunity to prove to those invisibly grinning Fellows of All Souls how well he can translate French, how well he can beat them at their own game of diplomacy. Chaguaramas was not a PNM victory. Everyone recognized it as Dr. Williams' personal triumph . . . Everyone, that is, except C. L. R. James who saw it as primarily the people's, whose spokesman Dr. Williams was. To show Churchill Chaguaramas, then, was the last thing necessary to assure himself of his achievement. The achievement could not be real until it had received the applause of the right people.

But that was not the end of the speech. The more vehement and histrionic the early rebellion, the more relentless the late swing toward absurdity. After the passage on Churchill, the speech moves to its anticlimactic climax:

> It is only left now for Her Majesty the Queen to visit us. After all we are an important part of the Commonwealth, and if Her Majesty can go to Australia, to India and to Pakistan, to Nigeria and to Ghana, she can also come to the West Indies.

Two interpretations are possible of this wonderful passage. The first is that Dr. Williams may have been welcoming the pomp and circumstance of a royal visit engineered by his own genius, as the ultimate proof of the greatness of his personal achievement, since it is difficult to see how he envisaged that the presence of the Queen per se could help the people of the West Indies in any way whatsoever. Indeed, he had earlier in the speech described the house slaves:

> Always better treated than their colleagues in the field, they developed into a new caste of West Indian society, aping the fashion of their masters, wearing their cast-off clothing, and dancing the quadrille with the best of them.

He even mentioned postrevolutionary Haiti with its court, its title, "its Duke of Marmalade and its Count of Lemonade, exploiting the Negro peasants." Indeed, nearly twenty years before, he had written of the colored West Indian middle classes:

> The visit of a Prince of Wales, the honeymoon of a royal couple find them ready to display their loyalty to the throne, their affection for the mother country.[9]

Eight years after 1961, Dr. Williams accepted the award of Companion of Honour at the hands of the Queen, thus fulfilling both halves of the Afro-Saxon psyche, that of rebel and that of conformist to values which as rebel he despised— or rather, said he despised.

The second possibility is that Dr. Williams may have realized the deep love which his generation of West Indians, nourished on the buns, slogans, and lemonade of countless Empire Day celebrations, have for royalty and intended to use Her unsuspecting Majesty as a gimmick to strengthen the devotion of his worshipers toward himself. Royal visits had provided excellent bread and circuses during the era of direct British rule, culminating in the fifties, when they had been relentlessly employed, first to prop up the foundering Crown Colony system and, failing that, to effect a smooth transition from colonialism to neo-colonialism. One of the biggest sins of Guyana's [People's Progressive Party] of 1953 was its refusal to pay even lip service to the throne. Some members had even picketed the Princess Royal, telling her "Limey Go Home," in spite of the fact that her propinquity to the throne had been most carefully explained. Among the sedition charges brought up against Nazurdeen in 1953 was his alleged declaration "that the Queen was nobody but only a symbol of imperialism and that all the white capitalists in the colony [British Guiana] were her stooges."[10] Perhaps remembering the Ordeal of Teacups and Cutlery at Oxford which preceded admission to a fellowship, Dr. Williams realized that certain games had to be played by the rules. Trinidad therefore needed royalty to bless its independence. Not surprisingly, the independence games have retained most of the features of the Empire games.

Thus, absurdity has led to rebellion which in its turn is a reinitiation into fresh absurdity. This is distinctly the Mohun Biswas syndrome, which demands that he forever leave and return to the colonial monkey house. The difference between Naipaul and Dr. Williams is that the former uses irony to probe and analyze the pain of his own loss, cultural orphanage, forced ambivalence, and futility, while the latter exploits irony as a means of reassuring himself of his own moral and intellectual superiority . . . This has led to a failure in self-knowledge, an inability to reconcile the broken halves of the psyche, and the necessity either to retreat from a people growing daily in awareness or to perform feats of self-justification over television and radio.

It is not surprising, then, to find Dr. Williams concluding from time to time in *From Columbus to Castro* that West Indian history is absurd. Exasperated at the continual efforts which were being made to keep the planter class alive, he finally explodes: "West Indian History is indeed nothing but a record of the follies and foibles of mankind" (p. 229).

This closely resembles Naipaul's now famous passage in *The Middle Passage* which states that "the history of this West Indian futility" can never be satisfactorily told, because "History is built around achievement and creation; and nothing was created in the West Indies."[11] *From Columbus to Castro* certainly reinforces such a conclusion. In it the West Indies are seen as a theater in which word, deed, religious idealism, belief, morality, custom, the very foundations of humanity itself, rotted under slavery, sugar, and the plantation system. Dr. Williams catalogues this decay, while at the same time trying to show that in West Indian history the entire history of Europe stands condemned.

In this respect he plays the role not only of schoolmaster but also of judge—two closely related roles, since they both carry with them the dual joys of castigation and condemnation. Thus (p. 11) Dr. Williams judges the world as each country sends its actors across the West Indian stage:

> For over four and a half centuries the West Indies have been the pawns of Europe and America. Across the West Indian stage the great characters, political and intellectual, of the Western World strut and fret their hour. . . .

The theater image is a trifle imprecise. Dr. Williams seems to conceive of the West Indies more as a universal assizes,

over which he himself presides as Grand Inquisitor, using
West Indian history as so much evidence for or against the
whole of Europe. Concerned with the moral implications of
slavery, he judges each personage according to how he relates
to the African, acquitting him if he can acknowledge black
humanity and condemning him if he shows any ambivalence
in the affair. It is Lestrade's role in Walcott's *Dream on
Monkey Mountain* that he seems to be fulfilling.

Thus, in Chapters 16 and 17 Dr. Williams looks at how
the entire cities of Liverpool and Manchester, built up by
the proceeds of the slave trade and slavery, first support the
trade and then argue just as bitterly against it, on the
grounds that it helps preserve the archaic mercantile system.
Nelson, Britain's loftiest hero, is tried and defrocked as one
who was against any sort of abolition (p. 261). Pitt the
Younger is tried and found wanting. After examining Pitt's
inconsistency on the issue, Dr. Williams concludes, "The
great minister stood self-condemned"—which, of course,
saves Dr. Williams the trouble of having to find further
evidence to condemn him himself (p. 263). Hume, Jefferson,
Chatham, North, Colbert are all guilty. Cowper is guilty of
weak sentimentality, Wordsworth of apathy, and the eighteenth-century purveyors of the myth of the Noble Savage
are duly ridiculed as absurd. Gladstone, in whose gentle
footprints Dr. Williams himself was due to follow when he
became Privy Councillor and Companion of Honour, is also
sentenced and with him the entire flawed Liberal tradition
of which he was a cornerstone. The mortality rate is certainly high. Wilberforce seems to come off a little better
than he does in *Capitalism and Slavery*, perhaps because Dr.
Williams does not dwell so insistently on what his enemies
had to say. But he is condemned as too wishy-washy and
gradualist in his conception of change. Canning is berated
for his attempt to serve humanity and mammon at the same
time (p. 297). Among the few redeemed are Clarkson,
Schoelcher, and Adam Smith who were reasonably consistent in their attack on the morality or economics of
slavery.

But a peculiar danger generally awaits all Grand Inquisitors—a danger of moral self-righteousness. Two examples will suffice. First, there is Dr. Williams' judgment of Canning (p. 297):

> The British Government's middle-of-the-road policy of gradualism was explained by the Prime Minister, Canning. There were knots, he said, which could not be suddenly disentangled and must be cut. What was morally true must not be confused with what was historically false . . . It was not, nor could it be made, a question merely of right, of humanity, or of morality.

But Canning, as Dr. Williams should know well by now, was simply articulating the dilemma of the Prime Minister anywhere and the classic British Conservative tradition of slow concession to change. Politics are, and have always been, a perilous sacrifice of morality to expediency in the pragmatist and a painful conflict between morality and expediency in the men of conscience. Most politicians solve the matter by doing away with conscience and identity altogether. This is really the most elementary lesson in politics. Politicians become the world's most consummate comedians when, having renounced morality and identity, they insist that a moral interpretation be accorded their every action.

Then there is one of Dr. Williams' more damaging observations about Wilberforce (p. 298):

> The British abolitionists relied for success upon aristocratic patronage, parliamentary diplomacy, and private influence with men in office. They deprecated extreme measures and feared popular agitation. This conservatism was largely the result of the leadership of Wilberforce, who was addicted to moderation, compromise and delay. He was a member of the secret committee of 1817 set up to investigate and repress popular dis-

content, in the days which foreshadowed the Peterloo Massacre.

Wilberforce, like Canning, seems from this passage merely to have been a product of the narrow and undemocratic pre-1832 English tradition, and one ought not to blame him too much for his "moderation" and "compromise." If one judges Dr. Williams' regime in Trinidad by the same absolute—cold morality—one may be tempted to arrive at the same conclusion; that here is one who "deprecates extreme measures and fears popular agitation"—except, of course, that which he initiates himself; one who has set up a committee and passed laws "to investigate and repress popular discontent" and to inquire into subversion; one who compromises over change, believing, as he says he does, in gradual but distinct reform. The self-righteous indignation of the historically maimed mars his vision, which too often remains one of outraged innocence at European hypocrisy and makes him less aware of the limits of his own rebellion. This is one of the pitfalls of protest politics, as it is of protest literature of any kind. Rebellion, if immature, can lead to a defeat rather than a liberation of consciousness.

This criticism is also true of the last quarter of the book, which treats the recent past. For example, Dr. Williams, to highlight the significance of the thirties, tabulates (pp. 473–74) the unrest of that decade in an interesting passage, which appeared before verbatim in *The Negro in the Caribbean* (see p. 93 of that work):

The road to revolution had been marked out. The revolution broke out in the years 1935–1938. Consider the chronology of these fateful years. A sugar strike in St. Kitts, 1935; a revolt against an increase in customs duties in St. Vincent, 1935; a coal strike in St. Lucia, 1935; labour disputes on the sugar plantations in British Guiana, 1935; an oil strike, which became a general strike in Trinidad, 1937; a sugar strike in St. Lucia, 1937; sugar troubles in Jamaica, 1937; a dockers' strike in Jamaica, 1938. Every British Governor called for warships, marines, and aeroplanes; total casualties in the British colonies amounted to 29 dead, 115 wounded.

That paragraph, as it stands was good enough for the forties, but hardly for the seventies. It ought to have been succeeded somewhere by a similar tabulation for the fifties and sixties, which would tell the reader something about the continuity of both distress and rebellion. Consider the chronology of these fateful years. Political, racial, and social upheaval in Guyana, 1962–64, followed by states of emergency, hunts for arms and subversive literature, the presence of British soldiers and warships, arson, labor disputes, long strikes, looting, murder, *mauvais langue*, the total poisoning of race relations on all sides, liberal cases of all varieties, commissions of inquiry serving little purpose and evading essential issues, mass emigration of skilled labor, civil servants, and graduates . . . Constant unrest in Jamaica: poverty, weekly shootings by both police and black youth, anti-Chinese riots in 1965, searches for arms, emergency in Kingston, restriction of freedom of movement and assembly; sporadic outbreaks of arson, strikes too numerous to mention, many of them quite serious, and culminating in a serious spate of labor unrest in 1968; the bulldozing of thousands of squatters from West Kingston to make way for a new industrial complex and flats for party members; the migration of these squatters to Maypen Cemetery from whence they are also driven by social workers, fire hoses, policemen, and soldiers; the celebrated Rodney affair acting like a regional catalyst; riots and arson in October 1968; increasing use of the army as police force . . . Consider Trinidad of these times, which Dr. Williams, strangely, refuses to do: strikes of all kinds . . . state of emergency in 1965, anti-Communist witch hunt, revealing hardly any Communist witches; the ISA to control labor through legislation unfavorably balanced to the advantage of the employer; demonstrations of all sorts; the Solomon affair; gas stations probe; the army revolt of 1970, shootings, calling out the army, marines; appeal to the British and the Yankees, abused over the Chaguaramas issue, to send help to a beleaguered Trinidad government in 1970; treason charges, sedition, another state of emergency, murder, arson, Draft Public Order Act. In the midst of all these things, an independence which few can take seriously. Obviously.

The list can go on and on, since this is but a short catalogue of the bacchanal of the sixties. The total dead and wounded, the total minds shattered in the dark, the total teeth and ribs broken, the total homeless have not been catalogued as yet. The total frustration hasn't been measured, though Dr. Williams probably has figures on that too, which he means to release before the next elections.

From Columbus to Castro, a work so rich in fact in its chapters which treat of the slave trade, the abolition, the decline of sugar in the nineteenth century, and the growth of gigantic companies in the twentieth, has virtually nothing to say about the post-World War II period. How is one to assess its worth? The first few chapters on Spanish and French imperialism in the West Indies are old hat and can have been derived from almost anywhere. The chapters on abolition rehash arguments with which the student of *Capitalism and Slavery* is by now quite familiar. However, more details are given, though no one can say where most of these come from, since the writer declines the reader this privilege. The chapter on the Haitian revolution, a clear paraphrase of C. L. R. James's *The Black Jacobins*, is, like Dr. Williams' treatment of all black rebellion, annalistic rather than analytical.

As the book proceeds, the reader familiar with the rest of Dr. Williams' work finds himself wondering what is really going on. Passages he has read before, entire chapters almost, seem to repeat themselves. Chapter 18 is a simple paraphrase of Sewell's *The Ordeal of Free Labour* (1862) and adds little new to what Dr. Williams has already said in *British Historians and the West Indies*. Also, material that appeared before in Williams' book on Trinidad appears here once more. Chapter 19 on indentureship again repeats work done in *History of the People of Trinidad and Tobago*. Perhaps that is why it contains no close examination of indentureship in Guyana or Surinam, despite the regional scope claimed for the book. Here, as in the book on Trinidad, little attempt is made to assess the effects of indentureship on the society. The problems of acculturation which faced Indian society in the West Indies, the questions of religion and language, of race relations and conflict are simply ignored, though one would have thought that some notion of these matters were necessary in a history book whose object is "the cultural integration of the entire area." An opportunity is lost to examine human relations in Trinidad during this exceedingly rich late nineteenth-century period, the latter-day struggle of French and English cultures for the souls of black folk, the international spectrum of races, languages, currencies, and customs that was nineteenth-century Port of Spain. Thus, *From Columbus to Castro* repeats here the main failing of the book on the people of Trinidad and Tobago, in that one never really sees the people of Trinidad or Tobago. Indeed, no one could ever guess from this book that the people of the different islands are profoundly different in temperament.

Chapter 20 of *From Columbus to Castro* contains passages which are almost a word-for-word transcription of passages in Chapter 12 of the *History of the People of Trinidad and Tobago*. Chapter 22, that hastily written chapter on the 1865 rebellion in Jamaica, is a brief summary of what Dr. Williams has already done better in *British Historians and the West Indies*. Some of the succeeding chapters, especially Chapter 26, repeat huge chunks from *The Negro in the Caribbean*. Chapter 25 is an impressive sketch of the growth of American influence in the region, but this analysis is not carried beyond the early forties, so that the reader cannot gauge what the position is today. Indeed, the more one reads, the clearer does Dr. Williams' secret design for over three quarters of the book become. The real aim is humanitarian rather than economic—to present a package-deal summary of most of what he has written before, in words as near to the original as possible, with a hundred or so new

pages as a lagniappe, which, at the modest price of twenty-
two dollars and fifty cents, would save the already hard-
pressed citizen the money he would otherwise have to spend
if he wanted to acquire the separate volumes of Dr. Williams' most prolific career.

One's wonder widens as one proceeds. In a book which
has been exceedingly rich in facts and statistics about sugar
throughout the ages, the reader learns nothing about Trinidad's oil or the bauxite of Guyana, Surinam, and Jamaica,
interests which are far more important today. There are
works available on these things, some of it done by some of
the very people whom Dr. Williams' Preface apparently
aimed to discredit. An analysis of the functioning of the multinational corporation in the area would have helped as a
basis for understanding the perils which attend attempts at
disentanglement of the regional economy from the metropolitan snare and might have led to a less vacillating attitude toward the Castro regime in Cuba. Nothing much is
said about tourism though it is becoming of increasing importance in the lives of these islands, threatening to split
tiny impoverished societies asunder for the nth time in history.

No analysis is offered of the political movement toward
a nominal independence. The emergence of trade unionism
is barely mentioned. The formation and failure of the British West Indian Federation are hardly ever treated. Dr.
Williams' real energies seem to have been consumed by his
tremendous efforts at looking backwards. Thus, he has little
to say about the present. The struggle for the franchise and
the important features of political consciousness which it
revealed in the different islands are not treated. Marryshow,
Critchlow, Manley, or Jagan might never have existed, for all
we are told of them in this book. Yet the book calls itself
The History of the Caribbean: 1492–1969. It is probably
meant to be the first volume of a really serious study.

Chapter 28 on Castroism is disappointing. It simply mirrors, rather than explains, Dr. Williams' ambivalence, as a
Caribbean leader, on the only country that has seriously

attempted to make independence a meaningful concept. The chapter hinges around a series of quotations pro but more generally con Castro's Cuba. More often than not, Castro is depicted as an impractical dreamer who doesn't care for economists and indulges in "planless planning," which leaves his economy in a mess. While Dr. Williams does try in the final chapter to make up his mind about the meaning and implications of Cuba, he seems to be more concerned with stressing the superiority of his own, ironically, gradualist policy of steering decidedly between the Cuban and the Puerto Rican examples. The last two chapters ought to provide the economists with a field day, since they will better be able to trace the disparity between what Dr. Williams says that he is doing and what he is doing in fact. The least charitable of his critics see his late attempts to recognize Cuba five or six years after he defined that country as enemy number one as simply another election gimmick which is meant to indicate apparent concessions in the direction of socialism while the basic structure of the economy remains the same. The more generous of his critics see his new attitude toward Cuba as part of a genuine attempt to initiate gradual but definite change in Trinidad. Whichever is true, it is clear that the youth are not really with the Prime Minister and that whatever efforts are being made now, have almost certainly come too late.

The most important thing about Cuba seems to have been the lesson which she has taught the rest of the Caribbean: that change is important, that some sort of rapport between the leader and the masses is necessary, and that, above all, self-criticism is an important feature in independence. These are elementary lessons, but there is little evidence that they have been learned anywhere in the rest of the Caribbean. Dr. Williams has had tremendous insight. A book like *Education in the British West Indies*, published since 1950 (written four years before), makes it clear that the entire education system needs to be restructured and lays down lines along which this restructuring should take place. There should be a greater emphasis on vocational and technical training. The area should understand the irrelevance of Oxford and Cambridge to local needs of agricultural development, an arrested urbanization, and the development of technical and commercial skills. A West Indian university should "consciously *and belligerently* undertake to guide its society along the lines marked out by the objective economic movement and in the direction to which the demands of the people are pointing."[12] The university will have to join the mass struggle if its academic education is to have any meaning.[13] However, if it is to have direction, "the governing body should be *controlled by the political representatives of the people*."[14] Thus, not only was the university to play a full part in nationalist politics, but politics was to control and shape the destiny of the institution.

Dr. Williams clearly did not envisage the possibility that both the politics and the academic endeavor of the area could be sterile, that the last thing postindependence politicians desire is that their authority should be challenged by either people or university. Everything which he wrote in the forties reads like a piece of bitter irony these days. Education has continued to be along the lines of metropolitan academism, churning out each year a fresh crop of GCE ordinary-level students whom the civil service cannot use. Education in agriculture was to have been accompanied by a vigorous policy of land reform, according to Williams' book. Fourteen years after his accession, there has been neither education in agriculture for rural areas, nor substantial land reform. The question of the sugar lands hasn't begun to be asked. The university as an institution has no obvious commitment to anything under the sun; and those few lonely souls who try to stop their own alienation by attempting to bridge the widening gap between the campus and the community, those who attempt to climb the fences which are being constructed with gruesome symbolism around the campuses of the UWI, get caught up in the barbed wire. Lecturers have been expelled for alleged subversive activity, and in the Trinidad of 1970, university personnel have been detained on most fantastic charges and released because Dr.

Williams himself, now in his disguise as Minister of National Security, could discover no adequate grounds upon which to hold them. Some university people, at times the most innocuous of souls, have received poison-pen letters and phone calls from people who have eventually identified themselves as supporters of the Prime Minister of Trinidad, all because they tried to involve themselves at grass-roots level. It is so throughout the area. Dr. Williams quotes Che Guevara's criticisms of Cuban economic policy, without noting that the most remarkable fact about these criticisms was that they were allowed to be made before the Cuban people and the world. It is not possible anywhere else in the West Indies for one so close to the center of power to admit failure.

But without self-knowledge, there can be no self-development. It is not therefore surprising that Dr. Williams in his last chapter is in constant despair about West Indian identity. The despair is probably as much personal as social. The passage (p. 502) that sums up his thoughts on a Caribbean identity is worth quoting in full. The region, he says, has indeed produced writers like Lamming, Walcott, Césaire, Fanon, Naipaul, and Brathwaite:

> Nevertheless artistic, community and individual values are not for the most part authentic but, to borrow the language of the economist, possess a high import content, the vehicles of import being the educational system, the mass media, other films and the tourists. V. S. Naipaul's description of West Indians as mimic men is harsh but true. Finally psychological dependence strongly reinforces other forms of dependence. *For in the last analysis, dependence is a state of mind.* A too long history of colonialism seems to have crippled Caribbean self-confidence and Caribbean self-reliance, and a vicious circle has been set up: psychological dependence leads to an ever-growing economic and cultural dependence on the outside world. Fragmentation is intensified in the process. And the greater degree of

dependence and fragmentation further reduces local self-confidence.

That definition of the vicious circle in which the region seems to be caught is one of the finest I know outside of Naipaul. Recently, indeed, Naipaul himself has made a similar observation:

> The small islands of the Caribbean will remain islands, impoverished and unskilled, ringed as now by a *cordon sanitaire*, their people not needed anywhere. They may get less innocent and less corrupt politicians; they will not get less hopeless ones. The island Blacks will continue to be dependent on the books, films, and goods of others; in this important way, they will continue to be the half-made societies of a dependent people, the Third World's third world. They will forever consume; they will never create. They are without material resources; they will never develop the higher skills. Identity depends in the end on achievement and achievement there cannot be but small. Again and again the millennium will seem about to come.[15]

This is the message of *The Middle Passage* taken to even gloomier extremes. It cannot be denied, though it can be qualified. No one anywhere can escape the tyranny of the mass media, and it is perhaps somewhat comforting to note that the entire bent of European literature suggests that the West Indies are not unique in their quest for identity. Identity depends in the end on self-knowledge, not on achievement. This is why people like Dr. Williams and his entire generation, who have *achieved* so much, are still uncertain about their identity. It isn't simply a question of the poverty of the area; it may be more a matter of failing to recognize roots, whatever these are. If the education system is irrelevant, it can be changed at least partially and along lines that Dr. Williams himself defined over twenty years ago. If increased tourism is to blame for a steady corruption of values, a more careful approach to the social effects of this aspect of the economy needs to be made.

For Williams simply to acquiesce in Naipaul's definition of West Indians as mimic men is, first of all, to fail to see that Naipaul was in that book talking particularly about West Indian politicians. As usual, Dr. Williams does not apply the lesson to himself, but sufficient has been said above to show that the statement does apply to him as much as it does to any part of the society. For Naipaul to state absolutely that West Indians will never create because to create one must have identity and to have identity one must create seems to be a sacrifice of truth for absurdist paradox. Were Trinidad all that sterile, it could not have produced Williams, Naipaul, James, Padmore, Sparrow, Spoiler, Mannette, and a host of others. Barbados, we have sometimes to remind ourselves, produced both Lamming and Brathwaite, whose contribution to our knowledge of self, and therefore to our identity, have been immense.

It is really quite naïve to view our economic dependence as an insurmountable barrier in the path of identity—unless the only identity recognized is the economic one. In this respect, Dr. Williams' final definition of the Caribbean predicament is much more important than Naipaul's. His statement, however, needs to be qualified with the observation that the lower classes in the West Indies have always been more certain of roots, religion, and self than the twisted products of a metropolitan education. When they mimic, they often make something of what they copy. Thus the black power mass movement of 1970 in Trinidad is very superficially interpreted if it is seen only as an imitation of the American thing. It is as Trinidadian as Canboulay, the Butler marches, Carnival, and the brilliant political calypsos which have been sung in 1970. The masses were transforming soul culture and international rhetoric and slogans, quite often improvising in mid-stride. The Rastafari cult, visible symbol of the worst kind of colonial neglect, has produced an artist such as Ras Daniel Heartman, a man with a deep sense of both tragedy and triumph, and has been a visible influence in the work of all serious Jamaican artists, including her talented musicians. Recently, Jamaica's substantial contribution to world jazz as well as to her own musical identity has been noted by James Carnegie.[16] All kinds of things are going on in the West Indies, which Naipaul and Williams seem not to consider important, although these things do indicate that in spite of a terrible past, West Indians do possess considerable freedom of mind. The politicians are really some distance behind the people. Finally what is always important about both Dr. Williams and Vidia Naipaul is what they omit, as well as what they say.

History, as a number of West Indian artists seem to be depicting it, is the study of human survival in the teeth of suffering. Finally, Naipaul the novelist has a more complex vision of West Indian history than Naipaul the social commentator, who tends toward an almost histrionic despair. A friend of mine describes Naipaul as a man who travels about the world looking for despair. The despairing vision of both Naipaul and Williams derives in part from their closeness to a European way of seeing. By not studying the West Indian people in any true depth, Williams ironically reduces their history to a Carlylean study of the lives of a number of significant individuals. Naipaul accepts the Froudian formula that there are no true people in the West Indies. Had Naipaul bothered with J. J. Thomas' *Froudacity* he might have qualified his opinion. Dr. Williams fails, not in not having appreciated Thomas, but in remaining too long in the late nineteenth-century ambivalence toward the world of the colonizer which was very much Thomas'. Both Dr. Williams and Naipaul seem finally to regret their position as poor relations at the European feast.

The most unfortunate thing which could happen to *From Columbus to Castro* would be for it to be regarded as the bible of the new era. It is distinctly a *fin de siècle* performance, a work that marks the spiritual end of a generation, the last will and testament of an era. The fact that Dr. Williams is much better at making statements about the past than about the present proves this. The very context in which the book was first welcomed to Trinidad also proves this. What was noticeable about Kamal Mohammed's panegyric was not only the adulatory 1956 catch phrases which he showered on Dr. Williams, but his lament that he is the last survivor of that original young brigade. When Kamal Mohammed told Dr. Williams, "Like a modern Moses you resolved to lead your people out of the house of Bondage,"[17] he may well have been aware that when Moses quit the scene, the Israelites were still in the wilderness. He may also have been aware of the politically disconcerting tendency which Dr. Williams shares with the biblical cross-country walker, of disappearing for long periods from the people to talk to his personal god, then descending from Sinai with a shining face and a mouth full of divinely inspired rhetoric to dazzle their eyes and puzzle their minds with strange new laws. This time the long sojourn on Monkey Mountain has produced *From Columbus to Castro* and the new Charter, "the most profound concept in contemporary political, social and economic thought."

The real point of Kamal's speech was his consciousness of the fact that with the New Year reshuffle and the final dismissal of O'Halloran and Montano, the pillars of the business interests in the party, the fact that he was an Indian was the only real reason he still remained in the Cabinet. William Demas, after all, is *the* real man in Carifta. Kamal, feeling his unimportance to the now empty nest, and perhaps knowing Dr. Williams' capacity for loneliness and authoritarianism, was fairly lyrical with his praise. The climax to his declaration of loyalty is, however, slightly tinged with self-interest: "I feel a great sense of humility, pride, and thankfulness as the only Minister of Government who is still with you."[18] One wonders which feeling was strongest, humility which the moment required, pride at having survived where even the blue-eyed boys seem to have perished, or gratitude for benefits derived . . . Kamal's speech was, like *From Columbus to Castro*, more a funeral oration on the passing of the old regime than a fanfare of welcome to the new.

The last thing which needs to be commented on is the citation of the party motto—"Great is PNM and it will prevail"—as part of the dedication of the book to the party. This motto, cited in English in the book, is still cited in Latin, as well as on the front page of the party newspaper—"Magna est PNM et prevalebit." Few better examples of worse taste can be uncovered in the party's unwholesome history than the motto of the party itself. The original Latin motto has the word "veritas" (truth) which the PNM have replaced by the letters PNM. In other words, the implications of the motto is one of Orwellian 1984 absurdity—*the party is truth and truth is the party.*

Nowadays, with the nation itself daily questioning the credibility of the party, the party motto is beginning to sound like its epitaph and that of its philosopher-king. It is the fact that the truth prevails which has eroded the moral ground from under the party. It may win further elections for want of an alternative, but it will be leading no one. Insofar as Dr. Williams is concerned, two attitudes seem possible. One is tempted to pass on him the kind of absolute judgment which he has passed on all and sundry in both history and politics. In this respect a quotation from Acton, quoted in Elsa Goveia's *Historiography*, seems particularly apt: "A man is justly despised who has one opinion in history and another in politics, one for abroad and another at home, one for opposition and another for office."[19]

This, however, is too absolute and implies that Acton understood neither history nor politics. The statement does not take into account the capacity of history itself to undermine belief or of politics to defeat morality. It should not be a matter of indulged contempt but one of austere silence, that the senior historian of a people, who has found Caribbean history—his own past—absurd, should have himself contributed so richly to the perpetuation of such absurdity. The 1930s generation has run its time and is slowly taking its place as just another link in the common chain. The 1950s generation will soon begin its mistakes. The people of the forties seem to be quite bewildered, caught as they are, between the embarrassing frenzy of an aging rebel and the posturing of youth, who also cannot recognize themselves as simple common links in the chain. In the struggle for power which characterizes the end of this era, as of any other, what is being lost is the sense of historical continuity. Regrettably, a deficient work such as *From Columbus to Castro* cannot restore it. It will help to integrate neither the people of Trinidad nor of the Caribbean area. If it does by mistake, then we are even more absurd than Dr. Williams or Naipaul has imagined.

REFERENCES

1. K. O. Laurence, "Colonialism in Trinidad and Tobago," *Caribbean Quarterly*, Vol. IX, No. 3 (Sept. 1963), p. 53.

2. E. V. Goveia, "New Shibboleths for Old," *New Beacon Reviews No. 1*, John La Rose, ed. (1968), p. 37.

3. S. Wynter, "Reflections on West Indian Writing and Criticism," *Jamaica Journal*, Vol. II, No. 4 and Vol. III, No. 1 (1968/1969).

4. E. E. Williams, *Inward Hunger*, London, 1969, p. 46.

5. E. E. Williams, *My Relations with the Caribbean Commission 1945–1955*, p. 11.

6. G. R. Mellor, *British Imperial Trusteeship 1783–1850*, London, 1951. On p. 540 of *From Columbus to Castro* Williams does mention Mellor's book, with the dry comment that it propounds "the idealist conception of history," a fault of which Williams himself will never be accused—though the ironist, such as Williams is, is quite often a frustrated romantic idealist.

7. E. V. Goveia, op. cit., p. 34.

8. E. E. Williams, *Massa Day Done*, Port of Spain, 1961.

9. E. E. Williams, *The Negro in the Caribbean*, Washington, D.C., 1942, p. 60.

10. *The West India Committee Circular*, Vol. 69 (1954), p. 48.

11. V. S. Naipaul, *The Middle Passage*, London, 1962, p. 29.

12. E. E. Williams, *Education in the British West Indies*, New York, 1968, p. 75.

13. Ibid., p. 77 (italics mine).

14. Ibid., p. 82 (italics mine).

15. V. S. Naipaul, *New York Review of Books*, Sept. 3, 1970, quoted by David Renwick in "Why Constantine Resigned," *Sunday Guardian* (Trinidad), Sept. 27, 1970, p. 21.

16. J. Carnegie, "Notes on the History of Jazz and Its Role in Jamaica," *Jamaica Journal*, Vol. IV, No. 1 (March 1970), pp. 20–29.

17. K. Mohammed, *Express* (Trinidad), Sept. 3, 1970, p. 5.

18. Ibid.

19. E. V. Goveia, *A Study on the Historiography of the British West Indies*, Mexico, D.F., 1956, p. 174.

GORDON ROHLEHR *was born in Guyana in* 1942. *He was educated at the University of the West Indies, Mona, Jamaica, and at Birmingham University, England, where he took his doctorate on the theme "Alienation and Commitment in the Novels of Joseph Conrad." He returned to the West Indies in* 1968 *to lecture in English literature at the University of the West Indies, St. Augustine, Trinidad. He has written extensively on West Indian literature and culture and has been published in* New World, Bim, Caribbean Quarterly, Moko, Tapia, *and* Savacou. *He has also, under the auspices of the Government Broadcasting Unit of Trinidad, presented a series of twenty-five half-hour radio programs on calypso music from* 1940 *to the present.*

Merle Hodge

THE SHADOW OF THE WHIP: A COMMENT ON MALE-FEMALE RELATIONS IN THE CARIBBEAN

The man-woman relationship is nowhere a straightforward, uncomplicated one—it is always perhaps the most vulnerable, the most brittle of human relationships. And in the Caribbean this relationship has been adversely affected by certain factors of our historical development, notably, I think, by the legacy of violence and disruption with which our society has never adequately come to terms.

Caribbean society was born out of brutality, destructiveness, rape; the destruction of the Amerindian peoples, the assault on Africa, the forced uprooting and enslavement of the African; the gun, the whip, the authority of force. Yet the Caribbean area today is not particularly noted for any large-scale, organized violence. Caribbean governments sit securely and complacently, with or without popular support.

But the violence of our history has not evaporated. It is still there. It is there in the relations between adult and child, between black and white, between man and woman. It has been internalized, it has seeped down into our personal lives. Drastic brutality—physical and verbal—upon children is an accepted part of child rearing in the Caribbean.

"Gavin," threatens Laura of *Miguel Street* to one of her children, "Gavin, if you don't come here this minute, I make you fart fire, you hear." And C. L. R. James in his novel *Minty Alley* describes a hair-raising scene of violence upon a child which contains not an inch of exaggeration.

Our capacity for verbal violence is limitless. Teasing and heckling are taken to lengths which would shock in another society. For example, we award nicknames on the basis of hopeless physical deformities—"Hop-and-Drop," for example, for a polio victim who walks with a pathetic limp. Our expressions of abuse would fill catalogues. Quarreling is a national pastime—quarrels are spectacular: a great deal of energy and artistry are applied to body movements, the ingenuity of insults, the graphic recitation of the antagonist's crimes; a good quarrel will provide a morning's dramatic diversion for a whole neighborhood, for quarrels often emerge onto the street as if in search of an adequate stage.

And the fact that a physical fight between a man and a woman—or more accurately, a woman-beating—may erupt into the open air and rage for hours without any serious alarm on the part of onlookers for the safety of the woman, without attracting the intervention of the law, is a strong comment on our attitudes:

> Never never put yu mouth
> In husband-and-wife business.

runs the refrain of one calypso, a word of warning to the sentimental, to those who may be naïve enough to think that a woman minds being beaten by her man. It is the message of many a calypso. Another song recounts with mock disapproval a public "licking." The thinly veiled sexual imagery is a stock device of calypso, but here it illustrates effectively the idea of violence being part and parcel of the normal relations between man and woman: a policeman who would intervene is rebuffed by none other than the "victim" of the licking:

Constable have a care
This is my man licking me here
And if he feel to lick me
He could lick me,
Dammit, don't interfere.

Of course, calypsonians are mainly men, and men are largely responsible for perpetuating the myth of women thriving on violence from their men:

Every now and then cuff them down,
They'll love you long and they'll love you strong.
Black-up their eye
Bruise-up their knee
And they will love you eternally.

The idea is not far removed from the maxim coined in the era of slavery: "Battre un nègre, c'est le nourrir"—a beating is food to a nigger.

But of course, violence in its narrowest definition, namely, physical violence, is only a visible manifestation of a wider disruption, a basic breakdown of respect. For violence to women includes the whole range of mental cruelty which is part and parcel of women's experience in the Caribbean.

Every now and then our attention is drawn to this existing situation when a woman, known to her neighbors as a devoted, hard-working, self-sacrificing mother, of no particular wickedness, appears trembling and speechless before a judge for having killed her man.

And the familiar, almost humdrum details roll out again— a history of intolerable ill-treatment by the man both upon her and upon her children: neglect, desertion, humiliation, tyranny, unreasonableness, lack of consideration . . . the last straw falls and the woman runs at him with a kitchen knife.

It would seem that the precedents of this case stretch far enough back into our history to have entered our folklore— there is the folk song about Betsy Thomas who killed her

husband stone cold dead in the market and had no doubt
that she would be absolved of crime:

I ain't kill nobody but me husband.

In fact, our society implicitly acknowledges the permanent
situation out of which husband killings arise, in the leniency
the court generally affords to a woman who has been driven
to this act. Of course, killing your man is an extreme measure, but, again, it is a crisis which is but the visible tip of
the iceberg or, to bring our imagery home, the eruption of
a volcano that all along has been silently cooking.

The black man in the role of Dispenser of Violence is
very likely a descendant of the white slave-overseer asserting
an almost bottomless authority over the whipped. But there
is one fundamental difference, for whereas the overseer beat
and tortured his victim because he had power over him, the
black man ill-treating his woman is expressing his desire for
power, is betraying a dire insecurity vis-à-vis the female.

In the Caribbean the "war of the sexes" takes on a very
special character. It is not a straight fight between handi-
capped Woman on the one hand and omnipotent Man on
the other. From the very beginning of West Indian history
the black woman has had a *de facto* "equality" thrust upon
her—the equality of cattle in a herd. We became "equal"
from the moment African men and women were bundled
together onto galleys, men and women clamped to the floor
alongside each other for the horrifying middle passage. A
slave was a slave—male or female—a head of livestock, a
unit of the power that drove the plantation. The women
worked equally hard out in the fields with the men, were
equally subject to torture and brutality. The black woman
in the Caribbean has never been a delicate flower locked
away in a glass case and "protected" from responsibility. Of
course, the African woman in Africa is no delicate flower
either, wielding a tremendous physical force in her daily
chores of pounding, planting, etc., all the while carrying
around her latest child upon her back.

From the very beginning of our history on this side of the Atlantic, woman has been mobilized in the society's work force. But there was, of course, some division of labor or functions, and this is where the male-female trouble began.

In the first place, the whole humiliation of slavery meant an utter devaluation of the manhood of the race; the male was powerless to carry out his traditional role of protector of the tribe, he was unable to defend either himself or his women and children from capture and transportation, from daily mishandling. His manhood was reduced to his brawn for the labor he could do for his master and to his reproductive function.

And the function of fatherhood was limited to fertilizing the female. Gone was the status of head of the family, for there was no family, no living in a unit with wife and children. A man might not even know who his children were, and at any rate they did not belong to him in any sense; he was unable to provide for them—their owner performed the function of provider. The black man had no authority over his children, but the woman did. The children's mothers, or female child-rearers, were responsible for the upbringing of the race. Women became mother and father to the race.

And it is this concentration of moral authority in the person of the woman that has influenced relations between men and women of African descent in the Caribbean. For today the average Afro-West Indian is still reared more or less singlehandedly by a mother, or aunt, or big sister, or god-mother—the men have still not returned to the functions of fatherhood. Fathers are either physically absent—the prevalent pattern of concubinage and male mobility results in a man not necessarily staying put in one household until the children he has deposited there have grown up—or, even when the father is present in the home, his part in the bringing up of the children is a limited one. His role is not clearly defined and not binding. One of the roles he may play is that of Punisher, administering beatings at the request of the mother; but the strongest influence in the home is usually female.

The society may be called a matriarchal one—many of our ancestors were in fact brought from West African societies which were matriarchal in structure, although there this by no means implied an abdication of responsibility on the part of the males. But this meant that our women had precedents of matriarchy upon which to draw in the new situation of male defection.

The Caribbean, and indeed black America on the whole, has produced the new black matriarch, the strong female figure who is responsible not only for the propagation of the race but by whose strength our humanity has been preserved.

Most Afro-West Indians have grown up "fatherless" in one way or another, most have been reared under almost exclusive female influence. So in the society moral authority is female, an authority that may sometimes be harsh and driven to extremes by the situation of stress in which a Caribbean mother often finds herself—often ill-feeling against a deserting man is vented upon the children he has left in her lap.

Caribbean writing teems with the strong woman type. Many of Samuel Selvon's immigrants are our feckless, happy-go-lucky men now and then marshaled into responsibility by brisk, matter-of-fact women. The female figures of James's *Minty Alley*, the dignified, almost statuesque Mrs. Rouse; Maisie the wraith, invincible in any situation. The women of *Miguel Street*, bawling out, battering (as well as being battered by) or working to support their unstable men. And I have discovered that my own book, *Crick Crack, Monkey*, is full of strong woman figures and that men are, like Auntie Beatrice's husband, "either absent or unnoticeable"—even the heroine's succession of "uncles" do not constitute any solid presence. And I had once intended to give the children a grandfather—Ma's husband—but I had conceived of him as an invalid in a rocking chair, ably looked after by Ma!

Caribbean woman has developed a strong moral fiber to compensate for the weakening of the male. Hence the desire of the man to do her down, to put her in her place, to safeguard his manhood threatened by the authority of the female upstart.

The black man in the Caribbean is capable of deep respect for his mother and for older women in general. The worst insult in our language is to curse a man's mother. An "obscenity" flung in the heat of quarrel is, quite simply, "Yu mother!" Authority is female, a man will have instinctive qualms about disrespecting his mother or, by extension, her contemporaries, but he will take his revenge on the black female by seeking to degrade women within reach of his disrespect.

Young men at a loose end (usually unemployed—the devaluation of black manhood is perpetuated in economic frustration) will position themselves on a culvert, at a street corner, on a pavement, and vie with each other in the ingenuity of their comments to embarrass women going by. The embarrassment of woman is part of the national ethos, stemming, I am convinced, from a deep-seated resentment against the strength of women.

In Trinidad the calypsonian, the folk poet, is assured of heartfelt, howling approval when he devotes his talent to the degradation of woman:

> Clarabelle,
> She could chase the Devil from Hell
> With the kind of way she does smell
> Anytime she pass yu could tell.

Our folk poet is rarely given to flattering and extolling the qualities of womanhood—woman and her sexual attributes are almost only a stock dirty joke in his repertoire. And the calypsonian mirrors collective attitudes—he is the product of his society and sings to please his audience.

There has, however, been one major development in our contemporary history which promises to have a salutary effect upon relations between black men and women in the Caribbean. This is the advent of black power ideology.

An important element of the history of male-female relations in the Caribbean has been the imposition of European standards of physical beauty—the tendency of the man to measure the desirability of women by these standards, and the corresponding struggle of black women to alter their appearance as far as possible in the direction of European requirements for beauty but of course still falling short of these requirements. A large part of male disrespect for the black woman was an expression of his dissatisfaction with her, "inferior" as she was to the accepted white ideal of womanhood.

This bred a great deal of destructive dishonesty, a canker eating away at the roots of our self-respect. For these attitudes were especially destructive as they were to a large extent disavowed or even entirely subconscious. A man would vehemently deny that he could be the victim of this mesmerism. His cousin, yes, damn fool who went to England to study and could find nothing else to get married to but a white woman—but *he* would never be found putting milk in his coffee, unthinkable, *he* had a healthy attitude toward these white people.

It was indeed a difficult burden to bear—his very deep-seated resentment of whitedom and this hopeless involvement with them.

Today's ideology has begun to liberate us from this particular dishonesty. It has forced into the open, and at popular level (a success not achieved by the literary movements of the first half of the century), the discussion of our polarization toward whiteness, and it has effectively set about revising our concepts of physical beauty. The progressive abolition of hair-straightening in the Caribbean is a momentous revolution. It is part of the revaluation of the black woman.

And the revaluation of black womanhood inevitably also implies a restoration of black manhood, when the black man no longer forcibly evaluates his women by the standards of a man who once held the whip hand over him. It is one stage of his liberation from the whip hand.

And it is only when our lives cease to be governed by the shadow of the whip that we can begin to heal the grave disruption of relations between men and women that we have suffered in the Caribbean.

MERLE HODGE *was born in 1944 in Calcutta Settlement, Trinidad. She completed her primary and secondary schooling in Trinidad and in 1962 left that island to study French at the University of London. She traveled in Europe, lived in Senegal and Gambia, and in April 1970 published her first novel,* Crick Crack, Monkey. *She returned to Trinidad in October 1970 and for the next two years taught French, West Indian literature, and English at a government secondary school. She now lectures in French Caribbean and French African literature at the University of the West Indies, Mona, Jamaica.*

Clive Y. Thomas

BLACK EXPLOITATION IN THE CARIBBEAN:
IS THERE A CARIBBEAN ECONOMIC SYSTEM?

It is surprising that social scientists in the Caribbean have accepted the notion that social phenomena in the area have sufficient integrity to constitute a separate and identifiable economic system. This conclusion seems to have been reached without any attempt to examine the ideological and philosophical preconceptions inherent in the notion of an economic system *qua* system. This, I believe, has been partly due to the equally surprising fact that it is only in our very recent history that a variety and multiplicity of economic systems has been recognized in the social sciences.

Much has been written about Marx's contribution to social theory, but few can surpass his challenge to the classical notion of economic systems. The classical economists had not only assumed that all economic systems were the same, but they further argued that the laws which "explained" or "governed" their functioning were as universal as those of the natural sciences. It was Marx who offered the first fundamental challenges to this closed view by arguing that the then prevailing capitalist system, as a system, which the classical economists held to be singular and universal was in fact only one of several historically necessary systems, and as such it was neither universal nor immutable. In particular, Marx argued that the capitalist system was a "modern" phenomenon and that its laws of operation differed in essence from other recognizable systems such as feudalism, which preceded this capitalistic mode of organization.

For a long time after Marx, indeed right up to the 1950s, while a diversity of economic systems was conceded by social science theorists, these were limited to Marx's precapitalist sequential systems and to another comparative system—the socialist economy. Indeed, one could argue here that in the Marxian schema this was a further sequential development— a higher mode of organization than that of capitalist society— even though many "Western" social scientists would challenge this.

After the Second World War, the liberation struggles of the black Third World gained considerably in momentum. It was aided indirectly by the war which temporarily affected the military and economic potential of Europe. This, together with the subsequent Cold War conflicts between Eastern and Western Europe, made it difficult for the imperial powers to mobilize sufficient force to wage a concerted counteroffensive within their empires. The result was that in many parts of the European empires, the colonial peoples won victories which were recorded in their attainment of constitutional independence. This constitutional independence was formal and essentially a partial, if not Pyrrhic, victory. Very soon it was evident that the same poverty and exploitation which gave the impetus to revolt continued unabated.

This new set of historical conditions immediately opened up several old and new arguments among social scientists, which culminated in the consensual view that the characteristics of these newly "independent" states were sufficiently unique to warrant their categorization as a separate economic system. It was in this manner that the so-called category of "backward countries" was invented by social scientists. This system, while accepted as a legitimate one in the social sciences, has posed immense methodological and operational problems for traditional "socialist" and "Western" social sciences. For example, the argument has raged unceasingly as to whether this system is precapitalistic and whether its inevitable direction of development is to capitalistic or directly to socialistic modes of organization.

It is against this unfolding of "Western" ideology and social science that the first understanding of the functioning of the Caribbean economic and social system was converted into dogma and then policy. It is therefore pertinent at this stage to examine some of the more major defects of this Euro-American view which dominate social science ideology in our area and in most parts of the black world.[1]

The first point to note is that these theories about the nature and categorization of systems are all specific. There are specific concrete historical conditions which explain their emergence. The classical views of universal and immutable laws which governed and explained the operations of economic systems were counterparts to the paradoxical existence of "universal" empires and the development of radical, democratic, political ideologies which inspired revolutions on the basis of the universal brotherhood of man, i.e., of course, European man. Similarly, the recognition of the "socialist" system followed hard on the heels of the development of a socialist state in Russia after 1917. And, finally, it was the historical conditions which saw the movement for political liberation in the colonial territories frustrated by the economic dominance of Europe and America, which gave rise to the notion of "backward countries."

The second point to note is that since these views are all derived from specific, concrete, historical conditions, they are as limited or as general as the methodology inherent in the study of specifics. Certainly they are limited both in

[1] Many of the criticisms raised here owe much to my reading of Professor W. Kula's contribution to the UNESCO survey of social sciences research. *The Social Sciences: Problems and Orientations*, Mouton/UNESCO, The Hague/Paris, 1968.

time and space. For example, the discovery system of the backward countries which has been attributed to Western social science has led to their approach to the study of this system by way of adopting *existing* tools of analysis to its study rather than attempting to fashion new tools born "exclusively" out of the experiences of the new system. It is for this fundamental philosophical and historical reason that contemporary political economy is incapable of analyzing successfully the Caribbean experience. Worse, its very application constitutes one of the most successful areas of Euro-American ideological penetration and hence continuing colonization of our world.

The third point is that insofar as Euro-American scholars (and their Third World counterparts) approach the study of our societies from this methodological standpoint, then they are uncritically accepting the rationality of the Euro-American society as the only rationality possible. Their very efforts to analyze and study our societies from this frame of reference are attempts to justify the "superiority" of their own economic system over ours and to legitimize this method of ideological penetration. Thus Professor M. Godelier was right when he argued "ideology gains the upper hand the moment a society comes to consider itself the *only* point of reference."[2] There are no philosophical or scientific reasons why theoretical preference should be given to one frame of reference, in the form of one type of society, when considering others. Any attempt to do so is the surest sign of an ideological offensive. Indeed, one may further argue that the treatment of all societies as equal is also an ideological position unsupported by scientific evidence. When a scholar wants to treat all societies as equal, "he wants" to do so, for such is his . . . ideology.[3]

A fourth point which we may note is that these theories accept the European view that social science is a modern science. All that existed prior to Adam Smith was considered to be pre-economic, presocial scientist in approach.

[2] Ibid., p. 110 (italics mine).
[3] Ibid., p. 110.

Thus, for example, it is argued that our struggles as slaves were prepolitical. The desire was for improvement in conditions without any notion of political organization. Indeed, the slave revolt is often treated as a spontaneous, unorganized eruption. So spontaneous, so unorganized as not to be even worthy of labeling as a practical example of the political theory of anarchy. This, of course, also held true for European societies. The theologians and other scholars of the Middle Ages, the feudalists and the mercantilists, did not have an "economic theory" of their own explicitly formulated in their views. This limited view of the genealogy of the social sciences is a characteristic of Euro-American approaches to the study of social sciences. They take their existing social and political conditions as the most characteristic. As Professor Kula argues, "bourgeois thinking thus sees only its own genealogy and makes an absolute of itself."[4]

Finally, there is in the Euro-American social sciences a tendency to treat most motivations as economic and to analyze the economic system *qua* system as one independent of other aspects of society. Thus, landlords maximize rent, laborers maximize income and minimize leisure, and the total economy tries to maximize total output. Methodologically, these started out as simple approximations in order to arrive at simple though precise solutions to certain problems of partial equilibrium analysis. They have since grown to the stature of being considered the reality itself. And, as is always the case with appearances, it has influenced the reality through people's minds and their perceptions of themselves and others. A wish-fulfilling prophecy if ever there was one.

This reduction of all motivation to economic ones is not merely a vulgarization of Marx and hence absurd, but it also confuses the nature of the cultural colonization of the area. If an employer seeks to maximize profit, why should he discriminate on racial grounds? If a landlord has houses to rent, surely he seeks to rent it to the highest renter? And so on.

If there are warnings which can be drawn from this

4 Ibid., p. 110.

analysis of the notion on systems in the social sciences, they are not that we of the Caribbean have to be vigorous and bold in asserting our own interpretation of our area. To my mind, the key characteristic of our system is not that it is "dependent" or "developing" or "backward" but that it is an exploited system. If we assert that position, we notice how much of "modern" social science is designed to deny this reality. Thus, in the field of economics even the most radical sympathizers confronted with the dilemmas facing societies of our sort have argued from the wrong basis. For example, they might try to show how and why the price system must lead to a misallocation of resources; how and why free international trade will always redound to our disadvantage. These are supposed to follow logically from an economic analysis of the relevant economic variables. As such, there is no room for an explanation in terms of deliberate exploitation. The motives of perfect competition when they are removed must be replaced by the motives of deliberate improvement for the benefit of the metropolis. But to the growing army of sympathizers, poverty and unemployment follow logically in response to dehumanized changes in economic variables. It is not created by design. It is not a conscious human creation. It follows from free trade, in flexible price systems, and so on. But this is of course absurd.

B. THE EVOLUTION OF ECONOMIC POLICY

Against this background one gains a sharper insight into the evolution of economic policy in the region. As it was to be expected, it was not until after the Second World War that the colonial administration "discovered" there was a need to devise a conscious programed policy for economic reform via the use of the state mechanism. Prior to that the development of the economy was left to the unhampered activities of the dominant expatriate plantation owners. When the state passed laws, it was to minimize its own discretionary authority and to maximize the scope for the free play of what have been euphemistically described as "market forces" aimed at stimulating an inflow of foreign capital, skills, and technology. It was, of course, assumed that this was the only basis for developing the area.

The results of this are well known. The region became specialized in the production of staples for use in overseas markets of the dominant metropolitan powers, while it imported most of its consumption requirements (including food) and all its manufactures. This symmetry between the regional production structure and consumption patterns was made possible because the region's resources were under the almost exclusive ownership and control of foreign capital. In specific institutional form, the perpetuation of this position of the Caribbean in the international division of labor was centered on the plantation, which became not only the physical locus of such economic activity, but also was elaborated from slavery to constitute the psychological, social, and political matrix through which as a people we were policed, indoctrinated, exploited, and terrorized. Insofar as this matrix grew out of such economic conditions, naturally its major focus has been to exploit us by way of seeking to internalize the externally dependent characteristics of the economic system. In other words, the long historical process of underdevelopment of the region has been centered on the internalization, within the social structure and in our psychological and personality structures, of the external dependence of the region, as expressed in its external relations to the economies of the metropolis. The internalization of dependency or underdevelopment in the body politic of the region was necessary if the region's resources were to be systematically exploited with the minimum disruption caused by the use of direct violence against the population—particularly as, for all this period, at least right up to the end of the Second World War, the region was characterized by very acute labor shortages!

There are four broadly identifiable phases in the evolution of postwar economic policy. The first of these covered, roughly speaking, the period of the late 1930s to the late 1940s. Generally, we can see in this first phase a reflection of the dominant Eurocentric view of the area. This was strikingly reflected in the report of the West Indies Royal Commission of the late 1930s and the official pronouncements of the Colonial Office. From this vantage point the area was seen as incapable of any industrial development. Industry was, of course, associated with modernity and non-primitivism. The only solution for the area was to revitalize and develop plantation agriculture by complementing this system with an independent peasantry. The system for doing this was the "land settlement scheme" first proposed in 1897 and reconfirmed by the 1938 Royal Commission as "the only way of meeting the fundamental requirements of the British West Indies, and the Sugar Commission of 1930 endorsed their view."[5]

When put into effect, this policy has been a total failure. Presently the situation is that throughout the West Indies 79 per cent of the total number of farms account for only 13 per cent of the total acreage in farms, and all these farms are under five acres each. By contrast, 0.6 per cent of the total number of farms account for 55 per cent of the total acreage and all of these farms are over one hundred acres each. The land given away on these schemes, therefore, had no impact on the inequalities of land ownership. Of the land given away, we find such results as that in Jamaica, where, of all the land grants through the land settlement scheme, only 41 per cent included the most fertile soil type (alluvium) and over 50 per cent of the settlements were on land of less than five acres each. Further, nowhere was there any success in attempts to diversify the crop pattern or to increase yields of existing crops.

There are numerous studies analyzing the failure of the land settlement scheme. These have usually been analyzed in terms of the defects of size, soil type, and so on, indicated above. But this is only a very partial truth. The realities of the plantation system and its relationship to an independent peasantry have never been fully realized. To my mind, one

[5] West Indies Royal Commission, *Report on Agriculture, Fisheries, Forestry and Veterinary Matters*, Cmd 6608, H.M.S.O., 1945.

historical lesson is clear: the plantation system cannot co-exist with an independent peasantry. To the plantation the peasantry is always first and last a reservoir of cheap labor. As such, the creation of the peasantry and the degrees of freedom this class will be permitted over the country's material resources are ultimately dictated by the extent to which, through economic, social, and political control of the labor market, the plantation is able to make labor both cheap and available. The peasantry is therefore in perpetual conflict with the plantation. This is a life and death struggle. The birth of an independent peasantry can only be achieved on the destruction of the plantation.

In Guyana we see clear evidence of this. From the break-up of the slave system in the 1830s until now, the peasantry has been at continual war with the estate system. The early village movement, the establishment of a rice-growing industry are examples of the struggle to destroy the plantation in a situation where the myth of much available land is strong, and where the idea that these two classes should be competitive is less strong. The peasantry has not been successful. And the whole system of land grants, cultivation of rice, and the extension of the cattle industry have all developed at a pace in keeping with the plantations' basic needs for cheap and available labor. For a land settlement scheme to be successful, it must dispossess the plantation. Unless it does this, the scheme remains at best a welfare appendage of the estates.

The policy of land settlement coincided with certain "favorable" conditions in the region. Unemployment was relatively low because of the demands for labor caused by the war and its effects (particularly the construction of imperialist bases in the area), the high prices for primary products (for the same reasons), the "shortages" of foreign exchange, and the physical unavailability of capital equipment. By the 1950s, this policy became obviously insufficient even to its main advocate—the Colonial Office. For by this time, the combination of high rates of population growth (and particularly the labor force element) and the collapse of primary prices was sharpening the economic crises at home. The plantations aggravated this situation to an unconscionable degree by their rapid mechanization policies. They wanted to overcome the unionization induced "shortages" and the "high price" of labor. This alone might have led to a decisive economic crisis in the region had it not been for two factors, viz., the relatively easy emigration outlets afforded our population to Europe and America and the beginning of the new phase of exploitation of raw materials in the area—bauxite, oil, and tourism.

Ideologically, this second phase of economic policy coincided with the so-called "enlightened" Euro-American view of development which was a crude application of the international humanist view which treated all societies as equal. Since modernity was equated with industrialization, the industrialization of the area constituted the basic social drive. The Euro-American approaches were clearly exemplified in the Puerto Rican model. The basic aim was to maximize the inflow of foreign capital for industrial purposes. This was to be achieved by a system of "incentives" such as income tax and customs duty exemptions, accelerated depreciation allowances, and a local monopoly through the prohibition of competitive imports. Industrial establishments soon started to flow to the larger territories. Jamaica and Trinidad and Tobago began to boast of rates of industrial expansion exceeded only by Japan. The illusion behind this soon became obvious, as it turned out to be a thinly disguised attempt to reinforce foreign control of the region's resources. The economic consequences of this are many.

1. The local "value added" in these industries is small. This has been attributed to the alleged "small size" of the national market and the need to confine industry to the assembly of final products.

2. This value added is further reduced by fiscal incentives. Thus, although before tax, domestic value added averages less than 20 per cent in the region, after tax we often find ourselves paying continuously to have these in-

dustries, i.e., they take more than they create within the domestic economy.

3. Several of these industries are given monopoly status. In many instances, the domestic market is not sufficiently large to support more than one enterprise and the monopoly is "natural." However, this is considerably reinforced by the prohibition of competitive imports. Since monopoly status in the Caribbean economy is to a large extent unavoidable, it is clear that to confine these built-in advantages to foreign capitalists is to perpetuate some of the most exploiting characteristics of the functioning of the economic system. It is also of note that for a mixture of reasons, mainly an ideological preference for so-called "free" enterprise and a fear of foreign big business in our small economies, these monopolies are completely unregulated. There are no effective standards bureaus nor are there controls on profits, prices, or quality. The result, as the excessively high profit rates in the region show, is the systematic exploitation of the Caribbean consumer.

4. Enterprises such as these make no attempt to harness indigenous materials. From the standpoint of the American businessman, the region has no resources in comparison with his home territory. The result is that in the formation of investment criteria, indigenous resource availability has no explicit function.

5. This failure to give prominence to local resource availability has meant that technological innovation in the area has been severely limited.

6. Indeed, the technology employed is usually that of Euro-America. As such, it tends not only to be nonspecific to our resource environment, but worse, it forces our resource environment to confirm to this technology with disastrous results. Thus, for example, despite our relative abundance of labor, the production functions employed in the region are generally capital intensive. The result is that industry fails to absorb our growing labor force in adequate numbers and unemployment is now at the level of over 20 per cent of the region's labor force.

7. As with their metropolitan counterpart activities, industries coming into the Caribbean have been concentrated in the urban areas. This has led to the malformation of the city, with excessive unemployment, unbearable housing conditions, poor health, and an environment of constant crime where every hunger pang inevitably leads to a "hustle" or "choke and rob." The prosperous classes in the city have been forced through the erection of burglar bars and huge locks to make clear to all that their suburban houses and huge lawns are in fact so many prisons.

8. Despite this, the city has been able to bleed the countryside not only of its people, who come flooding to the city for jobs which are not there, but of the bulk of their income as well. The internal terms of exchange are always against the countryside, and this together with their relatively faster population growth rates has meant that farmers' incomes in the rural areas have not kept pace with their productivity increases.

This list can be added to almost interminably, but sufficient has been said to indicate the direction in which analysis should be developed in order to isolate other defects. At this stage, two further important points may be observed. One is that in structural terms the economy has not changed the pattern of its dynamic. There is still an excessive dependence on exports, foreign capital inflows, foreign decision making, foreign technology, imports, and foreign good will. Intersectoral links within the internal economy have not been developed. The result is that economic change is compartmentalized and isolated through vertical integration to the metropolitan center. The other is the motivation of the people. Insufficient job opportunities, dissatisfaction with existing jobs, the manipulation of jobs for party political purposes have served to demoralize large sections of the working class. People migrate whenever they can. Now, with the sealed-off opportunities for mass migration to Britain and the United States, those favored by these countries, i.e., the skilled, the educated, etc., are the ones who go, thereby causing an increasing dependence in the population structure itself.

The development of these weaknesses were paralleled by the inherent weakness of the social science theory which guided policy formation. As far as economic policy was concerned, this was a crude mixture of Keynesian economics with its emphasis on industry and industrial capacity and of neo-classicism and its particularist views on resource allocation, productivity, and factor incomes. It is perhaps not surprising that this policy was given its most systematic pronouncement by Sir Arthur Lewis, a Caribbean economist.[6] The pattern of resource allocation he devised was based, as he argued, on the observed resources situation in the area and the application of rational criteria aimed at maximizing output, income, employment, and investment in manufacturing. To do this, he argued, the region should foster industries which minimized the use of its scarce factors—land, capital, and foreign exchange—and maximized the use of its abundant factor—labor. He was then able to establish a list of industries for the region in descending order of priority. This list was the exact reverse of what he termed an ideal allocation system.

Ironically, industries were established on the basis of the ideal pattern, and yet the economic system of the area remains as incapable of satisfying the needs of the mass of the West Indian peoples as it ever was. If any "motive" or criteria could be attributed to the businessmen who allocate and accumulate capital in the puny manufacturing sectors of the area, it is certainly the degree of monopoly power they could exert in any particular line of activity. This, together with the emphasis on "screw-driver" operations has resulted in the creation of a manufacturing sector, which is, in effect, another way of distributing imports. It is a distribution sector, where instead of obtaining a license to run an agency, one obtains concessions to import almost finished items for assembly and distribution at home. A capitalist class engaged in manufacturing has not yet been created. For this

[6] Sir Arthur Lewis, *The Industrialisation of the British West Indies,* Caribbean Organisation, Trinidad, 1949.

class must be derived from exposure to a process concerned with production and not simple distribution.

This failure of a capitalist class to grow in manufacturing has reduced the capacity of the economic structure to prove itself flexible enough to cope with some of the pressing and profitable business opportunities. It has meant that the existing profit takers are so mercantile in outlook that they are unresponsive to wider social and economic conditions. The capitalist class is shrewder than its mercantile counterpart. It knows that production and the entire process of creating output are integrally linked with its ability to contain the Caribbean peoples, not through brutal submission in the form of long and persistent unemployment, but through the promise and allure of a new refrigerator, more fringe benefits, and higher paid overtime.

The third and fourth phases of policy have more or less coincided with each other, as they followed on the widespread recognition in the 1960s that the policy of industrialization by invitation was failing in two politically important areas. The first of these was in its inability to provide jobs for those seeking gainful employment in a situation of dwindling emigration outlets. The second was the sensitivity of the broad mass of the peoples of the region to foreign domination of their resources, as reflected in the upsurge of black power philosophy. These two phases have centered their strategies on the economic integration of the region and the development of measures for more national participation in the region's resource ownership, structure, and management.

Predictably, because there has been no transformation in either political or social structures, economic integration has been translated to mean trade liberalization, i.e., a movement toward freer trading ties in the region. To put this into effect, a regional free trade association, Carifta, has been formed. In terms of this regional agreement, closer ties are to be established through the removal of tariff and quota restrictions on intraregional trade. The emphasis, therefore, is on establishing the permissive conditions for exchange. Unfortunately, the region does not produce much of great

value that is consumed within the region. Intraregional trade
is 6 per cent of total trade, and of this, nearly 75 per cent is
confined to trade in rice and oil from Guyana and Trinidad,
respectively. The only areas which are in a position to gain
from freer trade, and which have in fact shown gains, are the
recently established multinational corporations which dominate in the manufacturing sectors of these economies. These
have been able to use the opportunities of a wider market to
rationalize their distribution across the region. In this sense,
and also insofar as these new manufacturing enterprises have
a very low domestic value added, their establishment can be
viewed as a device to maintain the exports of these enterprises to the region and to circumvent national import restrictions by the substitution of exports in the form of investment. Given the low domestic value added and the high
profit rates, much of the gains from integration has therefore
left the region.

This development was bound to occur, since integration
did nothing to alter the production structure of the region,
which is common to all the territories and which is heavily
specialized in favor of producing staples and raw materials
for metropolitan consumption and a tourist industry which
stresses the novelty of sand and sea. Insofar as economic
integration does not have as its basic premise—coming to
grips with the questions of resource ownership and use within
the region—then it cannot offer much to the solution of the
problems of underdevelopment, and exploitation trade liberalization, alias "economic integration," is a policy leading
to more, not less, dependence of our economic systems.

On the question of national participation in resource use
and ownership, three devices have been employed. The first
has been "Caribbeanization" of the higher administrative
structure of the foreign-owned plantations and multinational
corporations. In 1966 a United Nations manpower study dis-
closed that in Guyana there were over five hundred expatriates
employed as managers and professionals in the private sector.
These accounted for 88 per cent of the administrators and

managing directors of the six largest firms and about 38 per cent of the managers and senior executives.

The question which this situation raises is how far can a policy of replacement of these personnel by persons from the Caribbean go toward extending the scope of national control. Two factors seem to militate against this extension. First, local people employed in this way move into a particular institutional structure. They are absorbed into institutions with their own ethos, values, life styles, and patterns of doing things—all of which are derived from the fundamental fact that they are here to exploit our resources for foreigners. No matter what a national may claim in this situation, he cannot deny that the basic fact of his life is that he works *all* day, devotes *all* his skill and brains to servicing an enterprise which exploits his people. This is a fundamental feature of his life. The result is that he is driven to conform to the values and patterns of behavior of the enterprise. Instead of the local people making the enterprise local, they are themselves turned into an extension of the exploiting corporation or plantation. In other words, the effect is not to *nationalize* the corporations but to *denationalize* the local bourgeoisie.

Of course, such developments suit the owners and decision makers in these industries well. Indeed, I would go further and say that they have anticipated it and that is why they have been so responsive to the call for more local staff. They have a lot to gain. In the first place, as we have seen, local personnel in higher management offers no threat to the system because of the socialization process which leads them to accept, and execute, the values and functions of these institutions. Secondly, as this occurs the companies can still reap the advantageous publicity of saying that they are becoming more local, more national in their orientation through simply pointing to the number of locals who work for them. Thirdly, these institutions have arranged it so that the local personnel on their staff become exposed to the public and their labor force as a sort of buffer. The white expatriate is no longer visible, only his black Guyanese image. The workers direct their grievances to the local man and divert their attention from the expatriate owner. Thus it is not surprising that whoever makes the *basic decisions* about employment, wages, output, investment, conditions of work, and so on in these expatriate enterprises, it is always a local man who is exposed as the personnel officer, the front-line man, the cannon fodder in disputes with the workers.

The second process is equally fundamental and equally undermines the significance of Caribbeanization. This process can be described as "organizational substitution." As more and more local personnel are taken on locally to fill positions held by expatriates, so does the firm shift the decisions which were made by expatriates back to the head office. The local man fills the posts, they empty it of any decision-making significance. We take the form. They keep the essentials and the substance. The result of this is that localization of staff as it has been practiced does not extend meaningful participation to the masses of the local people. It does not contribute to expanding our knowledge of the operations of these industries at the higher managerial and professional levels. It supports the non-participatory system by absorbing our skilled elites into expatriate plunder. It creates a brain drain which takes place before our eyes. We do not see it because we associate brain drains with the crossing of the geographical frontier. As a consequence, such policies actively support it.

The second device has been to encourage the expatriate industries to issue shares locally as a basis for developing local ownership. There are a number of objections to this procedure which should be noted and which would serve to indicate that such participation is equally meaningless. First, the companies which go local often offer shares in such quantities as not to put in jeopardy their control of the company. Often the local share issue, when it is a new company, is designed to raise enough finance to pay for the construction of the firm's operations. The rest of the shares are purchased by the parent company in exchange for technical services, patent rights, etc. This means that local money pays for the enterprise, but foreign capitalists control through their parent company. In addition, despite the wide publicity associated with local share issues, a lot of which is really designed to build an image of being local, the bulk of the local shares issued are either taken up by a regular clique of local businessmen who are offered directorships and who tend to specialize in what they euphemistically describe as "partnering" local and foreign capital, or they are purchased by institutional buyers, such as resident expatriate banks, insurance companies, etc. In both cases, the broad masses of the people do not participate meaningfully.

A second objection is that in situations when the enterprise is already a going concern, i.e., already engaged in local production, the money used to purchase any increase in their local shares also serves to provide the firm with local money for expansion without any watering down of their control. Also, when this money is raised locally, it frees funds from the parent company for investment around the world, in the same way as profits from the local company is available for investment around the world.

Thirdly, it has always been argued that the virtue of foreign capital is that it contributes resources to the country which are in short supply. But many of these procedures of issuing local shares indicate that situations are created where foreign capital comes, woos local capital, uses it, and controls it for foreign ends.

Finally, the clamor for going local has only been directed toward the foreign companies. This is understandable, since the bulk of resources is in foreign hands. But it must not be forgotten that many of our local firms are tightly controlled within families and they are also reluctant to dilute family control by going public.

The most recent strategy is meaningful participation through government purchase of 51 per cent of shares of the big corporations. This, of course, has long been in practice in many of the neo-colonial states around the world. It offers no threat to foreign capital, and, as it has been argued by leading American industrialists, they would welcome this: "It ensures greater harmony between the governments and the companies. It exposes both to each other's point of view."

The truth is that 51 per cent does not ensure control, for two basic reasons. One is, lacking adequate exposure to the technical and managerial processes of the firm, 51 per cent has to be counteracted by engaging in management contracts with these enterprises which secure their continued control of management. Secondly, the marketing and technological processes are also secret, and the expatriate enterprise through this is able to further ensure that control is not lost through a mere purchase of shares.

The problem with this suggestion, like many others similar to it, is a failure to understand what the local expression of a multinational corporation is. It is essentially a plant. It is not a firm. It is true that there are titles such as directors, managers, managing directors, etc. But the local plant of, say, Reynolds, the Caribbean bauxite producer, makes no decision as regards the prices of bauxite, the output, the levels of investment, or the markets. All these are done at the head office, where decisions which normally define a firm are made. The apparatus which exists locally is just a participation in a multiplant firm. Therefore, meaningful participation is not simply to acquire a share in the local apparatus, but to ensure that inroads are made into the decision-making centers which exist in the North Atlantic.

It is for this reason that national control can only begin, and I insist begin, at the point of outright ownership. It is only when there is effective national ownership that there is opportunity to develop a strategy of control. In other words, the history of these institutions precludes a divorce of ownership and control. Foreign ownership means foreign control. Complete local control can only come about through complete local ownership. Buying 51 per cent avoids the issue and does not confront it.

Such is the position in the Caribbean today—a tendency

to avoid rather than confront issues. This reflects, I believe, the fact that the basic radical philosophies of the region have to deal with the question—given the way the neo-colonialist state performs, how can the *power* which it commands be transferred to the people? Being an "irrational" system, it is futile to expect to be able to reason it out of existence, yet this appears to be the central thrust of much of the intellectualized radicalism of the region.

CLIVE Y. THOMAS *is a citizen of Guyana who obtained his doctorate in economics at the University of London in 1964. After graduation he taught at the University of the West Indies, Mona, Jamaica, when in 1969 he was banned from that country because of his political views and involvement in the struggle against neo-colonialism and capitalism in the Caribbean. After leaving Jamaica, he took up an appointment as professor of economics at the University of Guyana. He has also been professor of economics at the University of Dar es Salaam, Tanzania, during the academic year 1972–73.*

Professor Thomas is the author of a number of books and learned articles. His books include the Dynamics of West Indian Economic Integration, Monetary and Financial Arrangements in a Dependent Economy, Central Banking in the Caribbean, *and a forthcoming study (*Monthly Review Press*)*, Dependence and Transformation: The Economics of the Transition to Socialism.

Eva Hodgson

BERMUDA AND THE SEARCH FOR BLACKNESS

The contribution of a black Bermudian to a "West Indian" or "Caribbean" anthology is at least a tentative statement of identification of that person with the West Indians and therefore runs against the grain of Bermudian psychology. For as any Bermudian knows (and, I suspect, many Caribbeans), Bermudians, under white tutelage, have always prided themselves on *not* being West Indian.

Geographically, Bermuda is not a part of the Caribbean area. Historically, the plantation system was short lived in Bermuda, and therefore we were not cursed with plantation absentee ownership, as were many of the Caribbean islands. As a result, Bermuda was more developed economically and therefore enjoyed a higher standard of living. Over the years the white ruling oligarchy found it expedient to remind black Bermudians of their higher standard of living with the clear implication that we were, therefore, inherently superior to West Indians—as if the material standard was significant in terms of human worth and integrity.

Many ambitious, aggressive West Indians with the initiative and shrewdness to attempt to improve their condition in life came to Bermuda. Inevitably they had the potential for acting as a leavening process on the (comparatively) rather smug, self-satisfied, and more easily intimidated black Bermudian. Hence it was very important politically to the white ruling class that black Bermudians accept the assumption of their cultural and human superiority. They would then view the aggressive West Indian immigrant as uncouth and unworthy of their support in any effort made toward social change.

I suppose, at a conscious level, the West Indian myth faded for me, the first time I left Bermuda. It is now a very long time ago, but even now, in retrospect, I cannot rid myself of the sense of embarrassment which I still have when I recall how appalled I was at my own ignorance about West Indians when I first met them in England. They were intelligent, sophisticated, and cultured. I think what impressed me most was their intellectual quality. Several of them were published authors. I knew of no black Bermudians who were; for that matter, I knew of no white Bermudians who were either. Perhaps one or two Englishmen settled in Bermuda may have been, but I did not know them. For as long as I can remember, to write books had always seemed to me to be an impressive achievement. My own respect for the published word was undoubtedly a reflection of the attitude of most black Bermudians. We have probably always overestimated education as a way of escaping from oppression. We did not realize the extent to which the process of education itself could be used as an instrument of enslavement. Freedom undoubtedly begins with the awakening of the intellect, but fortunately or unfortunately, what one reads is as important as reading itself. In any event, I was impressed by these West Indian authors.

In fairness to Bermudians, or at least in defense of them, we were, in part, victims of the rather vicious class system which prevailed in the West Indies. Many of those West Indians who came to Bermuda were obviously ambitious people who could not satisfy their social drives at home and came to Bermuda specifically to improve their social status. Those West Indians whom I met around the universities in England were generally offspring of the educated upper middle class. They had little reason to immigrate to, or to expose themselves to, the indignities of a segregated Bermuda.

I had to leave Bermuda, then, to meet West Indians to whom I could give my unqualified respect and admiration, unsullied by the Bermudian connotation of the words "West Indian." This was undoubtedly because of the deliberately cultivated attitudes in Bermuda. The functional value to white Bermudians of the divisive distinction between us as black people was a reality to which I gave insufficient thought until a West Indian in Great Britain rather scathingly commented that black Bermudians would always be slaves to whites because our "bellies were full."

But that is not a total excuse for my own basic ignorance. At that time in the rigidly segregated black schools of Bermuda, many of our teachers were West Indians simply because we did not have enough black Bermudians educationally equipped to teach adequately at even our low standards. And since, at that time, fortunately for black children, only black teachers were used in their schools, West Indians were imported. The first black secondary school we had in Bermuda had to have three West Indian principals before we were finally able to "process" a black Bermudian to play that particular role. Actually, the lack of education among black Bermudians was only partly a result of the assumption of white supremacy. White Bermudians themselves had little education, they imported most of *their* teachers from England. In spite of their wealth and advantages, only some of the offspring of the "Forty Thieves" (the leading white families in Bermuda) went to universities, but obviously *they* did not teach.

Therefore "Massa Day" was done for me as far as West Indians were concerned when I first went to England many years ago. Of course, whether or not Massa Day is done for either me or Bermuda depends very largely on how we define the term. Certainly Massa Day implies control or the exercise of power by the white man whom we, as blacks, for so long have called "master." For Bermudians, in my view, Massa Day is represented primarily by psychic control of the black man's mind. It is reflected in negative black concepts and in the acceptance of the assumption of white supremacy. This definition is of course applicable to some extent for all black people who have been exposed to racism and white oppression. However, when economic oppression and enslavement are very brutal and overt, it becomes cynical to stress psychic control as of primary importance. Mental control and economic control are, of course, interrelated. One breeds the other. Nevertheless, for Bermuda I would emphasize the psychological aspects. This is why, when I rejected the white man's definition of the West Indian, I could claim that, to that extent, Massa Day was done for me.

There is a touch of irony in the fact that it is a West Indian-born Bermudian who can be seen today as a possible symbol of the ending of Massa Day or of black power in Bermuda generally.

He, a black man (and I use the term here to define skin color, not psychic commitment), was made the leader of the government as well as the leader of the white party by the rulers of that party. In spite of its "integrated" superficial features of membership, I believe it is accurate to define the United Bermuda party (UBP) thus, since it unquestionably represents old white vested interests. Blacks in the party merely legitimatize the protection of these ancient white interests. To put the matter another way, only someone who is already something of a social outcast from Bermuda's white society would ever even contemplate openly joining the Progressive Labour party (PLP), Bermuda's black party. It is perhaps of some psychological significance that this man, a few short years ago, was insulted on the floor of the [assembly] because he was "obsessed," it was said, by the texture of his hair and the color of the skin.

The white man who insulted him thus in public, and did so even more crudely in private, today calls him "leader." Surely there has been a revolution in Bermuda, Massa Day must indeed be done! Many undoubtedly think so. Many others do not. There are those who would see this black leadership as merely another form of bondage. Perhaps it is. Nevertheless, the point should be made unequivocally that for a place with the very deep and intensely racist heritage of Bermuda, this black leadership—however unreal it may be presumed to be—is of very real symbolic and psychological significance. The assumption of white supremacy in Bermuda has been uncompromisingly intent on preventing any challenge to even its projected image of black subservience and inferiority.

The fact that white men who spoke contemptuously of him because of his color a few years ago must today recognize him as leader, no matter how purely symbolic, must be regarded as having psychological value. For even young children who have never experienced the full impact of a deep segregated society, to have a black man even as token government leader must provide for them a positive role model, so we can acknowledge the value of this gesture whether its significance is purely symbolic or whether it is indicative of something more substantive. In doing so, we are also recognizing the existence of change in Bermuda. However, it is hardly a revolutionary change since the exercise of real power has not actually changed hands, even superficially. The real decision makers are the same men, or their sons, as they were two decades ago. However, even if there is a twist of amusing irony in the fact that white Bermudians, who for so long have pitted black Bermudians against West Indians, should have chosen a West Indian for this psychologically significant symbolic gesture, it should have an additional advantage. It should intensify the black Bermudians' awakening awareness of his common interests with all of the West Indians. Although, knowing Bermuda as I do, it is hardly likely that such was the intent of the gesture.

White news media, and white fears, have dramatized the term "black power" and have, therefore, popularized it as a concept. But in the reality of the black world in Bermuda and elsewhere, it is by no means a new concept for black people anywhere. It is important for us as black people to recognize this reality, not only in order to keep our historical perspective correct but also in order to avoid any illusions about the effectiveness of recent rhetoric in the matter of real power redistribution.

My personal experience, as well as my personal observation, suggests to me that the reality of power distribution and its use make a measuring of ambivalence unavoidable at certain stages of black psychic development, even with those who do challenge the current distribution of power. . . . I am convinced that it is important that we recognize that the rhetoric of black power is not the reality and that it is equally important that we also acknowledge that psychic ambivalence in various forms and at various times is a very real possibility, even among the most vocal black power advocates. To ignore these realities is to hinder our own struggle to break the chains of mental bondage and psychic control.

My own "black power" consciousness was planted in my mind at a very early age by an uncle who died long before that term became a cliché. He got *his* black consciousness, of all places, straight from the Bible and passed it on to me. At any rate, he used the Bible to validate his concepts. "Princes shall come out of Egypt," he said, "and Ethiopia shall stretch forth her hand."

That specific memory is really merely symbolic of all the self-proud, race-proud attitudes which prevailed within my own immediate family, examples of which could be multiplied—all incidentally with Bible backing! The race pride which they instilled in me, via the scriptures, was intense. When others today find that religion produces "Uncle Toms," I can only conclude, from my own experience, that in the matter of racial integrity, one gets from religion or the Bible what one carries to it. My Bible-reading family carried to their religion an intense consciousness of black power and self-respect. And that's what they brought from it in their interpretations of the scriptures. They sensitized me to my own value. Nevertheless, they could not give me total protection from the effect of a viciously racist society. Ambivalence was therefore inevitable.

My own increasing black power consciousness and my conscious analysis of the racial situation developed most rapidly only after I left the oppressive totalitarian-like atmosphere of Bermuda. Many of us have to leave our own particular "plantation" to get a truer perspective of reality. But perhaps not all of us. For while I was abroad in England developing a black power consciousness and discovering West Indians, Bermudians at home were demonstrating black power, and that was a decade before Stokely Carmichael put the term "black power" in the headlines.

The first tentative black power mass movement in Bermuda successfully made a dent in the rigid segregation pattern of Bermuda. It was a boycott of the cinemas. The white man's initial effort to manipulate the minds of the black people in response to the boycott was to attribute the movement to West Indians! If he could successfully blame a "rowdy West Indian element" for the boycott, Bermudians, he hoped, would lose sympathy and fail to support it. This proved futile. The widespread support which the boycott received was actually more significant than the resulting token gestures of "integration."

The next major black power manifestation in Bermuda was the movement, initiated by black parliamentarians but given real momentum by a young man who returned to Bermuda after having spent several years off the "Bermuda Plantation." It was a movement which eventually, and very belatedly, resulted in universal franchise. The psychological importance of that movement to the black psyche was significant. Unfortunately, its implication for freeing the black man from mental bondage was not nearly so great, nor its effect nearly so long lasting as most white Bermudians had feared and as a few black Bermudians had hoped. The furor caused then always reminds me that "sound and fury" can be very illusory in contrast to real tangible results. In spite of the drama of that moment, it certainly did not herald the dawn of "black power" or the end of Massa Day. The ineffectualness of that movement in terms of breaking the chains of mental bondage was so tragically and clearly reflected shortly afterwards.

A number of black Bermudians, concerned about the distribution of power, formed a political party. However, instead of frankly acknowledging that the most important and fundamental need was a redistribution of power within the context of society with a historically racist development, they rather foolishly played with ideological theories. They revealed the psychic damage that they had suffered by being ashamed to recognize their own blackness and by hiding behind ill-conceived ideologies. They proclaimed that they were "integrated" and, as black men with the deepest racial scars often do, they got hold of a white woman to prove it. In terms of the development of a black power consciousness, that act, in my view, set black Bermudians back an incalculable number of years.

In spite of the concern which it caused the white oligarchy at the time, the psychologically unsound foundation of the initial PLP move was revealed in two ways. Those who were committed to an "integrated" front have since either disappeared from the Bermuda political scene or have joined the "white" party. The PLP itself only began to show real potential for growth when two things happened. First, its spokesmen stopped pretending that any society as racist as Bermuda could produce a genuinely integrated political party under real black leadership. Secondly, those black men most ashamed of their blackness, and most concerned to have white approval, left the party. But by that time both the psychological and political damage had been done. The initial refusal of the PLP to emphasize the need for racial redistribution of power was tragic for the development of a positive black self-concept. It was a greater tragedy because the UBP, formed later in response to the PLP, promptly did so. They recognized the essentially racial nature of the new party politics. They, of course, would; race had always been their criterion for action. They quickly attempted—successfully—to diffuse the irritations of long years of racism by widely distributing to black people invitations to political cocktail parties. Many blacks, overwhelmed by this sudden white attention, succumbed and joined the UBP. The whites wished to ensure that there be no challenge to their real power. They in fact did so at a lower cost than that to white Southerners in the United States immediately after the abolition of slavery, when black votes were bought with liquor. Much of the latent support which the PLP would have tapped if it had honestly faced the issues of racism were lost as a result. In many cases, the loss would be permanent. So Massa Day continued to prevail.

The next widespread black power movement came in the form of a labor union strike. The incident began as a simple labor strike against the management of the Bermuda Electric Light Company. However, since almost all organized labor in Bermuda is black and all organized management is white, it had racial overtones from the outset. Eventually it developed into open racial hostility. White Bermudians, certainly until recently, perhaps even now, always seem to me to reflect a generalized fear of black people, even although they themselves control the political, economic, and military power. Black Bermudians, probably because they feel that white folks have done their worst anyway, have never had this generalized fear that white folks have.

However, on that occasion, for the first time in my life, I knew that black people were afraid of the naked hate which they saw in the eyes of the white people whom they met on the streets of Hamilton. Previously, animosity had always been veiled. But then it could be cut with a knife. The immediate effect was to unite the sympathies of all black Bermudians behind the labor union in a clear manifestation of a black power consciousness in a way that had scarcely ever happened before. The Governor's broadcast speech at the time and the security measures taken at Tucker's Town (the Beverly Hills of Bermuda) suggested that white folks' fear and hatred had turned to sheer terror.

The fury of white Bermudians was intensified because a white woman doctor was the leading figure and official in the black union. She was a living challenge to many of their racist, reactionary assumptions. She was white, and the union was essentially black. That in itself was unforgivable. Added to that, she was a professional and the union members were, obviously, generally laborers. (Black Bermudians have only recently begun to have delusions of a class structure; white Bermudians have always had a rather rigid class system.) So that did not help. But the aspect which probably traumatized them most was that she was a white woman, and most of the union members were black men. What that must have done to their psyche! A black person can only make an intelligent guess about that on the basis of our history.

In any event, the whole white oligarchy intended to make her a scapegoat, who would pay for both her "sins" and those of the entire union. She was indicted for inciting a riot. But, in terms of black consciousness, an interesting thing happened. The union hired a West Indian lawyer to defend her. Bermuda was not his "plantation." His brilliant and eloquent defense of her was itself a demonstration of black power for those of us who heard him. But since the eyes of all Bermuda were on the trial, even those who did not hear him were gratified by his performance. In addition to that, the woman was acquitted. For most of us it was a real demonstration of black power. But there was something else which, to me, was of equal, though more subtle, importance. That lawyer was, after the initial impact, not a "West Indian," but a "Jamaican." Looking back on it now, I believe that it is true to say that for the first time, at least in so dramatic and widespread a fashion, the Bermudian stereotype of the "West Indian" was shattered. The man just could not be fitted into the Bermudians' preconceived category. Therefore he became individualized and personalized, and Bermudians had to readjust their blurred, vague, and very negative concept of West Indians.

I do not believe that I have overstated our deep-seated psychic response to the term "West Indians," particularly as words that had come to symbolize for us in Bermuda our intensely rejected blackness, our slave ancestry, and our African heritage.

I cannot pretend to measure the effect of that single experience on the very slowly awakening black consciousness of Bermudians. Perhaps none whatever that was lasting. But then, the psychic dimensions of our self-rejection are so deep and so all-pervasive that the whole strike experience was quickly forgotten by many black Bermudians a very short time later. Bermudians who were enraged and frightened by their perception of the deep racial hatred, animosity, and hostility in white Bermudians on that occasion were, very shortly afterwards, being flattered when the cold steel in their white compatriots' eyes turned into smooth political smiles.

In attempting to examine Massa Day in Bermuda I have emphasized the role of West Indians and the Bermudians' psychic response to them. I have done so because black unity is the only foundation of black power. White power holders have always recognized this factor. We ourselves have failed, tragically, to do so. They have always used every trick in the trade to sow seeds of division among us, and we have carefully watered and tended those seeds for them until they have flourished and blossomed into sturdy plants of black self-destruction. Our most serious psychological problem was with West Indians, but we felt equally condescending toward black Americans. We knew no Africans, but we viewed them through the eyes of the English authors of our school text books. And today we, as black Bermudians "integrating" with whites, condescend to and despise each other. "Integration" in Bermuda has become another instrument of division, this time among ourselves. It was inevitable because it was the "integration" of the powerful, psychologically free, with the powerless and psychologically enslaved. And it is firmly based on the continuing concept of white supremacy.

What hope do we have, then, that Massa Day will ever be done? Little, perhaps.

Yet black Bermudians like myself who have traveled widely or who, alternatively, have read widely and have become aware of the universality of our blackness, can take heart from one historical fact. The black power concept arose in America only after the "integrated" civil rights movement of the early sixties. The comment was once made about me in Bermuda that my own black consciousness (they called it "racism") arose out of my segregated school life. Although the seeds of black pride were indeed sown at a very early age in my youth, they did not flourish without the weeds of ambivalence until *after* I had lived in intimate ("integrated"!) contact with whites in Canada and England. I would hazard a guess that a survey of Bermudians' attitudes, particularly among those who have lived or studied outside of Bermuda, would support my general thesis. I do believe that the most important factor in an individual's black self-acceptance is influenced primarily by the attitudes of that individual's immediate family during his or her early years. But in addition to this early influence, there is this other. Those who have lived intimately or studied with whites during those critical years of maturation from adolescence into adulthood have most black pride and are most intent on a racial redistribution of real power. Those who are most ashamed of their blackness and who are therefore most flattered by the attention of their white compatriots or who are most satisfied to settle for the shadow, rather than the substance, of power are those who went to predominantly black colleges or those whose contacts with whites on a peer basis have come much later in life or not at all. I do not want to oversimplify the very complex dynamics of the formation and development of the self-concept. The general sense of self-worth or sense of inferiority which a child develops in his home environment, irrespective of the wider society, will have a bearing on how he perceives himself in relation to other people, and I dare say that there would be exceptions to my generalization. But for those of us who are concerned about the continuing self-rejection of black Bermudians, it is something we need to remember.

Only integration itself will prove that it does not, in fact, dispel racist attitudes or the assumptions of white supremacy, and it is certainly no substitute for black self-acceptance.

I find that black Americans often find West Indians and West Africans frustrating in their indifference to the dynamics and meaning of black power ideology. Both West Indians and West Africans suffer from the effects of racism, but they have not lived in daily contact with the perpetrators of racism as do black Americans. As a result, they are not nearly so likely to be vocal black power advocates when they arrive. Their American experience, if long enough, is likely to change that.

On the other hand, both West Africans and West Indians have had a better opportunity to develop their individual self-concepts without the abrasive face-to-face contact with white racist attitudes on a daily basis until later in life. It is an advantage which black children in segregated schools had, which unfortunately blacks did not appreciate or value as they should have. To expose our children to white teachers and their racist attitudes, as we have done, at so early an age fills me with serious misgivings and concern. White psychic control of black minds is operative in any event, but previously there was the possibility of some protection in those formative years.

An example in my own experience will illustrate the point. Between 1963 and 1967, when I was teaching, I wrote a great many letters to the editors of the local newspapers. It was clear from my letters that I did not give assent to the concept of white supremacy and that I did have a positive concept of my own blackness. The white power structure felt very threatened by my view of the world. As a result, throughout that period I was exposed to widespread criticism by whites for teaching "politics" in my classroom. It was evident that their concern was not about what I taught specifically, because they had no way of knowing, but they were concerned about the way I thought. They knew that no matter what I taught I would have an influence on the way some of my students thought. They went as far as having the black principal of the school, and at various times different black members of the executive council (imagine!), "warn" me about what I was doing.

The white Director of Education even implied on one occasion that if I wrote letters to the newspapers, I had better not teach. My experience was apparently by no means unique as there was once an education code in Bermuda which forbade teachers from writing to the newspapers. And during the franchise movement many teachers who spoke at those meetings were "warned." White Bermudians have always taken the business of psychic control of the black mind seriously, much more seriously than we have. There was a time when if a black American spoke on the radio the speaker would be cut off. Movies which showed a black person in any but a very subservient stereotype role were prohibited. And we know how scarce were movies with positive black images there were, and how "dangerous" they were likely to be, during the fifties and sixties.

But at least, at that time, black children had black teachers who, even if not consciously building black pride, were not consciously attacking it either. I say "consciously" because unwittingly we often do. For example, that black principal and those black members of the executive council undoubtedly believed that their "warning" was an act of friendship to me. In actual fact, they should never have passed on those "warnings" to me and should have made it very clear from the outset that they would not do so. But they themselves were not free.

Another teacher earned adverse headlines in a local Sunday newspaper because she had given her class notes on African history. As late as 1967 I was scored by white politicians as a "racist" because I urged black Bermudians to study their own history since there were already a number of white Bermudian histories being used in the schools. I was told that I should be asking for an "integrated" history of Bermuda. No one mentioned this, however, when the white versions of Bermuda's history were being distributed throughout the schools, something that certainly would not have been done for anything written by a black Bermudian. A black politician who "agreed" with this point of view and accused me of wanting to "regurgitate" past ills was later put in charge of the educational system and effectively killed any official efforts which were being made toward establishing an organized program for information about black people.

There is no doubt in my mind that the white Bermudian agrees with me that Massa Day, as far as Bermuda is concerned, is very much a matter of psychic control and control of the thought processes. It is for this reason that I have very serious doubts about exposing young black children to the psychic control of white teachers. A process that black children will have to deal with eventually, in any case, begins at a much earlier age when they are less able to do so. The very fact that black teachers have not been permitted into the white "integrated" classrooms of Bermuda suggests that whites are much more careful about the molding of the minds of their own children.

Black Bermudians, in their struggle and anxiety to achieve racial justice, have been too unaware of their own cultural and social strengths. We have been too anxious and too quick to "integrate" and eliminate those very aspects of our social lives which we should not have. We have unthinkingly adopted social values and assumptions which are the most destructive and inhumane aspects of the white societies—often only because they were white. Some of us were very anxious to have white teachers in our schools. But I am not at all certain that that is not a major step toward prolonging Massa Day.

An even more socially destructive feature which black Bermudians are attempting to adopt in their wild and thoughtless chase after "integration" is a social factor which is undoubtedly entrenching Massa Day and making any real sharing of white power even more of an illusion. It is the rather vicious and very wicked concepts of class stratification which many black Bermudians are currently attempting to dabble with.

Only in a society as intellectually unsophisticated and

naïve and above all as unread and as uncultivated (even though literate) as that of black Bermuda would attempt either to establish or intensify social stratification at this period in history. In almost every society in the world—save that of the South African—there is some effort being made toward social democratization. At the very least, lip service is being paid to the ideals of reducing or minimizing class stratification. The reverse is true among Bermudians. But then, Bermudians who are struggling to become our black "elite" are, intellectually, well insulated from what is happening in the rest of the world. Social discrimination between blacks is the price demanded for "integration."

The criterion for this social hierarchy is not wealth. We still do not have real wealth—and what does exist is likely to be subsidized by whites. It is certainly not "family" or ancestry. We all have a slave heritage, and Bermudian slave owners never gave special privileges to their mulatto offsprings as happened in many Caribbean islands. Neither is the criterion markedly occupational, although that may have a little relevance, since we are a nation of shopkeepers and are primarily concerned with providing services for tourists. The criterion which the newly class-conscious black Bermudians have established for their pattern of social stratification is, of all things, social contact with whites(!). Who belongs to the white, integrated(?) clubs becomes the crucial question. Said one young man with great pride, "Why, I was the first colored man to be invited to join the R—— Club."

One young black Bermudian who now lives abroad expressed shock on a recent return visit to Bermuda to discover this new, and very shallow, class-conscious mentality among his erstwhile friends. But it was only by this social development that white political control could have been maintained. Surely Massa Day in Bermuda is hardly "done" when black Bermudians contribute thus toward maintenance of white power and their own divisiveness. The response which attempts to defend this social phenomenon is one further manifestation of white mental control. The contention is that the call for black unity is "racist"; therefore some blacks should not unite with other blacks but should rather unite with (or "integrate" with) whites. The irony is that whites who have always practiced white supremacy continue to remain united and merely use their "integrated" blacks to give support and credibility to their assumptions of white superiority. Most blacks do in fact fear the charge of "racism." They have not exercised their own intelligence sufficiently to recognize that the real issue is whether or not we will continue to believe and act on the basis of a "racism" which assumes that whites are superior to, and therefore have the right to rule supreme over, blacks. Certainly this is the continuing assumption in Bermuda's political social and economic life. Whites who are in fact aware of the true situation merely use a certain group of blacks to validate their assumption. Blacks who have given their minds over to white control are indeed "racist," because although they are themselves black, they clearly believe in white superiority and white supremacy.

Social, political, and economic injustice is, in fact, likely to be intensified for many black Bermudians. It is a tragic reality that blacks who assume white superiority and are given what are, objectively, positions of power (even though often only mere tokens) acquire the power to say "No" to other blacks but never to say "Yes." They have the power to harm but not to benefit. They can "even old scores" with other blacks, but they are likely to lack the power to reward them. Patronage and prizes remain the prerogative of the white man. It is not difficult to understand why. Black men with "token power" have no illusions concerning where real power lies. They know the real limit of their own power; therefore they are cautiously careful in their use of it. They recognize that they are not likely to meet opposition if they wish to hurt or discriminate against other blacks, but if they wish to share in the power of patronage, they may indeed meet opposition from whites. Thus either they will not make the attempt, or they will bestow their patronage on whites. Thus their own sense of power will be reinforced by the exercise of negative power but undermined by any attempt to exercise positive power. In addition, blacks are themselves probably more interested in exercising their power to seek revenge than to do constructively positive things for other blacks. With their own acceptance of the assumption of white supremacy, they are also likely to prefer to bestow patronage on whites than on blacks.

This phenomenon is by no means totally new in Bermuda. It may now be more widespread. But in a rigidly segregated society, whites have always used blacks as instruments of token power in relation to other blacks.

There is a black secondary school in Bermuda through which for many years the white power structure has permitted blacks, whom they have chosen, to exercise a form of subsidiary control over other blacks. The men they chose were not unusually evil men. They did, however, often suffer from the negative power syndrome and used their power to express personal animosities. In my own lifetime I have seen more than one of those who were in power suffer the revenge of the very blacks whom they had hurt. The white man's pendulum swung, and power was given to those who once had been despised. It is a lesson of black history which we seem not to learn. While it is true that whites have escaped retribution for many of their social crimes, it is rash, in view of actual events in Bermuda, to assume that blacks will also inevitably escape.

Massa Day will be done only when we in Bermuda who have ourselves suffered discrimination insist on using our energies to acquire a share of real power, which we will then use to improve the economic and social life and the positive self-concept of other black Bermudians who need it most, rather than merely attempting to imitate the very shallow and false social values of white Bermudians.

Black Bermudian women should recognize that they have a special stake in retaining the social values of black Bermuda. Black Bermudian society has not only been classless but has suffered less from the neurosis of what is called "male chauvinism."

I am not suggesting that we did not experience some of

the phenomenon of the assumption of male supremacy. We were influenced by these assumptions of the white society. I am positive, however, from personal experience, that our black society was far freer of assumptions about female inferiority than are many others.

My American experience has brought this reality home to me with great force. My life in America has been thoroughly racially integrated. My life in Bermuda was not. But it was in America that I discovered that to be a woman could be a far greater liability and brought more demoralizing discrimination than to be black. Until I came into an integrated situation, I had never before been made so aware that I was not a man. I state it negatively, deliberately. For strong men can make me very aware that I am a woman and it becomes a compliment. Weak men, threatened by their own inner insecurities, make me aware that I am not a man, and that becomes both a threat to my essential personhood and an act of discrimination. Women in any black society should be very aware of what is likely to happen to their own development, self-fulfillment, and capacity for independent action as it (their society) becomes integrated or adopts white values. I am not, at this point, referring to the need of many very demoralized and racially scarred black men for white women. Calvin Hernton, in *Sex and Racism*, and Eldridge Cleaver analyzed this phenomenom better than I could. I am thinking now of the social phenomenon, inherent in the white society, which is being challenged currently by the white, middle-class women's liberation movement and such authors as Germaine Greer, in *The Female Eunuch*. Black Bermudian women, and, in my view, West Indian women, have no concept of the kind of demoralization and devaluing of their person that white women experience. They should inform themselves. For in an integrated society, the black woman will bear an even greater brunt of the effects of the disease. It speaks well of the strength, character, and sanity of the black American woman that she continues to play the constructive role that she does in this American society. For she, more than anyone else, bears the full brunt of the impact of the racism and sexism of an integrated society. In an integrated white society she is the prime recipient of black self-hate. And yet, in America she has continued to be a contributing, functioning member of her society. While white women in women's lib rail against the "male chauvinism," black women have continued to be the only source of real strength which black men, crushed by a white society, have had. And yet black women are likely to suffer most in the "war of the sexes" because black society, in attempting to adopt white values, may intensify the discord between black men and black women.

In Bermuda black women have always been accepted by black men as intelligent, functioning, contributing members of their black society. There are for example, more than six active black women politicians and only one white female member of Parliament. This white woman politician is operating out of the black community, and black women in Bermuda should, in their own interest, consider it a matter of urgency to study carefully the role of white women in white society and the role of black women in an integrated society and then carefully compare it with their own. To the extent that the adoption of white assumptions of male supremacy become a part of Bermuda's "integration," it is bound to create conflict between black men and black women, further conflict which we can ill afford. This, in turn, will prolong Massa Day, because it will be an added source of division and conflict among blacks.

Is Massa Day done? Is there black power in Bermuda? Or is the white man whom we, as blacks, have for so long called "Master" still in control and exercising unshared power?

In Bermuda there can be no doubt whatsoever that he is still firmly in control, politically, socially, and economically. Not even his political control has been seriously challenged by black Bermudians. On the contrary, his political power has been reinforced because he has been given a black mandate. For black Bermudians, bowing to the assumptions of white supremacy, have feared to take on the responsibility of power. Black Bermudians have done no more than challenge the manner in which white Bermudians have exercised that power. They (white Bermudians), in turn, have responded to that challenge by modifying their use of power. Only a few have seriously concerned themselves about the actual redistribution of power. Black fears grow out of a deep psychological conditioning regarding the assumptions of white supremacy and white superiority and a sense of black inadequacy and inferiority. It is only when black Bermudians have honestly faced the deep degradation of the black self-perception and the resulting implications will it be possible to acknowledge that it is only as we force ourselves to share in the actual exercise of real power that we will, all of us, have the assurance that it is indeed our birthright to do so.

It is for this reason, more than any other, that the PLP must gain a political victory in Bermuda. It is not because the PLP will usher in the millennium in Bermuda or necessarily ensure even the implementation of all of its own ideals. It undoubtedly will not. It is because it is only those within the PLP, be they black or white, who make the assumptions that black Bermudians, as well as whites, have both the right and the capacity to govern and to exercise power. Unless they do, Massa Day of psychic control will never be done. When they assume power, that alone will be sufficient indication that more and more black Bermudians and (improbable miracle) perhaps even whites have rid themselves of the racist assumptions of white supremacy. This alone will also give to the fainthearted and fear-filled the assurance that black Bermudians do have a right to power.

It is only when black Bermudians have the courage and the honesty to admit (even if only to themselves and with great pain and inner shame) to their own "white syndrome" that they will even begin to *want* to freely share in the exercise of power. They must acknowledge, as humbling as they may find it, that they love the white man more than they love themselves. That they value him more highly than they value themselves. It is a step which must be taken, and it can be taken because they are not alone, for throughout the Caribbean and the United States, for many, Massa Day is not done.

EVA HODGSON was born in Bermuda, attended the segregated schools there, and left her home to study in Canada, England, and the United States. She took her undergraduate degree at Queen's University, Kingston, Ontario, Canada, and her graduate degrees at the University of London and Columbia University. She is currently working on a Ph.D. in African history at Columbia University.

Miss Hodgson was actively involved in the changes that came to Bermuda's segregated society in the 1960s and was the first president of the Teachers' Association when the formerly separate black and white unions merged. She is the author of Second Class Citizens: First Class Men, a book on ten years of black political struggle in Bermuda. She now lives in New York City and teaches at Richmond College in New York and Essex County College in New Jersey.

Timothy O. McCartney

WHAT IS THE RELEVANCE OF
BLACK POWER TO THE BAHAMAS?

"Black is the beauty, red is the hog" is an old Bahamian saying that many black children used to chant at fair-skinned or white children when there was some controversy, frustration, or quarrel. Whether these children at that time believed that black was really the beauty is a matter of conjecture, but from the history books and the attitudes of former Bahamians, everything that was black—pickie hair, black devil, black skin, etc.—was surely not beautiful.

Today in the Bahamas there is much talk about blackness —in fact, there is loud vocal and graphic evidence that "blackness" is becoming a "mod" thing, as is evidenced by the colorful drawings of clenched fists, symbols, and slogans that can be found on decrepit buildings, walls, and lampposts throughout our island. Statements like "Soul City," "Black Souls," "Power to the People," "Down with Whitey" are seen everywhere, especially in our very underprivileged areas. Added to this scenery are scores of idle youth dressed in dashikis, bands around their Afros and hair braided in Guinea rolls or other exotic styles. With a lethargic mien and red eyes, due probably to being high on "herbs" ("grass," or marijuana) with fists clenched in the "black power" salute, passers-by are greeted with "Peace brother," or "Let's get it together" in strong American accents, or some of the very popular "bad" Bahamian words. Policemen are called "pigs" or the "fuzz" and "dig it" has entered our vocabulary. Many visitors, some of them black Americans, have commented on this scene, and several have said that as they walked through some of our "over the hill" streets, they wondered whether they were at 125th Street in Harlem.

What, then, are these manifestations all about? Are they an indication of a definite black power philosophy coming into being in the Bahamas? Are these youths only imitating and identifying with scenes from the American ghettos as depicted in the popular American movies? What are the reasons for the adaptation of the so-called "African" styles, which are, in fact, *not* African at all but commercial American exports, exploited, interestingly, by white Americans? Are these developments a modern-day growth phenomenon of black countries trying to assert their own brand of individualism? Is this what happens to black people (or countries) moving toward complete independence from their colonial masters? No matter what the reasons may be, black power is a force in the Bahamas, and whether we accept or reject all the many implications of black power would depend, to a large extent, on the understanding, objectivity, and non-emotionalism of all Bahamians and in particular the political and behavioral scientists in our country.

Many Bahamians appear to ignore these definite trends. Other Bahamians, by just hearing the words "black power," become very emotional. Indeed, the word "black" is still a word to be avoided by very sensitive black and white people. Many of the establishment claim that black power only attracts young people that are bored and blame the government for not providing adequate recreational facilities for them. Other Bahamians believe that only "criminal" elements of our society would adhere to black power beliefs because they are not prepared to gain recognition or economic stability any other way than playing up the racial issue.

Of course, Bahamians that are close to some of these black power advocates, regard some of these youths as responsible, concerned individuals, who are not only aware of the many socioeconomic disadvantages of the masses, but honestly want to do something about it. Then others believe, that black power advocates are immature, insecure individuals, who have never been exposed to anything and are mere "copycats" of what they believe black Americans are supposed to be. What is even more surprising is that the majority of these young people have never been subjected to racial discrimination nor have been deprived because of race in the Bahamas, and yet they are evolving a definite philosophy of blackness. As a spokesman for one of these groups explained to me recently: "Black power is a search for identity or roots and an attempt to engender black awareness and pride among the Bahamian people." When asked about the white or mixed or other ethnic group Bahamians and their role in Bahamian society, he simply stated that they would have to "think black." He explained that the majority of the people are black, so naturally our life style, education, and beliefs must be black. Another young college graduate (from the United States) expressed his ideas in the following manner: "Man, Afro-West Indians and Afro-Americans have always had conflicts as to their worth culturally, religiously, and socially. The only solution to our problems of identity is to reject the false values of the white bias, rediscover African roots, and from this create a new life style which would evolve into a definite black culture."

More significant is that there is now in the Bahamas a return to African names and a tremendous interest in African history. Recently, Oscar Johnson proposed a committee to study building a statue to the Afro-Bahamian woman, and some of his colleagues would like to see the statue of Queen Victoria moved from the public square in Nassau.

The *Bahamas Handbook* of 1970–71 wrote that "with the 'Black is Beautiful' slogan, Afro-Bahamians are discovering a lost heritage but perhaps it's been there all along." *The Vanguard* of November 1972 has an article by Errol Hasfal entitled "If It Ain't 'Bout Africa, It Ain't 'Bout Nothing" and Dr. John McCartney of the Vanguard Nationalist-Socialist party believes that the crux of the black power movement is an "authentic quest for freedom." He states "black power strives to make black men and women realize themselves without the hindrances of white society."

I am a behavioral scientist, more specifically, a psychologist. I study behavior, both normal and abnormal. I am also a citizen, a father, a grandfather, but more than that, a Bahamian strongly motivated by deep Christian principles and my involvement with the Bahamian community in terms of honesty, justice, and freedom for all. It is hoped that this essay will stimulate discussions among Bahamians who must find the solutions for themselves if they care at all for the future of this country as well as for the wider and more universal aspects of the human condition commonly identified with equality, self-respect, and human dignity.

I do not intend to be biased in my views, nor do I intend to engage, as Rex Nettleford has said, "as a young self-conscious person, to look 'narcissistically' in a sickly contemplation of my navel." Nor do I intend to propose views of typical colonial attitudes of self-hate and a perpetuation of the belief that nothing good can be achieved by black people.

I would like to invite the Bahamian people, especially our young people, to look critically at our society—its trends and its faults—and to have a respect for our history, both past and contemporary, and a sensible approach to the very emotional question of race.

I would like to divide this essay into three specific parts: (1) developmental history; (2) Bahamian black power; and (3) personal thoughts and probable solutions.

1. DEVELOPMENTAL HISTORY

The Commonwealth of the Bahamas is a black country. This is not to be understood as a racial or political statement, but simply a statement in terms of the ethnic origin of the majority of the population. While the Bahamas (and indeed the whole West Indies) have been colonized by whites, it is nevertheless the black people, introduced into our country as slaves, who have not only over the centuries vastly outnumbered their former masters, but have also given the area its cultural and ethnic characteristics.

This basic premise is one we have in common with all West Indian countries. Beyond that, the geographical, historical, economic, and political factors peculiar to each island have created a rich variety of different cultures that make it impossible to link the whole West Indies together into one homogenous whole. The Bahamas look back on a historical development considerably different from that of, say, Trinidad or Jamaica. Closer to the American mainland than any other of the West Indian islands, the Bahamas are traditionally more closely linked to and influenced by American history. The common factor, though, that makes the whole West Indies somewhat alike in its attitudes is the "white power" structure, ruling and exploiting these islands and people for nearly three hundred years.

The historical antecedents of slavery, colonialism, and social injustices are too well known to go into any details, but the history of the Bahamas is mainly one of Spanish, French, and British bartering, invading, fighting, and conquering. But while it appears that there were several blacks not only among the conquering colonial forces, but also among the buccaneers and pirates that haunted Bahamian waters, the black man played only a minimal part in that early part of our history.

The main influx of blacks came to the Bahamas in the latter part of the eighteenth century which saw a considerable wave of white immigrants from the United States. Loyalists, who did not fancy life in post-Revolutionary America, moved to the Bahamas, lock, slave-stock, and barrel, to begin a new life here. Thus, the bulk of the black population in the Bahamas consisted of slaves who accompanied their masters in their exodus from the now independent United States.

Not all blacks brought to the Bahamas, however, were slaves. After the British prohibition of the slave trade around 1808, many ships out of Africa carrying cargoes of captured blacks destined for slavery in the New World were intercepted and brought to the Bahamas where the captives were automatically freed upon arrival. There was a very strong colonial influence at this time, and even though it is recorded that the liberated blacks were not ill treated, the system of "whiteness," which connotated "purity" and "civilization" over "blackness" with all its negative implications, became ingrained in the general society.

During the early period of the Bahamas' development, the blacks slowly outnumbered the whites, lived in clustered areas, and existed mostly on small farming and fishing.

An unenviable reputation for thriving on other people's misfortunes gave the islands semblances of economic "booms"—wreckers and gun- and rumrunners increased the coffers mostly of the Bahamian white. Since the Bahamas were not agricultural, there were no massive plantations like those found in other West Indian islands. Hence, after slavery, there was no need for indentured imported labor to take the place of the freed Bahamians. The population consisted of blacks, whites (colonial administrators, European sailors who jumped ships, etc.), and, in the late nineteenth century, Greeks who were engaged in the sponge industry.

Some Chinese came to the Bahamas around 1925, and these operated small restaurants, laundries, and grocery stores. stores. The majority of people were black but the Bahamas existed and operated under a white power structure not too unlike the southern United States. The shame of it all is that the majority of the population has always been black people. There have never been any laws or legislation fixing the status of these black people, and yet, for almost all of these three hundred years, the black man in the Bahamas was subjugated to a position of inferiority that placed him solidly on the bottom of the social structure.

The discriminatory attitudes and practice were everywhere —in schools, banks, clubs, hotels. Very rarely did black and white Bahamians have any meaningful social intercourse. Sir Etienne Dupuch in his book *Tribune Story* states that "At the turn of the century we lived in a very complex society, every man had a place and every man was expected to know his place. There were three main groups—the colored people at the bottom, the Bahamian white people, largely descendants of loyalists who left the United States during the American War for Independence, and the British official class." Sir Etienne continued: "The colored people were split in groups, determined entirely by degree of color, starting with black at the bottom, through off-black, dark brown, brown, light brown, high yellow, and near white. Only 'leopards'—people with spots in their character—attempted to cross these invisible barriers. The Bahamian whites were split mainly in two groups—the Government House crowd, composed principally of people of Scottish extraction, members of the powerful St. Andrew's Society who received invitations to Government House—and the rest. On top of this structure sat the Governor and his English officials, the Governor like a great silent Buddha. In those days it was only necessary for a man to say that he was an Englishmen. That was his passport. Immediately he became a small Buddha and was put on a shelf just below the pedestal reserved for the big Buddha. Each group—right from the top to the lowest level—played one set against the other."[1]

We can clearly see, therefore, the various divisions of color, nationality, social class, and race that characterized our Bahamian society. "Naturally following the yearning for upward mobility, those who aspired to social advancement, even within their own set limits, got their bearings from the beacon that shone at the top—thence the deep-rooted British and white-orientated value system."[2] The most obvious effect of the white economic stronghold, the colonial administrative system, and the lack of education among

[1] Etienne Dupuch, *Tribune Story* (Ernest Benn Ltd., London 1967), p. 37.
[2] T. O. McCartney, *Neuroses in the Sun* (Executive Ideas of the Bahamas Ltd., Nassau, Bahamas 1971), pp. 158–59.

Bahamian blacks was that psychologically the black seemed a powerless, pathetic individual. The bad self-image of being black, the historical propaganda of white greatness, the white life style, and the influence of the American communication media caused the Bahamian to engage in fantasy and wish he were white. This inferiority plus the constant inequities of his life style were embedded into his psyche, but instead of being motivated toward instigating change, he only became a passive, "charming" native.

It was perhaps this placid, somewhat denigrating attitude and subservience of the Bahamian that caused rich white tourists to build winter homes here, not just the sun, sand, and sea. The non-violent attitudes of black and white Bahamians (even though a select white minority ruled with an iron hand) made the Bahamas an "ideal" climate for investors, residents, and visitors. Prosperity began to come to the islands, and even though the majority of blacks were content to remain as they were, there were black men of vision who were aware of what was happening in other parts of the world. The Bahamian began to save his money to educate his sons, and a few blacks left the island for the United States and Europe to study.

There were no significant political organizations or parties prior to 1953 (the Progressive Liberal party was formed in 1953) but there were stirrings among black Bahamians. A significant group was the Bahamas Citizens Committee, composed of men like Maxwell Thompson, Cleve Eneas (who was editor of the *Citizens Torch* newspaper), Charles Rodriquez, Kendal Isaacs, Gerald Cash, Bert Cambridge, Leon McKinney, and S. C. McPherson, to name a few.

In an editorial in *Citizens Torch* in March 1951, the implications of this committee came out loud and clear: "It is necessary that we must develop self-pride, and no one with self-pride voluntarily takes insults to his integrity. It should be insulting to each and every one of us to be barred from any place because we are black. It is regarded as weakness on our part when we permit such practices to be leveled against us without the raising of a single protest or taking some stand against it. It is a different thing altogether when people are discriminated against because of behavior, but in our town the insults leveled against us brand all of us as being ill-bred, ill-mannered, and lacking in good behavior."

The first real protest by the masses was in 1942 when a group of Bahamian blacks, in order to effect some sort of social change, rioted. The Bahamian black workers protested against discriminatory practices of an American-British company which had signed an agreement to build air bases in the Bahamas. This foreign company also hired white American labor and paid them more money than the Bahamians.

The workers formed into a group and marched toward Bay Street (the financial and business center of the Bahamas) chanting "Burma Road Declares War on the Conchy Joe."[3] Rioting broke out, causing considerable property damage; six people were killed and many were injured.

Later on, men like Milo Butler, Sr., went to the banks and demanded that they hire black Bahamians other than as messengers or maids. The tragedy of this particular epoch in our history was not the discriminatory practices based purely on race. The color of one's skin was most important, *not* the race. Many fair-skinned blacks passed and went to hotels and clubs and were more vicious and prejudiced than the whites. There were also many blacks that took an attitude of non-involvement—"If they don't want me in their place, then I won't go."

Maxwell Thompson wrote in the *Citizens Torch* of September 1951 that in the Bahamas we were "fed a type of educational food which has been different from that fed to the colored peoples in the Caribbean area. All except us are clamoring to assume responsibilities—all except us are taking steps to awaken our sleeping brothers—all except us are devising ways and means of emancipating themselves generally—all except us are getting away from individualism because experience has shown that this practice is harmful to group progress." More Bahamians, however, soon began to

[3] "Conchy Joe" is a derogatory term used against Bahamian whites.

become involved, especially as more returned home from school abroad with new professions and ideas.

A. J. Hutchenson, Jr., writing a column called "The Power of the People" in the *Citizens Torch* of September 1951, urged Bahamians to grasp political and economic power: "The vast section of the population of this country today have more power economically than they realize." Then, too, there was an influx of West Indians recruited for the Bahamas police force. These men brought new ideas of "liberation" movements that were taking place in their own countries and spurred on the Bahamian to think more positively about his country. It is interesting to note that the present Prime Minister's father is a Jamaican who came to the Bahamas as a policeman.

In 1956, on a resolution in the Bahamian House of Assembly, Sir Etienne Dupuch, morally backed by forerunners of the cause like Dr. C. R. Walker, A. F. Adderley, T. A. Toote, Bert Cambridge, to name just a few, was instrumental in helping to break down discriminatory practices, at least in public places. Bahamian whites and blacks still, however, maintained their rigid social lines and stereotype images. Meanwhile, there was focus on other aspects of Bahamian life that caused injustices to the masses.

In 1958 there was a general strike against four companies that almost crippled the country. This strike was started by the taxi drivers and maintained by the newly formed unions. The Colonial Office sent to the Bahamas the Secretary of State for the Colonies, Mr. A. T. Lennox-Boyd. Reforms, which moved from limited male suffrage to universal male suffrage, were put into effect and soon—through demonstration and pressure by women like Dr. Doris Johnson, Mrs. Rufus Ingraham, Mrs. Bertha Isaacs, Dr. Willamae Saunders, and others—included, by 1962, the right to vote for all Bahamian males and females.

By far the most significant change in this country's social structure came in 1967 when the Progressive Liberal party (PLP) was elected to office—the beginning of black government over a black majority. The reaction to this change was predictably strong on all sides. The apprehension among the white people was to be expected, even though many liberal whites and a strong expatriate group supported the PLP. Remarkably, many black Bahamians were less than enthusiastic about the prospect of a black government. The ingrained inferiority attitudes still prevailed even though the black Bahamian had voted into office a black government.

2. BAHAMIAN BLACK POWER

In April 1967, four months after the PLP won the election, two black Bahamian intellectuals, Dr. C. W. Eneas, Sr., an American-trained dentist, and Father Bonaventure Dean, a Catholic priest, educator, and prior of St. Augustine's Monastery (Benedictine), gave a series of talks on black power and black awareness, respectively. They believed that because of the "new" government image and the hysterical reports of the world press (especially American) as to what black power really was, the Bahamian should understand his *own* power in relation to other Third World concepts.

These two men were castigated by the Bahamian news media and populace. Even the politicians who needed this additional objective exposure were silent on the issue. Father Dean was reminded that he was educated in a "white" university and would not be what he was if it were not for the white man. Many benefactors of St. Augustine's College withdrew their financial support because of this "renegade" priest. Dean declared that Bahamians had to go beyond the "black is beautiful" stage to nation building, where the black man must assume the responsibility of making a significant contribution to his own country and to the world. He believed that "the categories of thoughts, concepts of beauty, life styles were too basically white." He thought that "one does not have to wear an Afro, but one has got to be proud of the fact of being black and black is not being white."

Dr. Eneas' paper was a passionate, objective treatise tracing the history of the black power movement in the world and relating it to the Bahamian revolution. He believed that black power had "caused some people to take a new look at themselves and others to organize themselves."

Of course, much has been reported on the black power phenomenon with much emotionalism and there is an indication that there is much confusion among Bahamians. Because of this emotionalism and bad image by the local and foreign press, many Bahamians would like to ignore what is happening, especially among our young people. To pretend that it doesn't exist would be to be like the proverbial ostrich, yet to place more emphasis on it than it rightly deserves would be foolish. Bahamians associate black power with riots, the Panthers, and violent means to achieve an end. Thus black power, especially in a Bahamian multiracial society, is thought to be a dangerous force that must be eliminated from our society.

The black Bahamian has always been in conflict with his own identity. He always disliked the term "Negro," which to him is too strongly connotative of slavery and submission. "Black" until very recently was—well, quite totally unacceptable. The only term he would settle for was "colored," probably because of its politely euphemistic sound, because a kind of exoticism could be read into it that was at least suggesting something fascinating, instead of "black" or "Negro" with their strictly negative implications. Because of the difficulty in racial nomenclature and the multiracism of Bahamian society, many Bahamians, black and white, are advocating eliminating these terms—"We are neither black nor white, we are Bahamians." Then, too, many black Bahamians viewed with suspicion and resentment another American import, American singer Nina Simone, in June 1970. A new organization, Mafundi Bahamia, spearheaded by Bahamian film star Calvin Lockhart and myself as president, sponsored Miss Simone in order to raise funds for Mafundi. Miss Simone interspersed her songs with black poetry and political statements that many in the audience thought to be offensive and inappropriate.

The next day all hell broke loose. Ed Bethel on the national radio station ZNS denounced Miss Simone's performance and told her to go home. The *Tribune* (the daily evening newspaper) reported that "60 per cent of her program was racist harangue and the other 40 per cent was racist songs, which is not what the audience came to hear. Her whole attitude was destructive to the good racial relations built here."

Headlines like BLACK POWER HARANGUE ANGERS AUDIENCE and WE DON'T NEED PEOPLE LIKE YOU IN THE BAHAMAS MISS SIMONE superseded important world events. Probably the most important comment was made in the *Nassau Guardian* by its columnist P. Anthony White, the talented black American-trained Bahamian journalist. In his column "For What It's Worth," White wrote that "Miss Simone brought to the islands one of the worst cases of unsolicited black brotherhood in recent years."[4] More significant, though, were his further comments: "In our way we have come far past America, and so Miss Simone could well save her efforts for Detroit, Harlem, Newark, Watts, or even the liberal confines of Washington, D.C. Those of us who protested against the singer's repulsive attitude and performance did so not particularly out of sympathy for the ridiculed whites who attended, for they must have well been able to analyze the situation for themselves. We protested, rather, because this was yet another instance of an American black who feels he is the idol of black men everywhere and that his 'suffering' immediately qualifies him to draft the blueprint for the liberation of Negroes the world over."

For a long time Mafundi Bahamia was termed a black power movement and many of its original members either resigned or dropped out of sight. Unfortunately, Mafundi hasn't been the same since, but some of the members are planning to continue the organization and try to fulfill its objects of providing means for Bahamians to "actualize their cultural potential."

It is true to state that the Bahamas are better off economically than most of the other West Indian islands. The over-

[4] P. Anthony White, "For What It's Worth," *Nassau Guardian*, Friday, July 3, 1970.

employment situation, the gargantuan tourist industry, the "offshore" companies, and the financial institutions have placed the Bahamas in an enviable situation. Although the political opponents claim that this economic bubble is slowly bursting because of the bad management of the present government, the potential of the Bahamas is probably still very great.

The present government is on a Bahamianization program, and immigration has become very strict on the number and type of expatriates taking positions in the Bahamas. The average Bahamian fears the "overforeignization" aspect of tourism and development. The basic needs of these islands at present still cannot be met by Bahamian professionals or workers. With seven hundred islands stretching from Florida to the coast of Hispaniola and a population of only about 190,000, the one and a half million tourists per year and the lax tax structure attract many foreigners and contribute much to the ambivalence of the Bahamian who needs it all but fears it.

The white economic structure in the Bahamas is also cause for concern. Most of the banks, hotels, and industries are controlled by foreign interests. Many Bahamians believe that they only get the "crumbs that fall from the master's table" and would like to see more Bahamians share in the wealth of their country. Money produces power; economic viability enhances security. Bahamians believe that we have already achieved political and social power, but there is still economic power (or "green" power, as the youths say) to be attained.

In studying the history of the Bahamas, there is no evidence of slave uprisings or groups of people openly fighting for some cause. During slavery there were even laws in the Bahamas that condemned cruel beatings and injustices to the slaves. Bahamian slave owners, mostly white but also black, had the choice of slaves from the boats that stopped in the Bahamas before going to the other West Indian islands. Bahamian historians use this as a reason for the peaceful coexistence of the blacks and whites during the slave era. As previously stated, many blacks who came to the Bahamas were the "house niggers" of American loyalists. These slaves lived quite well and their masters cohabited frequently with female slaves so that they could "improve" the strain and provide more manpower. The slaves' life styles were very European, and when Christianity was introduced, the converted "dropped the African shackels" and became "whiter than snow."

This development background, plus the rise in economic strength of the black and the quest for education, has produced a rather conservative Afro-Saxon person. When the PLP was formed in 1953, the members were regarded as radicals because it was the first time in Bahamian history that a black political party challenged the ruling white oligarchy. There are still no organizations in the Bahamas that can be compared to Tapia in Trinidad, Ratoon in Guyana, or the Rastafari in Jamaica. There have never been any "back to Africa" groups per se, and Marcus Garvey, although admired by some Bahamians, has never had any great influence on Bahamas thinking. Interestingly, last year a group of black Bahamians led by Kermit Ford, director of the Pioneer Bugle Corps, held a commemorative service to honor Garvey's birthday. Ford, a karate teacher, had lived in New York for many years. The Bahamas Democratic League (BDL), formed by Sir Etienne Dupuch in the late 1950s, was the first integrated political party in the Bahamas. They never won any political seats and the party soon petered out, because black and white Bahamians were not prepared for such a type of integrated party at this time.

The youth organization Unicomm (formerly Unicoll) was formed in the late 1960s to air the views of Bahamian students on vacation from foreign universities and also to provide a public forum on community problems. This group had young, intelligent men like Sean McQueeny, Perry Christie (now a lawyer), Franklyn Wilson, and John McCartney, to name a few, and some liberated women like Leila Mitchell. When these young people started "rocking the boat," the adult society condemned them as upstarts and viewed them with suspicion, especially when there was talk condemning the tourist industry and ideas about nationalization. In 1969, during the formal ceremonies to commemorate the Queen's birthday, members of Unicomm paraded with anti-British placards and burned the British flag. This incident caused quite an uproar, and some adults who secretly admired this organization became incensed at this "disrespectful" act and people really started to think that perhaps they were communists, as some had charged, after all. Shortly after this incident, some of its members became closely and openly allied with the present PLP. Claims that they had sold out and that they had become pawns for the PLP caused a break in the organization. At present, Unicomm has been inactive and voiceless even though some of its members belong to the new Bahamas Federation of Youth (BFY) that embraces most of the youth organizations in the Bahamas.

The BFY, formed in January 1971, is gradually growing in numbers and in effectiveness. It has become involved in many social projects in the community and held its second annual national convention this year. The president, Sammy Bain, is a strong black power advocate, even though he admits that only about three out of ten young people in the BFY think like him. Sammy Bain advocates a total break with Great Britain, eliminating the monarchy even as a figure head. He and his so-called "radicals" would like to see a socialist type of government, nationalizing all the big companies and industries and bringing more social benefits to the masses. Even though these ideas are the minority views of the BFY, this group, consisting of a sizable number of hard-working youths from all the Bahama Islands, could become a tremendous force.

Closer, however, to a black power cell than any other group in the Bahamas is a new political party called the Vanguard National Socialist party (VNSP) formed in 1971. The prime movers of this party are former Unicomm members who became disenchanted with the capitalistic leanings of Unicomm members and the present government. The VNSP is strongly nationalistic and advocates a type of "Bahamian socialism" giving power to the people—the majority, of course, being black. Its monthly tabloid, *The Vanguard*, quotes liberally such black power heroes as Marcus Garvey, Frantz Fanon, and Stokely Carmichael.

It believes that the present ruling PLP, although a black party, has not catered to the needs of the black man in the Bahamas. The VNSP wants a clean break with imperialism and a real rise to power of the black masses. The VNSP's chief advocate is Dr. John McCartney, a black Bahamian lecturer in political science at Purdue University. Dr. McCartney has been living in the United States for many years and has been completely caught up with the American black power movement. A recent letter by him, published in the Black Muslim newspaper, claimed that "We [the VNSP] are now being criticized in the establishment press more and more often, which means we are being more effective. The house-to-house campaign is proceeding beautifully. The 'enemy,' aided by its imperialistic lackeys, is still strong and we have no illusions about that. At the same time, Vanguard has gotten stanch support especially from the youth and is now a definite factor in Bahamian life."

The reaction to the VNSP has been varied. To some radical intellectuals, there has been strong appeal; but many poor people want to wait and see if the VNSP will release them from the injustices of black and white men. To aware black youths, it is the only real party; to the mostly adult society, the VNSP will fade out into oblivion like most "renegade" parties in the Bahamas.

Counter to these attitudes, the multiracial aspect of social and political life has taken on a new dimension in the past year with the creation of yet another political party—the Free National Movement (FNM). This party was formed by eight former members of the PLP (three of them former ministers) who became disenchanted with the PLP and particularly with the Prime Minister. When these eight left, they called themselves the "Free PLPs." Shortly afterward, there were talks with the then opposition "white" United Bahamian party and the local National Democratic party (which have never gained a seat in the legislature) and which is now defunct. These parties soon agreed to merge in order to provide a strong opposition and to defeat, by all means available, the PLP.

The FNM's first convention in February 1972 drew tremendous crowds that flabbergasted even the leaders themselves. Their motto, "All Together," has brought, for the first time in the history of Bahamian politics, a supposedly *workable*, viable white and black party.

The controversy over black awareness and Bahamianization continues to go on and has developed a very strong political orientation. In order to understand all this, one must examine the complex economic and social situation in the Bahamas.

The Bahamas depend almost totally on the tourist industry, with finance, banking, and "offshore" companies taking advantage of the favorable Bahamian tax conditions. The climate is excellent, the proximity to the United States is an advantage, the people up to now have been friendly, there is no income tax, and there have been no violent uprisings—so far. The stability of the Bahamas is vital to the United States because of their proximity to Cuba.

For reasons economists have never understood, the economy of the Bahamas has brought an affluence to their people unequaled anywhere in the West Indies. Yet the situation is a fragile one. There are no big industries, no strong agricultural systems, and no natural resources discovered so far. True, the Bahamas are surrounded by the most beautiful waters in the world, with abundant seafood, but there is no real fishing industry and only recently aragonite has begun to be mined off the coast of Bimini.

Since 1967 there has definitely been more self-awareness, especially among black Bahamians—artists, writers (to a small extent), musicians, and actors are all doing their "Bahamian thing." It would appear to me that the majority of Bahamians are leaning toward *Bahamian nationalism* rather than black power per se. The Bahamian, especially the intellectual, has never wanted to go back to Africa. He has also believed that he has been better off socially than his black American counterpart. There are many Bahamians who still look upon the philosophy of black power, its jargon, and its attitudes as negative black stateside imports.

Realistically speaking, there is much to be done in every aspect of Bahamian living. It should be noted, though, and this has been reiterated by our Prime Minister, that the Bahamas are for *all* Bahamians. The Bahamian at this present time, can qualify for any job, live anywhere, and do as he pleases without hindrances because of race or creed.

There are definitely many questions to be asked.

How can the black Bahamian rid himself of his bad self-image?

Are Bahamians, because of their non-violence, conservative attitudes, and capitalistic orientation, really black men with white masks?

What about the *mixed* Bahamian? Is he to subscribe to that old fallacious cracker idea that "one drop of Negro blood makes him a Negro"?

What about Africa? There isn't any country in the world that is so diverse with regard to races, color, and culture or so fraught with identification problems.

What directions do we feel are necessary from Africa that would benefit us here in the Bahamas?

What type of religion, dress, educational system should we adapt here?

What type of *language* should we speak?

What type of customs—family structure for example—should we adapt?

Do we feel that an infusion of African culture (whatever we may choose from the almost two thousand different tribes and classes of racial branches) is necessary for us?

What role do the white Bahamian and foreign whites play in the Bahamas?

Are the masses of Bahamians willing to listen to or reconstruct their lives according to, what we so-called radical intellectuals claim to be the only way?

3. PERSONAL THOUGHTS AND PROBABLE SOLUTIONS

Here are my personal views:

The fallacy of race and its problems, with their alarmingly exaggerated importance, have been man's most dangerous myth. I say this because when the nature of contemporary "racial" theories are scientifically analyzed and understood, they cease to be of any significance for social or any other kind of action.

Ernest Renan once said, "Ethnic facts, though they constitute the main problem in the early stages of history, gradually lose momentum in proportion to the progress of civilization."

What then has been scientifically established concerning individual and group differences?

1. In matters of race, the only characteristic which anthropologists have so far been able to use effectively as a basis for classification are *physical* (i.e., anatomical and physiological).

2. Available scientific knowledge provides no basis for believing that the groups of mankind differ in their innate capacity for intellectual and emotional development.

3. Vast social changes have occurred that have not been connected in any way with racial type.

Historical and sociological studies thus support the view that genetic differences are of little significance in determining the social and cultural differences between different groups of men.

Thus, to my mind, in the Bahamas there is need for tremendous improvement with regard to attitudes. Every political or social system has flaws and is capable of some improvement. We in the Bahamas stand to profit immediately by giving up acting on "racial mythology." We cannot, however, change the conditions of social friction and inadequacies merely by changing our moods. Changing our minds often amounts to no more than rearranging our prej-

udices. Black prejudice is just as vicious as white prejudice.
We as Bahamians must:

a. Reorganize our educational system so as not to project
any superiority or inferiority feelings among our children.
Bahamian history and total knowledge of our islands are
necessary.

b. The confusing ambivalence of being black hating white,
seizing power, depending on whitey, projecting blackness,
eliminating whiteness doesn't make much sense to me.

c. On the other hand, there must be liberation of the
Bahamian black, whether he be poor, middle class or high
class, from the chains of self-contempt, self-doubt and cynicism. Correspondingly, there will have to be liberation of
Bahamian whites and expatriates from their self-importance,
real and *functional*, and from the bondage of a culture which
they believe projects them as superior beings.

If black power advocates the enhancement of the black
man's creativity and the elimination of conditioned inadequacies with respect to himself and if it is to denounce oppression and wrong, then I can be called a black power advocate. If, on the other hand, black power is the projection
that being black is the only thing that has any relevance to
the Bahamas, if it is to set up a black hierarchy system totally
eliminating anything of value that is white, and if black
power is going to be the same as white power (that system
of power over blacks without any participation of the
blacks), then I am violently opposed to black power.

To dismiss these issues would be unrealistic, especially at
this present transitional stage in Bahamian development. As
long as the Bahamian refuses to acknowledge the priority of
identification, as long as he rejects the concept of self that
affirms him an integral part of society equal to every other
Bahamian, as long as he persists in superimposing foreign
values on those of his own system, both he as an individual
and society will suffer.

Probably not the least inhibitive factor stifling our development toward a more united Bahamas is our still-pervasive
mistrust of each other. Every group, whether defined along

political, racial, social, economical, or philosphical lines, feels both threatened in its position and compelled to defend its motives and above all, is convinced of its sole claim to the validity of its purpose.

In any system there will always be the "haves" and the "have-nots," whether it is a white power structure or a black power structure. To my mind, black neo-colonialism is as real a threat as the white exploiting organization.

In my opinion, the Bahamas have a culture that is just as valid as any other, and one that has evolved from the colorful mixtures of Europe and Africa. The hope for the future Bahamas lies in the rejection of racial nomenclature and an emphasis on a united Bahamas. I do not mean the rejection out of hand of any culture, any value at all, that is outside our own experience. If I favor nationalism, I don't have in mind that kind of jealously chauvinistic attitude that is blind to the existence, not to mention the merits, of anything beyond our borders. This brand of "partriotism" betrays the very kind of insecurity we need to overcome as a nation.

To liberate ourselves from the pervasive hold of foreign cultures does not mean that we have to become anti-American, anti-British, or indeed anti-anything. In the interest of our economic survival, if nothing else, this kind of hostility will be self-defeating and certainly would do nothing to further our self-awareness.

Bahamians are still terribly complexed—the many psycho-social problems that are around us attest to this fact. Black power, which is valid in its own right, appears to be another emotional "cop-out" for many of our people, especially youths, and if the leaders of our Bahamian community do not project a sense of objectivity and black pride, based on opportunity for *all* Bahamians, black and white, black power would become the most negative and destructive forces ever unleashed on Bahamian society.

TIMOTHY O. McCARTNEY *was born in the Bahamas and is now clinical psychologist at the Sandilands Rehabilitation Center, Nassau, Bahamas. He studied in the United States, Switzerland, Jamaica, England, and France, where he obtained his doctorate in clinical psychology, with* mention très honorable *from the University of Strasbourg. He returned to his native Bahamas in 1967 and immediately became involved in the field of mental health. He has written many scientific papers and is an elected member of the French Psychological Society (Société de Psychologie de l'Est) and a foreign affiliate of the British Psychological Society.*

Dr. McCartney is president of the Bahamas Mental Health Association and the editor of the Bahamas Mental Health Association's magazine. He also lectures at the Extra-Mural Department of the University of the West Indies.

John Stewart

WHERE GOES THE INDIGENOUS BLACK CHURCH?

I

From the appearance of the first Europeans to the present, organized religion has played an important role in the political and economic colonization of all the Caribbean. As the colonial masters for individual territories changed, so too did the official religion. In Trinidad under Spanish rule the mission preceded the plantation as a colonial institution. With the constant support of military troops Catholic priests extorted all the work they could out of native Amerindians, who, once ensnared within the regional domains of the mission, constituted in fact a captive labor group. The instruction in Catholic dogma received by the Indians was poor compensation for the absolute surrender of being—physical and spiritual—demanded of them by the entrepreneurial clergy.

Just as the Spanish introduced Catholicism, the British, under whom the plantation as a socioeconomic system achieved its highest development, introduced Anglicanism. The Amerindians were displaced by African slaves as the institutional shift from mission to plantation occurred, and although plantations in Trinidad did not affect any religious goals, the effectiveness with which Christian dogma and ritual specifications were coercively used in the maintenance and expansion of plantation slavery has long been well known. Today, a good deal of what constitutes middle-class creole culture originates directly from the religious systems introduced by Spain and England.

Less well known is the scope of the resistance against colonization by religion put up by the slaves and freedmen laborers themselves. In many cases their resistance was grounded in an unambiguous and straightforward interpretation of Christian teaching. Individual prophets such as Nat Turner and Gabriel Prosser in the United States and Sam Sharpe in Jamaica were inspired by their religious experiences while under servitude to lead violent rebellions against the slave masters. In Trinidad, however, resistance took one or the other of two non-violent forms: (a) persistence—often surreptitious—in the performance of African rites, and (b) development of an alternate Christian church.

Particularly important in the development of an alternate Christian church in Trinidad were a group of refugees from the U.S.A. who settled in the island during the early nineteenth century. They established a Baptist community and maintain to this day an independent church which remains committed to the fundamentalist traditions associated with that sect. The Independent Baptist Church received little official attention during the colonial period and survived largely upon the will and strength of its individual pastors. In recent times this Baptist church has been fully recognized by Trinidad's independent government and awarded some governmental support. This recognition may be too little too late, however, unless the Trinidad government can really bring itself to dispel the bonds of a dominant creole mentality and divert much more of the support currently fed to the Catholic and other Euro-American denominations to an indigenous institution. The individual pastor continues as the most important element in the survival of an organized Baptist church, but distaste for the fundamental ethics he preaches in an increasingly indulgent society makes his position an ever more tenuous one.

Ever since the eighteenth-century heyday of the West Indian sugar planter, a tradition of conspicuous consumerism in material things had been established in the Caribbean. And this tradition is still very strong among the class-conscious elites, the class-conscious and ambitious middle-classes in Trinidad. To adopt the latest in style and habit, to eat what is currently distinguished, to belong to the exclusive—these identify some common ideals among creole middle-class Trinidadians. And although there is little to be said against such ideals per se, it is to the society's disadvantage that most often the concern with consuming the best is seldom backed up by either an effort in basic production or respect for local production. For most creole Trinidadians, all that is best still comes from abroad, particularly from Western Europe and North America, and it may not be unreasonable to estimate that over four fifths of the Trinidadian's food, other material, and social fare is at present imported from these regions.

Even among the recent revolutionaries who sparked the 1970 rebellion, the habit of importation was so strong that while they attacked the Catholic Church as itself an institutional imposition most oppressive to black Trinidadians, much of the fervor of this attack was forged out of another import—black power rhetoric and philosophy as elaborated by well-known militants in the U.S.A. Black power in the U.S.A. has its roots and cradle in the black American church. But most of the Trinidadian rebels probably knew nothing of a native black church, and if they did, they probably held in ridicule—as is common among Trinidadian middle-classers—what little they knew.

In Trinidad the black church is essentially a lower-class Baptist church and as such suffers all the shortcomings commonly faced by lower-class institutions. It remains rural and poor, is stigmatized as ignorantly backward. Its leaders are unlettered and therefore regarded as religious quacks. The black lower-class church has neither prestige nor influence to offer the social climber and as a rule draws ridicule where others draw respect. The lower-class church in Trinidad is basically a fundamentalist church which has incorporated various elements from West African religions in its rituals (i.e., baptism by total immersion, spirit possession, call-and-response style in prayer, and devotional singing and dancing). Yet even among Baptists the traditional will to indulge in class discrimination is strong enough so that "London" Baptists may regard themselves as superior to "Independent" Baptists, who are in turn superior to "Spiritual" Baptists, who are a cut above "Shango" Baptists. "Shango" Baptists use sacred drums as accompanying instruments in their rituals, the "London" Baptists use organs. "Shango" Baptists make offerings of cake and meat to the sea, "London" Baptists make no food offering to any deity. The stratificational mode which differentiates one Baptist group from another is based upon these details and others which illustrate the incongruity between West African Shango and a London-style mentality.

In one respect, however, Baptist groups are all uniform—they are all strong on the messianic mode in doctrine and style. Consequently a pastor's rhetoric, his bearing, his voice, the quality of his home and family life, all the details which go to make up his personal charisma rank high among individual church classificatory features. Traditionally, the pastor must be a person of exemplary character, in whom spiritual knowledge and folk wisdom combine to a fine degree. The traditional Baptist community dwellers at one time relied almost totally upon him for inspiration to face the day, for guidance in the aspirations and fulfillment of their total lives. But against the new dispensation advocated by secular revolutionists, the influence of the church declines, and with it the effectiveness of the pastor in his role as community leader. In a recent visit to one village, it was obvious to the author that the decline in religion consequent upon the newly general involvement in the politics of independence has so far resulted in no new real benefits. Moreover, the church's declining influence seems likely to continue. With characteristic folk tenacity the village pastor takes what is given, suffers what he must, and continues absorbed in the problem of ultimate survival for himself and his people.

II

He is tall, and the black seams of his face tolerate a light gray stubble as he goes out in the early morning to move the cattle. He wears knee-length soft rubber boots, the rough shirt and pants of a peasant gardener, and a favorite felt hat colored to nondescript gray with the sweat of many years, its brim rolled back to leave his forehead open. He has a strong face. He has worked as a peasant gardener all his life, and the cumulative effect of this outdoor labor shows in the lean muscularity of his torso and arms. He is sixty-three and cannot remember a morning—barring the extraordinary days of private emergencies or bad weather—when he did not go out to move the cattle. As a young man he inherited a small herd from his father and has been able to slowly add to this. His oldest son will inherit this herd when he dies, but he is sure the boy will quickly sell the cattle. The boy is a mechanic and has a deep interest in motorcars. Cattle he finds merely tiresome. Changing times. For in this village, at one time, a father who had cattle to pass on to his son was considered most provident, most successful. Unlike many rural fathers whose sons have moved to the town and adopted new ways, Pastor Lea feels no loss, because, most important, his son carries forward the family tradition of being a servant in the Baptist ministry and is himself in charge of a budding branch church in the town.

Pastor Lea sings a favorite hymn to himself as he walks from his house to where the cattle are each night tethered. The sloping path is crowded with overgrowth of the wild shrubs and grasses, and he flicks casually with the cutlass he carries, edging the path in spots as he goes. The cattle are on the banks of a shallow ravine. He calls their names as he unties them—nine in all—saving the old bull for last. As they are freed the cattle cross the ravine to find the path which takes them up the adjacent slope. He cuts himself a switch and follows, keeping them on the move by slashing at their flanks whenever they linger to crop a tuft of grass or shrub. It is not a steep climb, but the morning is already balmy, and the back of his shirt is soon soaked with sweat.

He sings in fuller voice now. It is himself and the animals alone in the dew-damp morning, with the hot odors of the day not yet strong, his blood and muscles awakened refreshed from the past night's sleep. Just he and the animals in the quickening day, and he lets his voice come lustily, singing in praise of the good God who made the morning and his strength and gave him courage not only to walk upright in the village, but to live his years by the letter of the Holy Bible so that he may be teacher and example, leader in spirit and the flesh to his fellow villagers. It is a charge he inherited from his father. It is a charge that has been in his family ever since the second decade of the nineteenth century, when along with several others whose men had fought with the British in the War of 1812 they were relocated in the south-eastern forests of Trinidad. Some of the families had been slaves in the Carolinas, others in Georgia. He believes his family came from Virginia, where, he understands, the name is most common.

As freedmen in Trinidad, each of the refugee families was granted a small parcel of land, and, as a group, they were charged with developing an economically self-sufficient community. Along with the grant of land, refugees were given temporary communal shelter, a meager supply of food, and a few tools. Leadership, the responsibility for group control, was given to an ex-military sergeant and his former corporal. Conditions were harsh, but the refugees had brought a faith with them—the fundamental Baptist faith they had learned to practice in the southern U.S.A. And when military drill commands and other martial skills proved ineffectual in maintaining spirits in their struggle against the rain forest, the preacher, spokesman that he was for the supreme deity among them, emerged as the strong leader. He could convince them of an inviolable relationship between daily hardships and supreme success in an ultimate kingdom. Without this preacher, the refugee community might have dissolved in short time and disappeared like similar ones which had been settled in the northern part of the island.

Pastor Lea is fifth in the line of village pastors whose descent traces directly to this old preacher. He carries an image of the old man as strong-willed and determined, successful in a personal battle not to pretend immunity against temptations of the flesh but to resist them, not to deny human frailty but to strengthen the being. Pastor Lea remembers these qualities in his own father, who himself devoted an entire life to work, worship, and service to others through the church. And he believes, whenever his son looks on him, that the heritage can be no less evident.

Living conditions in the village are still harsh, a high level of economic self-sufficiency still something of the future. In the early days, villagers could, and did, feed themselves well. Yams, cassava, and bananas were easily cultivated; opossum, rabbit, and agouti were plentiful. They could provide themselves with rough but adequate and inexpensive housing from the cedars, mahoganies, and moras which grew tall in the forest. Through a rudimentary bartering system they managed to trade craftsmanship and healing skills among themselves, and practically all heavy labor was handled on a communal basis. It was no easy life, but compared to other blacks on the island the refugees were well off for not being totally dependent on the white massa and his sugar plantation. They cultivated an ethic based upon the ideal of total self-sufficiency and the notion that every individual was responsible for every other in the community. Pastor Lea remembers well, for instance, the practice known as "gayap"—the organization of communal work groups to carry out projects demanding much heavy labor.

If a man had a house to build, a field to clear, plant, or harvest, he did so by gayap. Early on the morning of the day when the project was to be carried out, he sounded a shell horn which summoned workers to the site. When all were gathered, the pastor offered a blessing before work was begun. Whatever the project might be, nothing proceeded until the pastor had offered a blessing. Male and female worked together on field projects, men alone on building projects, accompanied by drum and work songs. The host had vegetables, meat, and drink for a feast, but that did not prevent individuals from donating various foods themselves. While the work was in progress, the cooks fired their pots and prepared the drink. When the work was finished, all sat down to feast on the food that had already been blessed by the pastor. And so it went on. The next time this host would be a worker on somebody else's project.

But the people do not hold gayaps anymore. On the occasion of a death, neighbors and friends do give their assistance in preparation for the wake and other preburial activities, but in most other instances a villager can have nothing done which requires more than his individual labor unless he can afford to pay out cash. Nowadays houses are built by wage-earning carpenters, fields are cleared and plowed by rental tractors. The houses themselves are no longer built from hand-roughed timber—the forest now belongs not to everybody but to somebody villagers don't even know—but from concrete and glass, wrought iron, Canadian pine—all articles on the vast and increasing list of items which Trinidadians import to satisfy their material needs.

In no other instance was the will to self-determination among the refugees greater than in that involving the matter of spiritual independence. When they decided to organize a church, they asked organizational recognition and assistance from Baptist missions in England and the U.S.A. They got what they asked for and more, for soon the white missionary preachers were in among them, revising the ritual mode, "cleaning out" Africanisms from the established forms of worship, and generally passing themselves off as self-sacrificing pioneers of a noble religious tradition among crude converts. The refugees withstood much of this patronizing, but were tenacious in holding on to the church's purse string. And when one white civilizing missionary debarred all overt show of religious ecstasy during regular worship—a culture trait common in all black religions—many church members drew the line. They said either he was sent back to wherever he came from, or they would leave the church. Others who equated white style with godliness supported the missionary, and he was retained. The rebellious members withdrew and started their own church, inviting no outsiders to assist them. Today Pastor Lea proudly heads this independent church, in a tradition that devolved upon the family since one of his ancestors was a leader in the revolt that split the original body.

It is currently, however, increasingly difficult to maintain a high level of commitment to any form of worship among villagers. There is a growing tendency to express independence, not in the stubborn protection of a spiritual order, not in the stubborn crusade for any sort of order, really, but in an individual scramble for money and influence and a consequent withdrawal from any commitment to the welfare of the community at large. Pastor Lea cannot say why, but clearly times have changed, and nowadays it is every man for himself. The whole community spirit in getting things done is dying out. Take the case of the Shango for instance. He never approved their practice of offering blood sacrifices. He never believed their claim that all the gods they talked about came down to possess them, and he never weakened in his judgment that Shangoists give too much power to the devil. Yet, an old Shango community grew up right alongside his village, and from childhood he couldn't help but see and hear their drums, their possession trances, their feasting, and not all of it was sinful. In his own congregation, his own family, there were individuals who could claim Shango cured one illness or the other. And although he would be a spiritual antagonist to the Shango, he respected them for the good they could do.

Even more than the Baptists, the Shangoists were a closely knit people, often living like one big extended family with several members' houses surrounding that of the Papa's. In those days Shango members did not want for anything. They took care of one another. But right now the last good Papa they had is dead, and the houses are all rotting. Once in a

while they still have a feast, but most of the people who attend are outsiders, there to laugh and drink, enjoy the dancing as spectacle, and share the food. Nowadays people are
believing deeper and deeper in "every man for himself."
Everybody wants to make his own destiny, and just as the
Shango has gone down, so too members of the Baptist family do not come to him for much anymore.

It used to be that along with officiating at gayaps, the village pastor also consecrated marriages, conducted burials,
led visitations to the sick, baptized new converts, and generally carried out all the functions necessary as the church
ministered the needs of the people. His general role in the
community extended far beyond mere ceremonial performance. Families took their marital problems to him, dreams
were brought for interpretation, he was advocate and judge
where public morals were threatened or abrogated, he was
the spokesman for the village before government agencies.
His church was the dominant institution through which villagers practiced local-level politics and monitored the everyday
ethics which governed individual relationships. And in the
main, he was the church. The organization and the man were
indivisible. The church stood for the highest morals in family
life, did not condone sexual promiscuity or common law marriages, parental negligence, or disobedience among the young.
It did not condone secular dancing, sports, or any other activity which could be identified as indulgence of the flesh. And
the pastor had to be a stern example since his role required
the upbraiding, disciplining, exorcising—even among members of his own family—of those who broke the rules.

Pastor Lea firmly maintains a correct image and receives
good support from the elders, deacons, and mothers of the
church. To them the church has always been one religious
family. They show the same bearing as Pastor Lea, and like
him they ache for that time when the family was large and
vigorously healthy. But it is difficult to keep others, particularly the young, focused on their example. Disappearing is the
time when the prospects of being back-benched was enough
to counteract temptations to drunkenness, carousing, general

idleness, and obscene dispute. Instead, backyard stills flourish, city people frequent the village seeking to buy ganja, and more young men choose idleness over the labor which gardens and orchards demand.

The village is now fully caught up in a modern cash economy, and this has led to a reduction in the social role of the church which provides no jobs and in no way brings cash revenues into the village. There are no major capital investments in the village, no industry. The only nearby source of wages is the rural sugar estate which grows but does not process the sugar cane and therefore hires field workers on a seasonal basis only. Some villagers earn a wage maintaining government roads in the area, but all other wage earners commute to job sites on daily, weekly, and monthly schedules or, in some instances, emigrate altogether for several years at a time. Job sites range in distance from the nearest town eight miles away to Florida, New York, Toronto, London—anywhere where black citizens of a recently independent Caribbean country may find employment. The village is losing its young men rapidly, and the young women follow. The older men who are commuting wage earners spend little more than weekends in the village and with their commitment to wage-paying agencies, no longer feel intensely the jurisdiction of the church. Sundays they prefer to relax at games or convivial drinking rather than give themselves to abstinence and religious worship.

All this leaves Pastor Lea with a congregation composed almost wholly of old men, old and middle-aged women, and children. He does not have jurisdiction over the village to the same degree his father used to have. He no longer receives many calls to settle disputes within families or among neighbors. He is still fairly well respected and as firm as ever in his perception of the role of his ministry. His duty is to keep the spirit of a respectable God alive in the village through maintaining the structure of the church, modifying none of its ritual, and being himself a controlled, aloof, and dignified messenger of the Lord who yet finds spiritual grace in visceral and participatory worship.

As yet there is no discothèque in the village, no cinema, no gambling places. Sunday church still is the major social event of the week. Yet the latest in styles from New York, details of a "gracious" suburban life style elsewhere in Trinidad filter in, and villagers are less concerned with dreams or other indications of divine will these days than they are with the problems of political corruption and economic exploitation. Along with thousands of other Trinidadians who pay attention to the daily news, they can identify certain villains of corruption and exploitation as directly responsible for the social and economic backwardness under which they live, and the dominant concern is how to overcome the impotence which retards their bringing these villains to ruin. Government ministers are corrupt, but how can poor villagers get them to carry out their responsibilities honestly or get them out of office? By prayer? That's a joke. Political power submits to superior political power and if you are poor you have none. Sugar estates, oilfield companies, and other corporate industrial and commercial bodies are exploitative. How can poor villagers get out from under—by prayer? That's a joke. The "big boys" have money, and money can get anything done. What can poor villagers do? Well, if you can't change the game, join it. Personal corruption is not so hard to achieve once a man accepts the premise that all others are out to profit off his individual industry. Industriousness then loses its virtue, and the individual withholding or suppressing of industry becomes a first step toward protecting the self against exploitation.

On any given day, groups of young men who are seasonally unemployed, or in between jobs, or waiting for their first job may be seen idling beneath favorite trees in the village. Pastor Lea has an attitude toward them that can be paraphased as follows:

"They are rebellious because it is fashionable to be so, they are giving their lives to emptiness and waste out of laziness. Fundamentally, they are captives of an evil state of being which is currently rampant in the land. Too many Trinidadians each day lose touch with God, lose touch with their superior selves and sight of the ultimate kingdom. They are coming to be more and more just like the same white people who used to be slave masters. There is a madness in the air, telling people that they alone are to control destiny, that fate is to be in their hands. This madness was started by power-hungry white men and now everybody is picking it up. Flawed from the depths of their being with a jealousness of power, these people cannot see the deception into which they throw themselves. Those in government are arbitrarily passing laws to take what little people have, the police are quick to take people's lives with their guns, those who pay starvation wages for their jobs are telling workers to take it or leave it—and nobody is responsible to anybody. What can we expect young people to do? How can we expect them to feel? They are bound to be rebellious.

"Everybody is seeking to live like the white man who sends money to do his work for him, but there is a great deception here because money cannot produce trust, and a village or a country without trust among its people dies shamefully— with nothing to recommend its memory and a total loss of its place in an ultimate kingdom. It is sad that so many fall for the deception. Because human beings trust one another only when all are committed to a common higher ideal, and there are no high ideals anymore for too many people. Take what you can and cut your neighbor's throat to get it if you have to—that is today's standard of behavior. In the meantime, the white man, who is the biggest cut-throat of all, can have a laugh, being able to pay others to do his dirty work for him. The country, the culture is being destroyed but he doesn't mind, because he doesn't believe he will be destroyed with it. The Bible teaches 'whosoever saveth himself shall lose it.' But that is a difficult lesson to convey in these times."

Pastor Lea still tries encouraging the young to attend church where maybe they would catch a spiritual fire that would raise their vision from the everyday to the eternal, but he does not have much success. One or two sometimes attend out of respect for himself or older members of their families, but never with their hearts fully in it. His biggest problem right now is how to rekindle a concern for God among the young people of the village. He worries about this problem and may never come to a way to solve it, because he does not believe in a secular solution. He has heard about churches in the States where they bring in dance-band music to encourage the young, but he is not moved by such approaches. They only cheapen the church and cheapen the experience of God, he believes. He knows a solution will come through divine revelation one day, and as long as he keeps faith, he may see the change before his death.

III

On the crest of his dewy hill Pastor Lea is finished tethering the cattle. He has staked them with sufficient distance in between so none will encroach on the others' circumference. The stakes are driven deeply so the cattle may not get away to destroy a neighbor's garden. Across a farther gully a stand of poui trees are in full blossom, and in between their branches the backdrop sugar cane is quiet and tenderly green. As the pastor retraces his steps he can see smoke going up from his kitchen and several others along the arc of the village road. His cutlass held on one shoulder he starts a new hymn, singing lustily, but now primarily for the others who stir the smoke before him. His voice carries easily on the morning air. After breakfast he will return to the garden for a few hours of weeding, after that a rest before lunch. A short nap in the early afternoon and then he will change into his formal black suit for a visit with Sister Clara who is resting ill at her daughter's house. He will later meet the Mother and Deacons of the church about arrangements for food, candles, and other necessaries for this season's baptism, then offer instructions to the four candidates. It will be time then to return home, change, and bring in the cattle, have a light supper, and return to the church for evening service. Pastor Lea feels generally good about the day, albeit with a longing for the time when baptismal candidates could be counted by the tens, and evening service did not echo back the emptiness of so many vacant seats along the benches in the small church.

JOHN STEWART *was born in Trinidad. He did his undergradu-ate work at Los Angeles State College and his graduate work at Stanford University. In 1973 he received his Ph.D. from the University of California at Los Angeles. He has taught at Fresno State College, the University of California at Los Angeles, and the University of Illinois, Champaign Urbana. He is now a visiting lecturer in the English Department, California State University at Fresno. His publications in-clude the novel* Last Cool Days *and* Follow the Curving Road, *a short-story collection. For his novel he received in 1971 the Winifred Holtby Memorial Prize awarded by the Royal Society of Literature, London.*

Locksley Edmondson

THE INTERNATIONALIZATION OF BLACK POWER: HISTORICAL AND CONTEMPORARY PERSPECTIVES[1]

In a civil rights march through Mississippi in June 1966, Stokely Carmichael, then chairman of SNCC (Student Non-violent Coordinating Committee),[2] raised the cry: "We want Black Power." This was not the first appearance of the "black power" phrase in black America. Adam Clayton Powell, Jr., then a Harlem congressman, had employed this terminology twice in speeches in May 1965 and May 1966. In 1963 an "organization for black power" had been formed by Jesse Gray in New York. And, as shall be discussed in more detail, Richard Wright and Paul Robeson in the 1950s had explicitly used the phrase, though with reference to non-American situations.

If, however, Carmichael cannot be credited with coining the phrase, he is considered as the effective initiator of Black Power. This is the fact acknowledged by Martin Luther King, Jr., in his discussion of the events of 16 June 1966: "The phrase had been used long before by Richard Wright and others, but never until that night had it been used as a slogan in the civil rights movement."[3]

King at the time "confidently" asserted that "the call for 'Black Power' will rapidly diminish."[4] But, on the contrary, the cry for "Black Power" has rapidly escalated. While it is difficult to ascertain the extent and intensity of support for the slogan, it is clear that Black Power is now an entrenched phenomenon in the black American revolution.

I

This article does not propose to deal with the domestic American implications of Black Power[5]—used here in capitalized form to refer to the black American formulation—except where necessary to the development of an international and comparative perspective. Instead, the writer intends to analyze Black Power against the background of it pan-Negro articulations and in terms of its internationalizing potentialities.[6] Black America, Africa, and the Caribbean constitute the main arenas of investigation and the following analysis will embody:

1. Historical and contemporary treatment of the evolution and significance of certain global black nationalist ideologies.
2. A comparative study of their origin and diffusion.
3. Transnational perspectives on the situations in black America, Africa, and the Caribbean which may condition the future prospects of pan-Negro ideological initiation and diffusion.

A brief word may here be said about the importance of the historical dimensions in the present analysis. In a recent lecture C. L. R. James (who was closely associated with his childhood friend George Padmore in the Pan-African movement of the 1930s), after defining black power "not in the ordinary sense of the phrase but in terms of the emancipation of black people," observed:

> Black power is perhaps the most remarkable unplanned movement that the twentieth century has known because of consistency, steady development, and constantly growing ascension and expansion. . . . Stage by stage it has mounted higher and expanded wider until it has reached the peak where it is today.[7]

In developing this contention James proceeded to trace the evolution of black emancipation strivings through the contributions of W. E. B. Du Bois, Marcus Garvey, George Padmore, Martin Luther King, Frantz Fanon, Malcolm X, and Stokely Carmichael.

What is significant in James's analysis is that he has pinpointed the historically important phenomenon of the linkage of ideas and interests of black men the world over and the historical interrelationships of pan-Negro and pan-African aspirations. On these factors a British historian has commented:

> The first British Empire owed much to the triangular trade between Africa, the West Indies, and North America. The last British Empire has not been uninfluenced by another triangular trade not of pocatille, slaves, and molasses, but a commerce of ideas and politics between the descendants of the slaves in the West Indies and North America and their ancestral continent.[8]

So, too, the French Empire was not uninfluenced by a trade of ideas and politics between New World Negroes and Africans:

> What Shepperson pointed out for the British Empire was equally true for the French Third and Fourth Republics. French-speaking Africans and West Indian Negroes and Malagasies shared a common intellectual life which gave rise to the founding of the Society for African Culture in Paris, the publication of *Présence Africaine*, and the death of a man like Frantz Fanon from Marti-

nique in the cause of the Algerian Liberation Movement.
The concept of "négritude" is a joint production of Sene-
galese poet Léopold Senghor and Martinique poet Aimé
Césaire.[9]

Enough has been said to illustrate the significance of his
torical perspectives in this analysis of the internationalizing
capacities of Black Power. When we turn to the contempo
rary setting, we are confronted with certain realities of black
existence beyond the United States which have a direct bear
ing on the Black Power international outlook:

1. The almost universal phenomenon of colonialism
until recent times.
2. The process of political decolonization and the
facts of legal sovereignty—the formal arrival of politica
black power—in the greater part of the African and Carib
bean world.
3. The political repression of blacks by whites in cer
tain areas in southern Africa, the world's most regressive
area with regard to racism.
4. The Third World revolution against poverty and the
strivings for political and social integration.
5. The economic position and relations of the white to
the non-white world, and the lag between the attainmen
of political and economic independence.
6. The global struggle of the black man for dignity.

II

Thus Black Power has been regarded as a potential pan
Negro ideology without examination of the bases of such a
assumption. It would therefore be appropriate to commen
on the international implications of the black America
revolution and more specifically on the evolving global in
terests of the Black Power movement.

What, it may be asked, is the utility of analyzing Black

'ower, a phenomenon basically indigenous to the United
tates, with reference to outside contexts? Can Black Power
ave any bearing on the future of African or West Indians?

These questions may be approached initially by surveying
ome of the ideas in circulation within the Black Power
10vement. Take, for example, the following statements of
rominent Black Power leaders or organizations:

We must therefore consciously strive for an ideology
which deals with racism first, and if we do that, we recognize the necessity of hooking up with the nine hundred million [*sic*] black people in the world today.
That's what we recognize. And if we recognize that,
then it means that our political situation must become
international. . . . It must be international because if
we knew anything, we would recognize that the honkies
don't just exploit us, they exploit the whole Third
World—Asia, Africa, Latin America.[10]

Therefore . . . we talk of international black power
because the apex of power, guided by the United States,
revolves around the western, barbaric countries in relationship to the exploited peoples of the Third World.
. . . the Black Power we are talking about in the United
States has to become an international concept.[11]

We must learn how close America and Russia are politically . . . We must seek out poor-people movements in
South America and Asia and make our alliances with
them.[12]

Black Power is the coming together of black people
around the world to fight, wherever they are, for their
dignity, and to fight for the masses of our people who
are oppressed around the world.[13]

[Black Power] is a slogan used as a cohesive force for
black people in the United States and hopefully for
black people in the world.[14]

Such enunciations involve a variety of international angle: the relation of the black American struggle to Third Wor strivings; American power in the international system whic in turn is symptomatic of international white power; th anatomy of superpower behavior and the related consider. tion of a non-alignment response; the psychological revolu tion of black people in their search for dignity; the pan-Negr unifying potentialities of Black Power.

But to what extent are the expressed international inte: ests of a few prominent Black Power proponents illustrativ of a general international orientation within the as yet dive sified Black Power movement? And to what degree do th specific international themes expressed by these spokesme enjoy support at large within the movement?

While it may be true that some specific internation. formulations represent individual rather than collective held beliefs, the foregoing illustrative statements appear t be in harmony with widely held opinions. Especially signi icant is the fact that the Black Power movement now do not couch its thinking in exclusively domestic America terms, a fact which is clearly evident from the tone of th manifesto of the 1967 National Conference on Black Pow (full text in Appendix).[15] What is of initial consequence less the realizability of the hope of bringing black America fully within the Third World orbit than that such global. oriented concerns are being articulated.

In focusing attention on Black Power conceptions of th outside world, a salient background consideration involve the arrival of formal political black power in Africa. N only has this development aided in boosting black America aspirations and self-conceptions, but it also has had a cat lytic impact on black American nationalism and internatio alism.[16] James Baldwin in 1961 succinctly pinned dow this consideration: "Africa has been black a long time b American Negroes did not identify themselves with Afri until Africa became identified with power."[17]

Black Power, as a domestic American phenomenon, ca not be isolated from race developments in the outer worl

Indeed, well before its effective indigenous adoption, the idea of "Black Power" had made a limited appearance in black American vocabulary (or ideology), but with reference to the global, or external, contexts of the race question.

Writing in 1962 a Nigerian student of the Black Muslim movement summed up its ideology in the following terms: "The attainment of black power over the whole world is relegated to the intervention of Almighty Allah sometime in the future."[18] Almost a decade earlier, Richard Wright recorded his impressions of the then Gold Coast in his book *Black Power*, and in so doing counseled Prime Minister Nkrumah on ways and means of making black power a reality.[19] And three years after Wright's publication, Paul Robeson, in an interview with another black American, declared:

Yes, I think a great deal of the power of black people in the world. That's why Africa means so much to me. . . . Yes, this black power moves me. Look at Jamaica. In a few years the white minority will be there on the sufferance of black men. If they're nice decent fellows, they can stay. . . . If I could get a passport, I'd like to go to Ghana or Jamaica just to sit for a few days and observe this black power.[20]

Of additional relevance to the international view of, and background to, Black Power is the already evident infectiousness of the Black Power slogan beyond black America. Kwame Nkrumah recently hailed Black Power as "a vanguard movement of black people" which "opens the way for all oppressed masses" and which "heralds the long-awaited day of liberation from the shadows of obscurity."[21] There is a fairly well-developed black power consciousness among non-white minorities in Britain,[22] and a black power awareness among some Australian Aborigines,[23] black Canadians,[24] and southern African students in the United States. On the basis of interviews conducted among the latter it was speculated: "It may be that Stokely Carmichael will be as influential to this generation of African freedom fighters as Marcus Garvey was to Nkrumah's generation."[25]

The pan-Negro potentialities of Black Power can be assessed in terms of the global themes in circulation within the movement, the international racial context within which the black American assertiveness has evolved, and the initial dissemination of Black Power ideas beyond black America.[26]

III

George Padmore, writing in 1956, thought it significant that "the two most dynamic black nationalist ideologies . . . had their origin in America: Garveyism and Pan-Africanism."[27] For reasons later suggested, Padmore's observation requires amplification. But for the moment we shall raise some considerations concerning the undoubtedly striking black American role in the international diffusion of race ideas.

In the first place, Negro America gained quite early titular legal political freedom and equality, but after a century the American political system has failed to convert this nominal freedom and equality into actuality. Given this discrepancy, the black American has had a long history of agitation against his actual status. In articulating his needs and strivings, he was strategically positioned to attempt to effect a linkage of ideas and aspirations with others of his race who were in large measure similarly situated in terms of white domination. Secondly, white racism has from the outset been ingrained in the American political culture,[28] thus heightening the confrontation of white racism and black nationalism over time.[29] Despite the recent retreats of overt white racism on many fronts, it remains a powerful influence in the United States.[30] A reinforcing factor lies in the demography of racial balance, for unlike their numerically dominant Caribbean and African counterparts black Americans, who comprise less than 11 per cent of the American population, have always been confronted with the elusiveness of meaningful power.

Thus in the African and Caribbean situations, black nationalism could be articulated in anticolonial or majoritarian–democratic *political* terms to which a rigid racial emphasis was often subordinated. By contrast, in the conditions of black American existence, black nationalism has inevitably involved a pervasive racial emphasis in its political, socioeconomic, and psychological dimensions.

A related consideration—here there are many similarities with the Caribbean Negro—is the long history of direct black American exposure to the ideals and performances of Western civilization. With an intensive and extensive contact with the very civilization which enslaved him and more often than not disregarded his worth, the black American nationalist has been well situated to mount an intensive and extensive attack on the failings of Western civilization in its treatment of black men.

Historically, the Caribbean has played a highly significant role in the initiation of global black nationalist ideas, so we are not here implying the uniqueness of the black American role in such ventures. What we have tried to do is to suggest some considerations in viewing the very prominent and consistent part played by black Americans in the dissemination of such ideas. The conclusion seems warranted that if any pan-Negro ideology was to arise in the 1960s, it was most likely to originate in the United States. However, it is because of its origin and basic entrenchment in the realities of black American existence that Black Power, though conveying some ideas of relevance to the black world at large, is limited in its potential as an internationalizing force.

IV

This contention will first be developed through a comparative exploration of the origins of the major pan-Negro ideologies of the nineteenth and twentieth centuries. It is on this score that Padmore's comment on the "American" origin of Garveyism and Pan-Africanism requires elaboration.

Neither of these two ideologies, strictly speaking, was American in origin. It would be more correct to refer to their New World Negro origin, and even this characterization should not lead one to ignore the contributions emanating from the African continent.

Garveyism was as much West Indian as American in origin and style. While it is true that Garveyism in dynamic form arose to prominence in the United States, the following facts should be borne in mind:

1. Marcus Garvey's UNIA (Universal Negro Improvement Association) was initially established in Jamaica; its headquarters later was transferred to the United States.[31]

2. Garvey left Jamaica for the United States at the age of twenty-nine, after his race emancipation program was conceived and after his lengthy process of socialization into the West Indies race relations system. The latter influence at times led Garvey to carry over to the American race context some West Indian conceptions of color or shade stratification which were less relevant (though not as irrelevant as some writers suggest) to the American situation.[32]

3. In its American origin, Garveyism was activated and initially dominated by expatriate West Indians.

Thus it is not surprising that in death Garvey has been reclaimed by Jamaica as a national hero.[33] And viewing Garveyism as a philosophy of race, rather than the specific school founded by Marcus Garvey, it may be argued that the first prominent "Garveyite" was Edward Wilmot Blyden (1832–1912), another West Indian-born pan-Negro thinker, who unlike Garvey preached his vision from an African base having emigrated to Liberia at the age of eighteen.[34] Garveyism, therefore, was not exclusively a black American invention.

The same can be said of Pan-Africanism, a term used in this analysis to refer specifically to the organizational movement for continental African liberation launched in the early twentieth century and later evolving into a drive for African continental political unity. This is the narrow specific definition of "Pan-Africanism." By contrast, the broader term "pan-Africanism" (with a lower case "p") can be defined in Colin Legum's terms as "essentially a movement of ideas and emotions; at times it achieves a synthesis; at times it remains at the level of thesis and antithesis."[35] To illustrate this broader dimension of pan-Africanism, Vernon McKay refers to its "complex and varied" cultural, economic, and political aspects and adds that "It is related to the concepts of the 'brotherhood of Negro blood,' the 'African personality,' and *négritude* and at times has fostered . . . the racist concepts of 'Black Zionism,' 'black power,' and 'blackism.' "[36] These distinctions between "Pan-Africanism" and "pan-Africanism" have been employed in part to stress the point that the former is but one (and the most important political) manifestation of the latter and is thus interrelated in motivation to other pan-African ideas, including Garveyism. In addition, such distinctions aid in precisely analyzing a variety of interrelated concepts.[37]

The effective initiator of Pan-Africanism was a black American (W. E. B. Du Bois), but the initial organizational impetus came from H. Sylvester-Williams (1868–1911), a Trinidadian barrister. It was the Pan-African Conference of 1900, convened by Williams in London, which, in Du Bois' words, "put the word 'Pan-African' in the dictionaries for the first time. . . ."[38] And it was here that Du Bois "transformed Williams' limited conception of Pan-Africanism into a movement for self-government or independence for African people."[39] This later found more concrete and effective organizational expression in the first four Pan-African Congresses convened by Du Bois between 1919 and 1927 in which the primary actors were black Americans and West Indians. It was at the Fifth Pan-African Congress of 1945 that the movement for the first time came to be predominantly African-led, but even though by this time black American participation had lagged, West Indian involvement was still significant. Indeed, during the 1930s and early '40s, it was West Indians in Britain led by Padmore who were largely responsible for keeping alive the Pan-African idea, and through their contacts with emerging African nationalists—notably Kenyatta and Nkrumah—they aided immeasurably in facilitating the transition to African leadership. It was fitting that the Trinidadian-born George Padmore (by then Nkrumah's adviser on African affairs) was responsible for the organization of the two Pan-African Conferences which were held in Accra in 1958 and that on his death in the following year he was acknowledged as the "father of African emancipation"[40]—a designation also recently assigned to him by a biographer.[41] Thus, in origin as well as early promotion, the West Indian contribution to Pan-Africanism is at least as prominent as that of black Americans.

Dealing with cultural pan-Africanism, the major concepts of "African personality" and "négritude" can be treated simultaneously. As in the cases of Garveyism and Pan-Africanism, these concepts originated from a diverse international base. Blyden appears to have been the first to use the phrase "African personality" in a lecture delivered in Sierra Leone in 1893.[42] Shortly after, John Edward Bruce (1856–1924), a black American journalist who was in regular contact with Blyden and later became an active Garveyite,[43] explicitly used the phrase and also began to express the sentiment of négritude.[44]

The "African personality" idea in the English-speaking black world was destined to become primarily an African-promoted and African-applied concept, as witness the writings of Casely Hayford (1886–1930) of the Gold Coast,[45] and its subsequent active promotion by Nkrumah. However, neither Casely Hayford nor Nkrumah restricted their vision to black Africa. Nkrumah's pan-Negro allusions in this particular respect are perhaps less well known, but he did at least on one occasion raise this consideration. In a letter of 7 June 1962 to all the West Indian heads of government, pleading with them to work at maintaining the disintegrating West Indies Federation, he wrote:

> My excuse for making this appeal is the sincere conviction I hold that success in the establishment of a powerful West Indian nation would substantially assist the efforts we are making to redeem Africa's reputation in world affairs *and to re-establish the personality of the African and people of African descent everywhere*.[46]

In the meantime, the French-speaking concept of "négritude" was to come to prominence in pan-Negro aspirations. The term first appeared in 1939, coined by Aimé Césaire of Martinique in his poem *Cahier d'un Retour au Pays Natal*, thus paving the way for its subsequent popularization, particularly by Senghor. Négritude's contemporary exposition is a joint African-Caribbean venture.

But prior to négritude's explicit formulation, related ideas and influences had been in a process of pan-Negro diffusion. Mention has already been made of Blyden (the West Indian-African) and Bruce (the black American). A more influential development in the parentage of négritude was the Haitian cultural response to the American occupation of 1915. Also significant were the writings of the Afro-Cuban school which rose to prominence from 1920 to 1940. Marcus Garvey's role in these developments should not be overlooked: "He did not know the word 'négritude' but he knew the thing. With enthusiasm he would have welcomed the nomenclature, with justice claimed paternity."[47]

A closer study of black America of the early twentieth century will complete the link in the triangular trade of cultural pan-African ideas. In many of Du Bois's early writings this concern is prominent. Of more importance in the field of black cultural reconstruction are the contributions of Alain Locke (1886–1954), who is acknowledged as the mentor of the Harlem (or Negro) Renaissance. Black American writers (including the Jamaican-born Claude McKay) of the immediate post-World War I period had begun to give négritude literary expression during the heyday of the Harlem Renaissance. There is now no need to speculate that "it is likely that Césaire was aware of their work,"[48] in view of the following assertion by one of the leading members of that school:

> In France, as well as Germany, before the close of the Negro Renaissance, Harlem's poets were already being translated. Léopold Sédar Senghor of Senegal and Aimé Césaire of Martinique, the great poets of négritude, while still students at the Sorbonne, had read the Harlem poets and felt a bond between themselves and us. . . .
>
> The Harlem poets and novelists of the twenties became an influence in faraway Africa and the West Indies —an influence till today in the literature of black men and women there. To us, "négritude" was an unknown word, but certainly pride of heritage and consciousness of race was ingrained in us.[49]

V

In tracing the roots and initial promotion of certain dominant pan-Negro and pan-African concepts, we have documented their transnational origins. Almost simultaneously, various ideas associated with these concepts sprang from different quarters of the black world. Their initial motivation was to serve as black internationalizing forces. Garveyism, Pan-Africanism, négritude, and the African personality originated as forces of African racial rather than African continental relevance. A variety of ideas and formulations within each school evolved into a symbiotic relationship in Negro race aspirations.

Black Power, by contrast, is more explicitly American in origin and immediate relevance. It is true that some of West Indian origin have been prominent in the promotion of Black Power,[50] but such a contribution can best be styled "indirect" from the global racial standpoint. Although their

West Indian background has had an influence on their perceptions of race relations, their race thought and action essentially have been molded by their American experience. Even if Harold Cruse is correct in his contention that their West Indian background more often than not results in their distortions of the realities of the American race problem,[51] the fact remains that they have set out to address themselves primarily to the question of the black present and future in the United States. In any case, West Indian born activists represent but a handful of the recent crop of black American nationalists, the vast majority of whom have no direct links with the Caribbean. The same did not apply in the case of Garveyism, the most dominant prior manifestation of black American nationalism.

While dealing with the question of comparative pan-Negro ideological origins, mention can be made of the rise of other versions of black power outside the United States in recent years. For a brief time between 1961 and 1962 a new political party appeared in Jamaica under the banner of "blackmanism."[52] In 1959 Chief Remi Fani-Kayode declared in the Nigerian Parliament that "blackism is the answer to our problems,"[53] a view on which he has since elaborated:

> Blackism is a call to the states of Africa to unite. A positive, aggressive, and direct force. Naked and unashamed blackism, a force to weld together the states of Africa into one unified entity. Not a negative force activated against anyone, but a positive force for progress, strength, and power . . . I may as well copy the communist slogan: "Black men of the world unite, you have nothing to lose but your shame, humiliation, suffering, and the contempt of the white man." . . .[54]

Common to the formulations of Black Power, blackism, and blackmanism is that each has independently arisen as an indigenous response to situations in the United States, Africa, and the Caribbean. They have not effected a triangular linkage as did earlier forms of black political and

cultural nationalism. Indeed, no active effort has been made
to internationalize blackism and blackmanism, nor for that
matter is there any evidence of their effective slogan value in
the contexts wherein they originated. Only Black Power has
so far succeeded in emerging as a powerful rallying cry
within its domestic sphere and only Black Power has been
striving to become a major internationalizing influence within
the black world. But, as we have been arguing, Black Power
remains essentially rooted in the realities of black American
existence. Black Power was initially articulated in terms of
black American needs, and only after it began to gain root
there did talk of its internationalization emerge.

However, the questions of ideological origin and initial
motivations are not sufficient tests in assessing the potentialities for transnational ideological diffusion. The fact is that
there is, even today, an objective situational similarity in the
black world in its relation to the white. This is the situation
which James Baldwin trenchantly pin-pointed in his reflections at the 1956 International Congress of Negro Writers
and Artists held in Paris:

> And yet it became clear as the debate wore on, that there
> was something which all black men held in common,
> something which cut across opposition points of view,
> and placed in the same context their widely dissimilar
> experience. What they held in common was their pre-
> carious, their unutterably painful relation to the white
> world . . . the necessity to remake the world in their
> own image, to impose this image on the world, and no
> longer be controlled by the vision of the world, and of
> themselves, held by other people. What, in sum, black
> men held in common was their ache to come into the
> world as men. And this ache united people who might
> otherwise have been divided as to what a man should
> be.[55]

This underlying situational unity is manifested in the fact
that in the past, as in the present, the common situation and

needs of black people throughout the world have been characterized by their strivings for psychological reformation; for
political independence (which is not necessarily the same
thing as the acquisition of legal sovereignty), or—in the case
of black minorities—political power and equality; for economic advancement and self-sufficiency and social reconstruction.

It is therefore not surprising to find some older or revised
editions of pan-African and pan-Negro themes reappearing
in Black Power international philosophizing[56]: the Pan-
African notions of African liberation[57] and continental
unity,[58] the pan-Negro premise of global racial solidarity,[59]
reflections on neo-colonialism,[60] the Garveyite "Back-to-
Africa" theme (here articulated in terms of political support
and psycho-cultural linkage rather than repatriation),[61] the
conceptions of the African (as of the African-American) personality and négritude.[62]

But it is one thing to say that black men the world over
exhibit a situational unity in that they are all urgently trying
to acquire meaningful political and economic power and are
attempting to reorganize their position vis-à-vis the white
world and redefine their self-perceptions. It is quite another
thing to assume that black men will (or can) be united in
formulating specific goals, in drawing up priorities, and in
agreeing on tactics. The present situation in black America
is evidence enough of these divergences. There the creative
aspects of Black Power as a force for black unity co-exist
with its uncreative potential for black disunity. Looking
beyond black America, it would be natural to expect that
such divisions in black opinion will be accentuated. In assessing Black Power's internationalizing capacities, it is therefore necessary to examine more closely the African and Caribbean worlds of the 1960s. In this connection, the significant
contemporary development bearing on the further prospects
of pan-Negro ideological diffusion is the decolonization of
most of the African and Caribbean countries.

We earlier noted the impact of the African independence
movement on black American aspirations, on their growing

interest in Africa's future, and on the accompanying impetus to forge at least a measure of psychological linkage with Africa. In this sense the emergence of numerous political sovereignties in Africa has broadened and strengthened black American pan-Negro feelings.

The nature of the present Caribbean link with Africa is less easy to assess. The earlier political co-ordination of the African and Caribbean struggles for independence, as was manifested in the Pan-African movement of the 1930s and '40s, became weaker and weaker the nearer the prospects arose of actually achieving their goals. Now, in the era of actual or impending Caribbean independence, two factors appear to be at work which do not always move in the same direction. On the one hand, it is certain that Caribbean knowledge of Africa has increased in scope and advanced in accuracy. It is also likely that there is a growing Caribbean interest and psychological involvement in Africa as the dominant symbol of black power. But another factor is that West Indians now have political communities of their own, largely black-dominant numerically and formally black-controlled politically, in which the requisites of nation building and the related establishment of national identities become immediate.

Much, of course, depends on the solution of the relationships of national identity and racial identity. On the surface, the Caribbean appears to have progressed further than most in solving the issue of multiracial existence, and considering its historical conditions, the Caribbean area has managed to achieve a creditable degree of multiracial harmony. But many painful realities lie beneath the surface. The ideal of the multiracial (or—as some there prefer to say—non-racial) society is frequently propagated in the Caribbean, but the multiracial composition of Caribbean societies is based on a black majority which suffers most from economic and psychological insecurities.[63] Many of the racial factors submerged could well erupt in the future unless the pressing problems of economic opportunity and maldistribution are solved.[64] But whatever adjustments are required will have to be worked out in Caribbean terms.

The strengthening of Caribbean bonds with Africa in the foreseeable future will probably be in the area of formal political contact and supports rather than in the realm of mass race-unity response. Prime Minister Eric Williams was not merely officially reaffirming the ideal of multiracialism, but was addressing himself to the question of nation building as a matter of political immediacy when he stated:

> There can be no Mother India for those whose ancestors came from India . . . There can be no Mother Africa for those of African origin; the Trinidad and Tobago society is living a lie and heading for trouble if it seeks to create the impression or allow others to act under the delusion that Trinidad and Tobago is an African society. There can be no Mother England and no dual loyalties . . . There can be no Mother China . . . no Mother Syria or no Mother Lebanon. A nation, like an individual, can have only one Mother. The only Mother we recognize is Mother Trinidad and Tobago, and Mother cannot discriminate between her children.[65]

What of the new Africa in its relations with its descendants in exile? With the progressive unfolding of independence, the earlier forms of racial pan-Africanism which forged a bond between New World Negroes and Africans evolved through contraction into a stress on continental Pan-Africanism.[66] But simultaneously, the imperatives of nation building have frequently led to the subordination of the Pan-African ideal. In either case, the pan-Negro dimension has declined in significance.

We have been discussing some of the operative constraints on Black Power's internationalizing mission. This is not at all meant to suggest that Black Power formulations are by definition irrelevant to many African and Caribbean conditions. As was earlier maintained, there is a large measure of situational similarity—especially in economic and psychological spheres—between black people in the contemporary global setting. And as has been argued elsewhere, there are some Black Power programmatic and tactical formulas to which many leaders in the outer black world could well subscribe.[67]

But what is debatable is whether black Americans are in a position to set the pace and example for a fuller degree of Negro race emancipation. Unlike past times when the zeal of black Americans in the arena of race ideas was directed against institutionalized white power in most of the black world, now such global race ideas face formalized black power in the greater part of the black world. Some black leaders in Africa may indeed—as have some in the Caribbean —view Black Power activities as unfriendly acts. More certainly, many black Africans and Caribbean leaders will react unfavorably to Black Power's global leadership pretensions.

This focusing of attention on leadership response ignores one important factor, namely, the potentialities of Black Power diffusion to masses rather than elites in the outer black world. Certainly the fundamental antiestablishment and antielitist attitudes connoted by Black Power must be taken into account in explaining—what appears surprising to many observers—why some Black Power leaders reserve some of their harshest strictures for some black elites outside the United States.[68]

Earlier pan-Negro ideologies were essentially elitist in conception and dissemination. (Garveyism differs to some extent in that it was based in origin and style on a mass appeal and response, but in his conceptions of the outer world Garvey was first and foremost concerned with the transfer of power from white to black elites.) In the present, unlike the past, the question of black elite–mass domestic relations assumes prominence. The nature and conditions of these relations vary from area to area and from country to country. The debatable thing is whether, in these variations, a race solidarity slogan can achieve a meaningful degree of transnational unity in the way that Pan-Africanism, for example, once represented a conspicuous degree of concord in the quest for the specific goal of decolonization. Add to this consideration the nature of politics in the international system which acts as a source of (and in which are reflected) the tensions arising in the relations between black-controlled sovereignties, and the conclusion is inescapable that in an era of declining colonial white power and rising postcolonial black power, theoretical constructs of global black unity become more elusive in the undertaking.

Another limiting factor to the internationalization of Black Power derives from the pervasiveness and immediacy of the black–white American confrontation, on which we earlier commented. In view of a minority position in a predominantly white environment which has proved unresponsive and antagonistic, black American race consciousness vis-à-vis whites is a logical function of the conditions of black existence in America. (It is no accident that outside the United States the black power concept has found its greatest appeal among racial minorities in Britain, Canada, and Australia. The apparent attractiveness of the concept to southern African students in the United States is a function of the fact that unliberated South African blacks, while in a numerical majority, constitute a political minority.) Such heightened race-consciousness in the black–white context is not automatically transferable to other quarters.[69] To Ibos in Biafra, to the Afro-Shirazi in Zanzibar, to the southern Sudanese, to the Batutsi (or conversely the Bahutu) in Rwanda, to some Africans in Guyana, the immediately perceived racial (or ethnic) threat in recent years has not emanated from the white world. Many black American nationalists are tempted to view the outer black world predominantly "through the thick mist of race"—to use Langston Hughes's words with reference to his first visit to Africa[70] —but such a restrictive vision can often lead to unrealism and distortion concerning the totality of African or Caribbean problems, especially in the era of their independence. Indeed, back in the 1930s the Negro internationalist George Padmore "worried about the Negro American tendency to analyze African problems in an American light."[71]

We are not here minimizing the persistence of black–

white adjustments as significant and explosive national and international issues. It only requires certain incidents—like those in Notting Hill (London) in 1958 or Selma (Alabama) in 1965; the Sharpeville (South Africa) massacre of 1960; the murder of Patrice Lumumba (in Congo, at black hands but, as the feeling persists, at white instigation), and the various evidences of direct outside intervention in Congo (Kinshasa); the unilateral declaration of independence in Rhodesia and the hanging of black Africans by the white regime there; the initial invitation to South Africa to participate in the 1968 Olympics—to arouse a common pattern of strong emotional response throughout the black world. Despite this, the development and propagation of "a philosophy of Blackness"[72] as a co-ordinating force and organizing principle for all black people have severe limitations in terms of the immediate realities of, and perceived needs in, the varied quarters comprising the black world.

The upshot of the foregoing arguments is that Black Power encounters many difficulties in facing the realities of the black world beyond America. Indeed, it might be argued that in spite of what some Black Power spokesmen say about its internationalizing potential, they recognize its limitations in this quest. Far from trying to organize the non-American black world, they may well be interested primarily in getting back into this world from which they have been removed physically and spiritually. The endorsement by some Black Power proponents of revolution (Fanon-style); the "non-aligned" posture openly advocated by some (see note 12); their persistent condemnation of neo-colonialism; their "Back-to-Africa" spiritual mission; the effort to effect a black American linkage with the Third World—all these appear to support the previous assertion. In other words, the essential function of Black Power's internationalizing mission appears to lie less in its intended external effects than in its internal consequence to the black American struggle for political, socioeconomic, and psychological emancipation.

But there are significant implications emerging from the rise of Black Power in America of the 1960s, to which leaders in African and Caribbean political systems could well pay heed, for Black Power's rise brings into focus many generalized political, socioeconomic, and psychological issues bearing on the national integration question: the consequences of the arrogance and insensitivity of majority power and of the systematic deprivation of minority groups and their relegation to a position of inferiority; the dangers of institutionalized and non-institutionalized racism (or its variations); the degree of racial and ethnic assimilation necessary and feasible; the relationships between less and more privileged economic groups; the problems arising from the psychological insecurities and low self-esteem of a subgroup.

The American experience in almost two centuries of nation building has much to offer by way of instruction, both in terms of its successes and failures. The realities of multiracial and multiethnic existence in the Caribbean and Africa make it politically prudent that Caribbean and African leaders study closely other experiences, if only to try to reduce the possibilities of duplicating errors which have occurred elsewhere.

VI

This study began with a brief look at Black Power in its domestic environment and proceeded to look outward in its primary purpose of assessing the internationalizing capacities of Black Power. In conclusion, we shall return briefly from the outer to the inner context. One point will be dealt with, which is the major potential contribution that, in the author's view, Black Power's Third World vision can make to Black Power in America.

In the long run, Black Power efforts to effect this Third World linkage may well prove the most beneficial to the internal (and external) aspects of Black Power race throught. For the more that Third World strivings are promoted, the more it will be realized that not all problems of the Negro race can be analyzed at the black–white dimension. Carmichael, for example, can maintain a more harmonious dialogue with a white Fidel Castro (who has welcomed him to Cuba) than with a black Eric Williams (who has banned him from entering his country of birth); with Cheddi Jagan (of East Indian origin) than with his black political opponent Forbes Burnham[73]; with Ho Chi Minh than with Hastings Banda (of Malawi).[74] Moreover, as Carmichael and others are aware, white masses in Latin America comprise a significant part of this Third World with which Black Power is striving for co-operation. Oversimplified as many of Carmichael's political and economic formulations may be in his internationalizing mission, they could aid on the other hand in expanding the Black Power vision beyond the confining world of black and white.

The greatest long-run danger facing Black Power is that it may become too dogmatically ethnocentric, which could be disastrous in terms of both its internal appeal and export value. The urgent need of Black Power is to promote race consciousness, not racism; to nourish black nationalism, not black chauvinism; to aid in the fight for a more meaningful degree of black self-determinism; to work for a measure of race unity, not race exclusiveness; to strive for race emancipation while eschewing all forms of race domination. Black Power does not of necessity connote antiwhite power, but it necessarily denotes anti white-power. On the latter, a large measure of mutual sympathy will arise in the black world at large; on the former, black men will forever be disunited.

APPENDIX

Black Power Manifesto from the National Conference on Black Power

Black people who live under imperialist governments in America, Asia, Africa, and Latin America stand at the crossroads of either an expanding revolution or ruthless extermination. It is incumbent for us to get our own house in order to fully utilize the potentialities of the revolution or to resist our own execution.

Black people have consistently expended a large part of our energy and resources reacting to white definition. It is imperative that we begin to develop the organizational and technical competence to initiate and enact our own programs.

Black people in America and in Black nationalist groups across the world have allowed ourselves to become the tool of policies of white supremacy. It is evident that it is in our own interest to develop and propagate a philosophy of blackness as a social psychological, political, cultural, and economic directive.

The objective conditions for reversing the plight of the Black peoples reside within the Black communities of the world. It is of importance that efforts be undertaken to develop a communications system among the larger Black communities in America and the Black nations of the world.

The democratic process has failed to bring justice to Black people within the framework of the imperialist government of the United States and within the imperialist framework of white nations throughout the world.

Control of African communities in America and other Black communities and nations throughout the world still remains in the hands of white supremacist oppressors.

The colonialist and neo-colonialist control of Black communities in America and many Black nations across the world by white supremacists necessarily is detrimental and destructive to the attainment of Black Power.

It is therefore resolved, that The National Conference on Black Power sponsor the creation of an International Black Congress, to be organized out of the soulful roots of our peoples and to reflect the new sense of power and revolution now blossoming in Black communities in America and in Black nations throughout the world.

The implementation of this Manifesto shall come through the convening of Regional Black Power Conferences in America and in Black nations of the world.

It is recommended that these International and Regional Black Power Conferences be held before the end of this year, in the spirit of unity exhibited during this National Conference on Black Power. The Regional Conferences shall be convened by the co-ordinated efforts of delegates to this National Conference on Black Power in each region, working in conjunction with the Committee on Continuation of the National Conference on Black Power.

These Regional Conferences shall begin to structure methods of attaining operational unity in their regions in preparation for the convening of a Second Annual International Conference on Black Power in a year's time, to be held in a Black setting.

The International Black Congress shall act in concert with the Committee on Continuation, which shall convene the Second Annual National Conference on Black Power to establish a method of electing delegates to the National Black Congress.

The International Black Congress shall be inaugurated within the next year and a half, at which time it shall replace the Committee on Continuation in the convening of future International Black Power Conferences and in the implementation of programs for the realization of Black Power.

[The Manifesto reproduced in full above was the only *official* document approved by the Conference held in Newark, New Jersey, 20–23 July 1967. The other resolutions adopted (e.g., those described in note 61) were *advisory* to the continuing bodies set up by the Conference.]

NOTES

1. Some of the following arguments were first presented in my "Black Power, Africa, and the Caribbean," a paper prepared for the University of East Africa Social Sciences Conference held in Dar es Salaam, 2–5 Jan. 1968, and since circulated in the Makerere Institute of Social Research *Conference Papers* (1968).

2. SNCC, founded in 1960, recently announced that it had "terminated" its relationship with Carmichael "with regret and no pleasure" (New York *Times*, 23 Aug. 1968). This development should not be construed as a diminution in Black Power ardor on the part of either SNCC or Carmichael, who is closely associated with the Black Panthers, a rival militant Black Power group. (See report on the deteriorating relations between SNCC and the Black Panthers in the New York *Times*, 7 Oct. 1968.)

3. Martin Luther King, Jr., *Where Do We Go From Here: Chaos or Community?* (New York, 1967), p. 29. Chap. 2 of King's book gives good inside account of the immediate origins of the slogan. See also Paul Good, "The Meredith March," *New South*, XXI, No. 3 (1966), 2–16, and "A White Looks at Black Power," *The Nation*, 8 Aug. 1966.

4. Martin Luther King, Jr., "Black Power," *The Progressive*, XXX (Nov. 1966), 15–17.

5. Of the numerous relevant writings, special attention should be paid to Stokely Carmichael and Charles V. Hamilton, *Black Power: The Politics of Liberation* (New York, 1967), and Nathan Wright, Jr., *Black Power and Urban Unrest: Creative Possibilities* (New York, 1967). Wright organized the 1967 and 1968 National Conferences on Black Power. Carmichael has since become much more revolutionary in his formulations.

6. Not much has been written on the international and comparative aspects of Black Power. I have attempted some such analysis in "Black Power, Africa and the Caribbean" (note 1, above). See also the special issue, "Black Power and Africa," *Africa Today*, XIV, No. 6 (Dec. 1967), in which is included my "Black Power: A View from the Outside," some relevant analyses, in Floyd B. Barbour, ed., *The Black Power Revolt* (Boston, 1968); Inez Smith Reid, "Black Power and Uhuru," *Pan-African Journal*, I, No. 1 (1968), 23–27; The Times News Team, *The Black Man in Search of Power* (London, 1968), Chaps. 1 and 2, parts of which previously appeared in *The Times* (London), 11–16 Mar. 1968. The major Black Power statements of international relevance will be documented below when necessary.

7. C. L. R. James, "Black Power," public lecture at Makerere, 21 Aug. 1968.

8. George Shepperson, "Notes on Negro American Influences on the Emergence of African Nationalism," *Journal of African History*, I (1960), 229.

9. St. Clair Drake, "Negro Americans and the Africa Interest," in John P. Davis, ed., *The American Negro Reference Book* (Englewood Cliffs, N.J., 1966), p. 679, note 33.

10. Stokely Carmichael, "A Declaration of War," transcript of speech, 17 Feb. 1968, in Oakland, California, published in *The Running Man*, I, No. 1 (May–June 1968), 17–21.

11. James Forman, "The Concept of International Black Power," *Pan-African Journal*, II, Nos. 2 and 3 (1968), 93.

12. Excerpt from publication of the SNCC Chicago office, quoted in the *International Herald Tribune* (Paris), 18 Aug. 1967.

13. Stokely Carmichael, in an interview published in the *Sunday News* (Dar es Salaam), 5 Nov. 1967. (In an earlier interview in Guinea, Carmichael conceived of Black Power "in its simplest form" as "the coming together of black people throughout the world to fight for our liberation by any means necessary," *Africa and the World*, IV, Nov. 1967, 19. See also interview with Carmichael published in *The Nationalist* [Dar es Salaam], 6 Nov. 1967.)

14. Carmichael interview, *Sunday News*, 5 Nov. 1967.

15. Held in Newark, N.J., 20–23 July 1967, this was, in the words of its chairman, Nathan Wright, "the first major national dialogue by 1,300 [a more recent figure given by another Conference official is 1,094] Black Americans on the creative possibilities inherent in the concept of Black Power." The first such Conference, at which there were roughly 100 participants, was convened by Adam Clayton Powell in Sept. 1966 in Washington, D.C. A third Conference chaired by Wright was held in Philadelphia, Penna., 29 Aug.–1 Sept. 1968, at which there were between 3,000 and 4,000 participants (official reports unavailable at the time of writing). One New York *Times* report has it that at the 1968 Conference "it was announced that the Government of Tanzania . . . had issued an invitation to the Conference to hold a meeting there."

16. See, e.g., Rupert Emerson and Martin Kilson, "The American Dilemma in a Changing World: The Rise of Africa and the Negro American," *Daedalus*, XCIV (1965), 1055–84; Harold R. Isaacs, *The New World of Negro Americans* (New York, 1964); Thomas F. Pettigrew, *A Profile of the Negro American* (Princeton, 1964), pp. 10–12, 191–92; St. Clair Drake, op. cit.

17. Quoted in Lewis Nkosi, *Home and Exile* (London, 1965), p. 81.

18. E. U. Essien-Udom, *Black Nationalism: A Search*

for an Identity in America (New York, 1964), p. 313, first published in Chicago in 1962.

19. Richard Wright, *Black Power* (London, 1954). See especially Wright's concluding open letter to Nkrumah (pp. 342–51), excerpts from which are given a full-page reprinting by Nkrumah at the beginning of his book *Dark Days in Ghana*.

20. Quoted in Carl T. Rowan, "Has Paul Robeson Betrayed the Negro?" *Ebony* (Oct. 1957), 41.

21. Nkrumah, "The Spectre of Black Power," *Granma* (Havana), 17 Dec. 1967; also in *Africa and the World*, IV, No. 39 (1968), 9–12.

22. *The Observer* (London), 6 Aug. 1967; "Black Power in Britain," *Life*, 16 Oct. 1967, pp. 8–17; *East African Standard* (Nairobi), 30 Apr. 1968; The Times News Team, op. cit.

23. Charles Perkins, "Black Power," *The Union Recorder* (published by Sydney University Student Union), 13 June 1968, pp. 110–13. Perkins, who is part Aborigine, was until recently regarded by many as "the Australian Martin Luther King." See also "Black Power May Emerge in Australia," *The Nationalist* (Dar es Salaam), 23 Aug. 1968.

24. Murray Barnard, "For Negroes in Halifax, Black Power v. Ping Pong," *MacLeans* (Toronto), Nov. 1967, p. 1.

25. John Strong, "Emerging Ideological Patterns Among Southern African Students," *Africa Today*, XIV, No. 4 (1967), 16.

26. SNCC, among the major black American groups, has been the spearhead of Black Power's internationalizing mission, and the two most prominent international Black Power spokesmen are James Forman, Director of International Affairs for SNCC, and Stokely Carmichael, who in 1967 visited eleven countries (Algeria, Cuba, Denmark, France, Guinea, North Vietnam, Sweden, Syria, Tanzania, the U.A.R., the U.K.). Very recently, Carmichael left the U.S. for Senegal expressly "to unite the black peoples of Africa with those of the United States" (*The Nationalist* [Dar es Salaam], 7 Sept. 1968).

27. George Padmore, *Pan-Africanism or Communism?*
The Coming Struggle for Africa (London, 1956), p. 319.

28. This stands in inherent conflict to the egalitarian
ethic also deep-rooted in the political culture, but, as Sey-
mour Martin Lipset argues, this contradiction "has if anything, forced many Americans to think even more harshly
of the Negro than they might if they lived in a more explicitly ascriptive culture. There is no justification in an
egalitarian society to repress a group such as the Negroes unless they are defined as a congenitally inferior race" (*The
First New Nation: The United States in Historical and
Comparative Perspective*, London, 1964, p. 330).

29. On the general development of black American nationalism, see Herbert Aptheker, "Consciousness of Negro
Nationality: An Historical Survey," *Political Affairs* (June
1949); Essien-Udom, op. cit., Chap. 2; C. Eric Lincoln,
The Black Muslims in America (Boston, 1961), Chap. 2.

30. This is given blunt official acknowledgment in the
March 1968 Report of the President's National Advisory
Commission on Civil Disorders.

31. Garvey, who was in the U.S. from 1916 to 1927
(when he was deported), had initially planned a brief visit
to launch the UNIA there and intended to return to "perfect the Jamaica organization." But because of conflicts in
the Harlem UNIA branch, some of its members asked him
to remain on as its president; see *The Philosophy and Opinions of Marcus Garvey*, comp. Amy Jacques Garvey (2nd
ed., London, 1967), Pt. II, pp. 128–29.

32. It has been argued that one of Garvey's major
tactical errors was in transferring to the United States the
white (upper-class)–colored (middle-class)–black (lower-
class) cleavages which were West Indian, not American,
phenomena (see, e.g., Edmund Cronon, *Black Moses*, Madi-
son, Wisc., 1962, pp. 9–11, 191; E. Franklin Frazier, *Black
Bourgeoisie*, New York, 1962, p. 105; David Lowenthal,
"Race and Color in the West Indies," *Daedalus*, XCVI
(1967), 613–14; Padmore, op. cit., p. 91). But in the two
situations there were only differences in degree. The major

difference was that in terms of American (unlike West Indian) intergroup (white–black) relations, shade factors were irrelevant in the caste system. But in terms of intragroup relations, shade was not at all irrelevant in black America and the differences with the West Indies system narrowed. See, e.g. Frazier, op. cit., pp. 116–17, 164–66, and *The Negro in the United States* (New York, 1957), Chap. 12; Isaacs, op. cit., pp. 137, 145; Gunnar Myrdal, *An American Dilemma* (New York, 1944), pp. 693–700; Malcolm X, *Autobiography* (New York, 1966), pp. 1–8, 374.

33. In 1956 a bronze bust of Garvey was erected in Jamaica's National Park. In 1965, three years after Jamaican independence, Garvey's remains were brought back from London (where he died in 1940) and enshrined as Jamaica's First National Hero. At that time the Jamaican government established a £5,000 Marcus Garvey Prize to be awarded in 1968 to "the person who, in this generation has contributed most significantly to the field of Human Rights."

34. See, generally, Edward Blyden, *Christianity, Islam and the Negro Race* (London, 1887; Edinburgh, 1967), and Hollis R. Lynch, *Edward Wilmot Blyden: Pan-Negro Patriot, 1832–1912* (London, 1967). Like Garvey, Blyden was a proponent of a New World Negro repatriation; his vision was one of global black race unity, and he was even more bitter than Garvey in his denunciations of mulattoes, so much so that Lynch (p. 251) speculates that Blyden probably boycotted the 1900 Pan-African Conference because of his suspicion of the mulatto leadership of Du Bois and others. Lynch also states that "although so far no reference has been made to Blyden by Garvey, it seems likely that the latter . . . was well acquainted with the writings and ideas of the former."

35. Colin Legum, *Pan-Africanism* (New York, 1962), p. 14.

36. Vernon McKay, *Africa in World Politics* (New York, 1963), p. 93. Like Legum, McKay deals with "Pan-African" political, economic, and cultural aspects. (Note that McKay's reference to "black power" is not a reference to the subject

of the present analysis but to the exaltation of African and Caribbean "black power" by Wright and Robeson referred to above at notes 19 and 20. "Blackism" is discussed below in Section V.)

37. The foregoing distinctions are derived (with minor modifications) from George Shepperson, "Pan-Africanism, and 'Pan-Africanism': Some Historical Notes," *Phylon*, XXIII (1962), 346–58.

38. W. E. Burghardt Du Bois, *The World and Africa* (enlarged ed., New York, 1965) p. 7.

39. Rayford Logan, "The Historical Aspects of Pan-Africanism, 1900–1945," in American Society of African Culture, ed., *Pan-Africanism Reconsidered* (Berkeley, Calif., 1962), pp. 37–38. See also Legum, op. cit., pp. 24–25, and Padmore, op. cit., pp. 117–19.

40. C. L. R. James, *The Black Jacobins: Toussaint L'Ouverture and the San Domingo Revolution* (2nd ed. rev., New York, 1963), p. 399.

41. James R. Hooker, *Black Revolutionary: George Padmore's Path from Communism to Pan-Africanism* (London, 1967), p. 140.

42. Lynch, op. cit., pp. 54–55 (note 37). See also Robert W, July, *The Origins of Modern African Thought* (New York, 1967, Chap. 11, "The First African Personality: Edward W. Blyden."

43. Bruce regularly contributed a column to Garvey's *Negro World* and in 1920 was knighted by Garvey for services to the UNIA.

44. Shepperson, "Notes on Negro American Influences . . . ," pp. 309–10.

45. See July, op. cit., Chap. 2.

46. This letter and related correspondence was published by C. L. R. James in a pamphlet, *Kwame Nkrumah and the West Indies* (San Juan, Trinidad, 1962).

47. James, *The Black Jacobins*, p. 397.

48. Rupert Emerson and Martin Kilson, eds., *The Political Awakening of Africa* (Englewood Cliffs, N.J., 1965), p. 21 (note 2).

49. Langston Hughes, "The Twenties: Harlem and Its Négritude," *African Forum*, 1 (1966), 17–18. My treatment of the origins of Négritude has benefited from these studies: Albert H. Berrian and Richard A. Long, eds., *Négritude: Essays and Studies* (Hampton, Virginia, 1967)—particularly the essays on Du Bois, Locke, and Price Mars of Haiti; G. R. Coulthard, *Race and Colour in Caribbean Literature* (London, 1962); and especially Abiola Ircle, "Négritude or Black Cultural Nationalism," *The Journal of Modern African Studies*, III, No. 3 (1965), 321–48.

50. In addition to Carmichael, who left Trinidad at the age of eleven, there were at mid-1967 at least four other such Black Power proponents holding major offices in SNCC and CORE (Congress of Racial Equality), the two leading nationally organized Black Power organizations: Lincoln Lynch, associate director, CORE, born in Jamaica; Roy Innis, chairman, Harlem CORE, born in the Virgin Islands; Ivanhoe Donaldson, director, New York office of SNCC, born in Jamaica; Cortland Cox SNCC field secretary, who lived in Trinidad (William Brink and Louis Harris, *Black and White: A Study of U. S. Racial Attitudes Today*, New York, 1967, p. 60). Lynch, I understand, has since left CORE to form a new Black Power organization (official details unavailable). Innis, who succeeded Lynch as associate director, was elected national director of CORE (succeeding Floyd McKissick) at its reconvened 1968 national convention, at which was adopted a new constitution advocating black nationalism (New York *Times*, 17 Sept. 1968).

51. Harold Cruse, *The Crisis of the Negro Intellectual* (New York, 1967), deals extensively with historical and contemporary relations of West Indian-born and native black Americans. See especially pp. 422–38, 550–59, where he assesses the "undercurrent of West Indian-American Negro rivalry" in present day black American nationalism.

52. This was the People's Progressive Party founded by a Jamaican barrister, Millard Johnson. (On its origin and philosophy see Katrin Norris, *Jamaica: The Search for an Identity*, London, 1962, pp. 57–64.) In the 1962 General

Elections the party gained slightly over 2 per cent of the total vote; it thereafter disintegrated, and Johnson left for Africa.

53. McKay, op. cit., p. 127.

54. Remi Fani-Kayode, *Blackism* (Lagos, 1965), p. 13; quoted by E. U. Essien-Udom, Introduction to *The Philosophy and Opinions of Marcus Garvey*, Pt. I, p. xxiv.

55. James Baldwin, *Nobody Knows My Name* (New York, 1963), p. 35.

56. References for the following illustrative statements of Stokely Carmichael and James Forman (notes 57–62 and 68) are to be found in notes 10, 11, 13, above.

57. CARMICHAEL: ". . . if we are going to talk about the liberation of Africa, then we prepare for a revolution." FORMAN: ". . . the kind of struggle for liberation which is going on in the southern half of Africa is extremely important and must be supported." In 1967 H. Rap Brown, then chairman of SNCC, twice sent letters to the United Nations offering black American troops to support African guerrilla movements in southern African liberation struggles (*Africa Diary*, 24–30 Sept. 1967, p. 3584; *Uganda Argus*, 7 Dec. 1967).

58. CARMICHAEL: "Many of them [i.e., African leaders] are not concerned with a united Africa. And that is absolutely absurd."

59. CARMICHAEL: ". . . the African world stretches wherever the African has been scattered." Or: "Our struggle lies in the unification of those 900,000,000 [*sic*] people" of African descent throughout the world. "Our base of course will be Africa—it's our motherland." And: "Once the African states accept . . . that this struggle is an integral part of the general Pan-African struggle, they should assist these liberation movements in the United States, in exactly the same way as they already assist the liberation movements in southern Africa . . . There is absolutely no difference of principle involved. It is all one struggle for African liberation."

60. CARMICHAEL: "The [African] continent today is controlled by the white man, particularly the United States."

FORMAN: "Many of us are willing to take these skills and put them in the service of the continent . . . This purpose is to free Africa to some extent from the neo-colonialism that exists." See also the Black Power Manifesto in the Appendix, para. 8.

61. CARMICHAEL: "We are an African people with an African ideology, we are wandering in the United States, we are going to build a concept of peoplehood in this country or there will be no country." When asked if he favored the return to Africa of black Americans: "No, not a complete return. At least not at this point. The best protection for Africa today is the 50,000,000 [*sic*] African-Americans inside the United States . . ." FORMAN: "It is paramount to get rid of the concept that we are Negroes, Afro-Americans, or even African-Americans; we are Africans living inside the United States. . . ." The 1967 National Conference on Black Power adopted resolutions on the teaching of African languages and establishment of Institutes of African Studies; cementing ties with the OAU (Organization of African Unity); establishment of a Black Youth Exchange, Student-Teacher Exchange, and International Employment Exchange Service with African countries; and promotion of African-American Home Hospitality programs for African visitors.

62. CARMICHAEL: "It seems also that the motherland has a responsibility to safeguard the humanity of Africans in countries where they live outside of Africa. They also need cultural organizations that will begin to revive and place the culture of the African back on the pedestal where it belongs." See also the Black Power Manifesto paras. 3 and 9; W. A. Jeanpierre, "African Négritude—Black American Soul," *Africa Today*, XIV, No. 6 (1967), 10–11.

63. See, e.g., David Lowenthal, "Race and Color in the West Indies," *Daedalus*, XCVI, No. 2 (1967), 580–626; Rex Nettleford, "National Identity and Attitudes to Race in Jamaica," *Race*, VII, No. 1 (1965), 59–72.

64. This is no doubt recognized by those Caribbean governments which have banned Carmichael's entry in person or through the printed word. I understand from a reliable

source that the governments of Trinidad and Tobago, Guyana, and Jamaica have prohibited Carmichael's proposed visit, apparently because of his remarks on the prospects of guerrilla warfare in the Caribbean (see Carmichael interview in *The Observer* [London], 23 July 1967). The Jamaican government has prohibited the importation of all publications authored or co-authored by Carmichael, Malcolm X, and Elijah Muhammad (*The Jamaican Weekly Gleaner*, 31 July 1968, p. 34).

65. Eric Williams, *History of the People of Trinidad and Tobago* (Port of Spain, 1962), p. 281. But the Rastafari cult in Jamaica thinks otherwise (Norris, op. cit., Chap. 5; M. G. Smith et al., *The Rastafari Movement in Kingston, Jamaica*, Kingston, 1960).

66. On the evolutionary relationships of pan-Negroism and Pan-Africanism see Legum, op. cit., pp. 40–44; St. Clair Drake, op. cit., pp. 691–700; Ali A. Mazrui, *On Heroes and Uhuru-Worship* London, 1967), pp. 58–59, 209–30, in which the theme of "pan-proletarianism" is mentioned.

67. See my two analyses referred to in note 6, above.

68. CARMICHAEL: ". . . the African continent today in general is ruled by clowns who are more concerned about big cars than the welfare of their people." And: ". . . the African leaders are not prepared to sacrifice. They are engaged in bourgeoisie tea party revolutions." FORMAN: ". . . within the concept of International Black Power there is revolutionary Black Power and there is reactionary Black Power. We must not ignore the fact that some of our brothers and sisters who are leaders of certain African countries, like certain people within this country, are espousing the policy of reactionary Black Power." (It was reported that during Carmichael's 1967 visit to Tanzania, President Nyerere privately asked him "to moderate his . . . criticism of African leaders" *Uganda Argus*, 28 Nov. 1967.)

69. President Nyerere was also reported to have privately asked Carmichael "to moderate his 'hate whites' message . . ." (*Uganda Argus*, 28 Nov. 1967). It is uncertain if Nyerere used these precise terms. Nothing that I have seen

in Carmichael's 1967 speeches and interviews reported in the East Africa press can be construed as a "hate white message." But I gathered from a reliable source that Nyerere was not fully receptive to Carmichael's uncompromising racial emphasis.

70. Quoted in James Farmer, "An American Negro Leader's View of African Unity," *African Forum*, I, No. 1 (1965), 70.

71. Hooker, op. cit., p. 18. Thus, when Carmichael in 1967 criticized African liberation movements on their failures and in so doing drew on examples from black America, the African National Congress of South Africa (based in Tanzania) replied that "his attacks . . . reveal profound ignorance," and added: "The struggle in South Africa cannot be fought with bottles" against a "well armed and cruel" enemy (*Sunday Nation* [Nairobi], 12 Nov. 1967).

72. Black Power Manifesto, para. 3.

73. During a recent visit to Uganda, Guyana's opposition leader Jagan said in an interview: "The majority party . . . has been completely silent on the Negro question in America . . . My party supports the line of leaders like Stokely Carmichael . . ." (*The People* [Kampala], 30 March 1968).

74. When visiting North Vietnam in August 1967, Carmichael said: "We are not seeking the end of the bombing or the end of the U.S. policy of aggression in Vietnam. We want to see the Vietnamese win the war, defeat the United States, and drive it out of the country" (*Keesing's Contemporary Archives*, 14–21 Oct. 1967, p. 22304). James Forman recently cited Banda as an example of "reactionary Black Power" (see note 11, above).

LOCKSLEY EDMONDSON, *a native of Jamaica, is senior lecturer in the Department of Government, University of the West Indies, Mona, Jamaica. After his undergraduate studies in the social sciences in England, at the University of Birmingham, and his graduate studies in political science in Canada, at Queen's University, he taught at the University of Waterloo, Ontario, Canada (1963–67); at Makerere University, Kampala, Uganda (1967–70); and at Cornell University (1970–73), before joining the University of the West Indies in October 1973.*

From September 1972 to January 1973, on leave from Cornell, he was acting director of the Center on International Race Relations and visiting associate professor in the Graduate School for International Studies at the University of Denver. He has published numerous articles, essays, and reviews—mainly in the area of international race relations—his most recent article being "Caribbean Nation-Building and the Internationalization of Race," in Wendell Bell and Walter Freeman, eds., Ethnicity and Nation-Building, *to be published by Sage Publications in 1974. He is now completing a major study,* Race and the International System.

INDEX